Date: 1/28/21

BIO SODERLIND
Soderlind, Lori,
The change : my great
American, postindustrial,

The Change

Living Out
Gay and Lesbian Autobiographies

David Bergman, Joan Larkin, and Raphael Kadushin

Founding Editors

The Change

My Great American, Postindustrial, Midlife Crisis Tour

Lori Soderlind

The University of Wisconsin Press

Publication of this book has been made possible, in part,
through support from the Brittingham Trust.

The University of Wisconsin Press
728 State Street, Suite 443
Madison, Wisconsin 53706
uwpress.wisc.edu

Gray's Inn House, 127 Clerkenwell Road
London EC1R 5DB, United Kingdom
eurospanbookstore.com

Printed in the United States of America

This book may be available in a digital edition.

Library of Congress Cataloging-in-Publication Data

Names: Soderlind, Lori, author.
Title: The change: my great American, postindustrial, midlife crisis tour / Lori Soderlind.
Other titles: Living out.
Description: Madison, Wisconsin: The University of Wisconsin Press, [2020]
| Series: Living out: gay and lesbian autobiographies
Identifiers: LCCN 2019050469 | ISBN 9780299328306 (cloth)
Subjects: LCSH: Soderlind, Lori—Travel—United States.
Classification: LCC PS3619.O3775 Z46 2020 | DDC 818/.603—dc23
LC record available at https://lccn.loc.gov/2019050469

Book epigraph © 2020, 2005 June M. Jordan Literary Estate Trust. Reprinted by permission. www
.junejordan.com. From June Jordan, *Directed by Desire: The Collected Poems of June Jordan*, edited by
Sara Miles and Jan Heller Levi (Copper Canyon Press, 2005).

This is a memoir. It is a fact-based personal narrative created through careful notes, research, and
memory. Some of these memories may contain embellishments, to aid storytelling, but no facts have
been changed. Names have been changed to protect the privacy of some who did not expect to turn up
in the pages of a book. All photos in this book are by the author.

For **Suzanne**

There is no chance that we will fall apart.

There is no chance.

There are no parts.

June Jordan,
"Poem Number Two on Bell's Theorem"

Contents

1

A Prelude

I had been thinking for a long time of driving out into the middle of the country with my dog. Names on maps and highway signs had been tempting me all my life, and I figured I would do it one day; I would go off on a simple kind of "where the heck's Paducah?" meander across the continent with no particular story to tell. Just curiosity. I would search for junk-shop treasures in little towns I had never heard of. I would find all types of new places to drink coffee. My dog, Colby, was getting old; if we were ever really going on this journey together, it couldn't wait much longer. And we were definitely going. Eventually. But time passed and nothing happened and the dream remained a dream.

Until the night of the crisis. Apparently, a crisis was needed if I was ever going to leave, and when a crisis is needed, one will come. Believe me. In short—and I hesitate to say this, but it must be said—one night in the early summer of my dog's thirteenth year, I cheated on my girlfriend. And after that, leaving was easy. After that, I had to flee.

Of course, to say I "cheated" is a bit of an exaggeration; the violation occurred strictly in theory. I did not touch anyone's body and no other body touched mine. That's part of the confusion of the whole affair; there was no affair, really. The trouble was in my mind. I was a woman of a certain age, with a fine life constructed around me like church walls; if anything was missing, I thought, it was only a little time to wander off, to feel more like myself for a while. But my mind has a mind of its own, and one night, inside those church walls, my mind was torridly unfaithful. To have felt so determined to act on impulse, to break the agreement I had built my life on—that woke me up. Yes, it did.

Also, I should add that when I say I "cheated on my girlfriend," the word "girlfriend" doesn't quite fit either. I had been with my partner about thirteen years (just a bit less time than I had been with my dog) and I was nearly fifty when the crisis arrived; fifty was not as old as Colby in dog years but still, I was hardly a "girl." So when I confess that I cheated on my girlfriend one night, technically not a word of it is true. But words are as flawed as I am, it seems. They mean well; they fail. What matters is, I really was in trouble.

The nonevent I've called "cheating" occurred on a June visit to my family's cabin in northern Wisconsin, which also involved a drive, though not quite such a long one. A prelude. I probably never would have "cheated" if I had never left home, but then there I was, in peril, in Wisconsin. My family has roots six generations deep in Wisconsin, which makes the cabin one of the few things in this world that feels absolutely certain. Everything else—and everybody, I see now—comes and goes, no matter how beloved. It's all fungible. But not the cabin. The cabin sticks. It's like the one true thing, though I shouldn't say this; I fear it might burn down now.

Colby and I drove out to the cabin that June just as I had driven so many times before, at least once a year all my life and lately often more. It's a 1,200-mile drive from New York, where I live; it takes twenty hours to get there. The route passes Cleveland and Sandusky; Angola and South Bend; Gary, Indiana, and Rockford, Illinois, a chain of mysterious places I had, over fifty years, wondered about but never seen. Not really. On our way to the cabin that June, Colby and I stopped for the night in Erie, Pennsylvania, a city we normally would have seen nothing of beyond the motel parking lot; we were only there to sleep, after all. But on this trip, I did something different, and everything changed. I might have known this one change would open up a floodgate. I might have kept on doing every-thing just the same instead, had I known. But on this trip, faced with unsatisfying motel-brewed coffee in a tiny foam cup, it occurred to me that I wanted something better for myself, that in fact I deserved more, and that if I looked, I could find it. I might even find what I wanted—a real coffee shop with scones and everything—right in downtown Erie.

Which begged the question: Did "downtown" Erie exist? And if it did, why had I never seen it? For all I knew, Erie, Pennsylvania, was in fact nothing more than a knot of motels and chain restaurants along the interstate. It's entirely possible to be somewhere without ever being there at all. But my addiction to caffeine set me off that day in search of "real" Erie, wherever that was, and if there was no real Erie I might at least find a Starbucks. Then, before I found any of this, something else happened: I made a fateful turn and traffic whisked me off to a place called Presque Isle State Park. And boy, that was another place entirely.

The moment I entered that park, Colby sat up in the back seat and started panting like he knew something good was going to happen or, maybe, like he had to pee; I was never absolutely certain what Colby's panting might mean, but it always meant something. I figured I better pull over.

Presque Isle State Park has a gorgeous beach, so unspoiled and peaceful. How had I not known? Why had I never been there? We went for a walk on that beach, where Colby limped spritely across the sand ahead of me, pulling on his leash like a geriatric reindeer tethered to my reins. Arthritis in his legs had slowed but not stopped him. He pulled me right to the water and stepped in to take a little sip of Erie—a Great Lake once so polluted that it caught fire. The fire was big news in 1969. Fires in other Great Lakes and rivers were in the news too; they burned with alarming frequency in those days. I remember thinking as a girl, "But Mommy, water can't burn," then realizing it wasn't the water that was burning, then feeling terrified. Humans can really mess things up. Colby took a long drink from the lake, then I steered him around the big, terribly dead fish carcasses washed up in the sand, which his nose hunted avidly but his dim eyes couldn't see. Across the bay stood boxy concrete buildings with smokestacks, which looked to me like the last gasps of once enormous and water-fouling industries. Or sewage plants, possibly. It would spoil the memory to know.

I found a driftwood log to sit on and my dog lay beside me. I felt such affection in that moment for the lake and the park and the lost city of Erie;

I was overwhelmed with a feeling of love that I can, in hindsight, attribute partly to low blood sugar and partly to a rush of warm, spring air. But I'll take love where I find it. And I felt love. Oh, my dear Erie; she was so beautiful. People in Erie must feel like the luckiest people in the world. If I lived in Erie, I would spend all my early summer mornings sitting on this quiet beach and I would be happy, I thought. And then, I felt a terrible sadness.

Because of course I never would live there, which put true happiness just out of reach. The sinking feeling was familiar. Small waves tapped at the sand. Colby panted.

"You know, Colby," I said, "you and I really need to take that drive around the country." We walked back to the car.

Colby and I were driving to the cabin that June to host Girls' Week, a biannual reunion for me and four high school friends. No husbands or kids, or in my case no same-sex partners, were allowed at Girls' Week. We left our families for this get-together—and they left their families in such intriguing places, like Idaho. Like Port Huron, Michigan. Where's that? We had grown up in New Jersey; they had gone off to these exotic lands. Every couple of years, though, we would meet up at one of our homes, just us Girls, and within moments of arrival they would silence their cell phones, unhook their bras, and start drinking. The Girls can really party. Soon, the decades would look like a joke we had played on each other; time collapsed and let loose our original selves and soon after that, truths would surface. Longings secreted deeply away nosed up for air. Theirs, that is; not mine. I thought I was fine. I had known some struggles; I had been a bit unhappy lately, sure, but that was to be expected at this phase of life. Surely, it would pass. On the other hand, if I had a husband and kids and lives like they had, I would have lost my mind. I was smug about that. I was wrong to be.

After a few days with my old friends at the cabin, I had become a bit unmoored. Girls' Week was always unmooring. I suppose that was the point. I recall lots of weepy hugging and words like, "Only you understand me." There had been some naked swimming and a cellphone dropped in the lake, not once but twice, as if its owner was determined to cut her ties forever. There had been confessions and suggestions and promises made;

one of the girls wanted to see what it would be like to kiss me, and I obliged. This was not cheating. This was silly. This Girl wanted something, maybe excitement, maybe affection; maybe she wanted an easy explanation for her life's disappointments, as easy as to say, "Oh! Look! Now I'm gay!" But she wasn't. Soon, that Girl got bored and moved on to other mischief. The party continued. We had been running like this for days, with no filters, no judgments. And then we ran out of beer.

A morning restocking expedition led me to Trig's supermarket, where I purchased supplies and was harrumphing back across the parking lot with a gallon-sized wine box in one arm and a half case of light beer in the other. As I tripped along, bear-hugging these packages and scanning the horizon for my car, I glimpsed a certain unmistakable shape off in the periphery. I turned, and there she was: someone I had once loved, loading her groceries into a Jeep. I recognized her before she even looked up and the shock of it made me weak. Could it be? Oh, so sweet, the flush of hope this ghost awoke in me. We had been girls. Shopping carts clattered across the pavement. The sun was in my eyes. When at last she turned and looked my way, I squinted hard and saw that it really was her, my friend, though her face was older than the face I had known long ago. Fuller, looser. Beauty changes. Still, it was a wonderful face and, caught unaware, the face looked so tenderly sad that I felt I had to kiss it. And I mean, seriously kiss it. My mouth on that mouth and maybe that body pressed against her car. And yes, that. Yes. The urge was startling and visceral and it made me dumb. I stood for a time just staring and thinking stupid things before I said a single word to the woman. Two words, actually. I said, "Oh! Hello!" And stood there. She stepped closer.

I say I had once loved this woman but again, the truth is confusing. When we were teenagers, we had spent part of each summer together and of course, back then, every summer was perfect and lasted forever. A child's forever is a grain of sand. She was beautiful, but not like a picture; I saw something in her that I did not always see when I looked at people. This beauty, when I saw it, sometimes simply made me laugh. I was happy to see her, in a way that gives real power to those words. I never imagined I would lose this friend, or more to the point, that we would stop seeing each other, that we would forget. But change comes, sometimes gently.

We grew up and apart. Over decades we had kept in touch at least enough that I knew she was married, that her children were nearly grown. I had seen her sometimes across the years and the connection, however brief, had still charmed me; the feeling would remind me of something I had not realized I had forgotten. I would feel that for a while before slipping back into the business of real life, which was fine. I was fine. I was certain.

Then I saw her in the raw light of Girls' Week. And something had changed.

This time, I felt that recognition—Was it hope? Sure, yes, a sense of possibility, the sense that everything would always move toward better, better—and I wanted to know why that sweet feeling had never come and stayed, and for the first time I was sure: It never would. I was nearly fifty. The time to build had somehow passed. Lately, I had been waking each day further altered, a longer jowl here, a gray hair there. Sometimes a gray whisker. Other things were happening too; shocking things. Things that hardly any woman will discuss but everyone should know: the hormones, the crazies. The heat that would have consumed me in flames if the flop sweat hadn't put the fire out. This is frank stuff; I'm talking perimenopause. I'm talking about truly merciless change that all who survive it understand; some do not survive intact but instead disintegrate, then become someone else entirely. I swear it's true. Watching my body start this ride, I had confronted something hard about time: it would run out. And Colby was growing old—he would be fourteen!—and in time, he would die. It seemed impossible. It made me sad for all the things I would not share with Colby after he was dead, and for all the other things I would miss myself after I died—which I would do, eventually, I had realized.

I would die. Colby would die. Good god, we were all going to die; we were all, every one of us, right there and then, dying.

Usually, I kept that chain of thought tucked tight inside my chest, where it couldn't do much damage except maybe cause a heart attack, which seemed unlikely. I was fit. That day, when I saw this woman in the parking lot, I nearly panicked. It felt primal, beyond words; I needed something I did not have. And also, I needed to cover her mouth with my mouth and wrestle our clothes off. That seemed like it would help. It felt urgent and obviously right.

We stood there in the parking lot, the Other Woman leaning on her Jeep's tailgate and me clutching my liquor, and she lit a cigarette; my god, that's suicide. Why? She told me she had been depressed recently, or something, that her life had been a waste of time maybe, that she had not done anything worthwhile (unless you count the kids, and they do count, of course they do) and now it was probably too late. She may have choked back a tear. I'm not sure because I was thinking too much about her mouth, which from time to time let a stream of smoke out, which did not stop me from wanting to kiss her.

"I feel so alone, some days, I can't stand it," she said, biting her lip. And I thought, wow. Look at that lip.

Then this happened: after we talked for a minute, she touched my arm. Right there on my skin. It was the arm holding the wine box, I think. She looked into my eyes. I mean, deep into my eyes. My eyes are like green-brown flowers; I offered her the flowers. I looked at her. She said, "I'm so glad to see you." And, oh yes, I knew what that meant.

It meant it didn't matter that she was married. To a man. With two (or was it three?) teenaged daughters. Or that she was a very conservative Christian woman who sometimes taught Sunday school. When that old friend touched my arm, I knew: We were gonna do it. Weren't we?

"Come by the cabin tonight," I told my old friend. "If you want." Then I smiled as fetching a smile as I could muster and I said, "Just come right in. Door's always open."

"Maybe," she said as she crushed her cigarette. "Okay." And as she slipped into her car, she said, "Hang in there."

That night, the Girls wandered off early to pass out in bed, and I found myself pacing the cottage floors, alone—unless you count Colby, which you should. We were anxious. Colby followed me around, panting. He was a Portuguese water dog, all fluffy and black except for the gray that had recently invaded his snout and ears. How strange to have loved a creature from birth to old age, the whole biological arc in a swift pass of years. I petted his head. I swept back my own graying blonde hair. Through the window I saw the lake and the moon, and in the glass, my reflection. I wondered if—no, I didn't wonder; I knew, I knew—she would come. We were going to do it. I couldn't remember the last time this had happened for me, with anyone—the panting anticipation of new love, new sex, yes that of course but also, to be honest, the chance to be so intimate with anyone, to connect with a body in just the way my old friend and I surely needed. And we needed it, that was clear. It was almost like a sacred and ordained truth that we could and should touch the places words, however well chosen, don't reach. We would either have to fuck or maybe, *maybe*, read each other poetry, but odds were on the body, I thought.

As a side note, I'll betray almost everyone I know and confess one of the darker points Girls' Week revealed, and because it betrays nearly everyone I know it will surprise almost no one: sex itself, as a thing to do, had become one of life's great disappointments. A plurality of my friends at the time insisted on this as a life cycle fact—after reaching a busy peak not long after high school, adult humans do not have sex except to procreate. Other points of view: it's nice to keep your husband happy; it's hard to find time; it's a relief to not do it because sex is work. Feeling anything, really, is work. What grown-ups do is watch porn. Bottoms up! The Girls laughed and drank. We didn't have many secrets, us Girls, but it was best not to press talk of this further, because the truth beneath all this can blow up your life. I had felt a kind of time bomb in my own life and had tried valiantly to restrain it. The bomb had slipped its leash. I paced. Then I sat by the cabin door for a spell, waiting. Then I checked to be sure the door was unlocked, which it was. Eventually, I went to bed.

In the morning, I woke to loon song rising from the water, passing through the cabin. For a moment that clear light buoyed me, and all was as it always had been and always would be and it was perfect. The one true place. Then I remembered. Colby lay on his own little bed on the floor, looking up at me. I couldn't quite make myself look back. The adrenaline and the booze and maybe a little hit of pot I may have taken with the Girls the night before had crept gently out of my system and my body felt more or less normal. I glanced around to confirm that I was alone, and that the world was in order, which it more or less was, and then I thought: "Oh dear god. What was I *thinking*?" I sat up and sighed. Colby sat up and wagged his tail, relieved to see that the crisis, whatever it was, had passed. But he was wrong on that one. This is what separates dogs from humans, tails and disgusting dietary interests aside; dogs are in a persistent enlightened state of "now" but people—or let's just say, I—could worry the past and the future half to death, and my troubles, I knew, had only started.

In hindsight, the sudden fixation I had on getting my old friend into bed was like the stab I sometimes feel in my throat when I'm about to get a bad cold. There is nothing to do at that point; the stab announces the process has begun. Similarly, it seems a catastrophe was incubating in the middle of my life, and a sudden stab announced it. Something was wrong. I felt neglected and sad and, left untended much longer, the pain I was feeling might cause me to do something embarrassing at least. At worst, such pain might be dangerous.

Curiously, that's exactly how I came to see the whole country, once I got out there; things do fall apart. We fight hard against it, but change is relentless, and change accelerated by what economists call "creative disruption" had really scrambled things up in the world as many of us had known it, or believed it to be. The country I saw when I went out to see it was watching itself change, and was just as confused as I was about changing and just as uncertain that survival was assured. On the road home from Girls' Week, what had seemed so illuminated on my way west looked frankly ruined, drained of its potential. I stopped for the night at a dog-friendly hotel in a sad-sack commercial strip in a very small city near Cleveland. The hotel was large, four stories with a full floor of meeting and banquet rooms, and it was dreary, about exactly as old as I was and in bad need of renovation. It was just about empty too. The hotel was limping along, and the steak house across the way had boards on its windows; high weeds had sprouted in its vast, vacant parking lot. The Quality Inn down the road was also shuttered, though a sign in the window promised it would reopen on a date that had passed. This did not look like the world I had grown up in. It didn't even look like the world I saw a week before. It was all so forlorn and desperate and in need of loving. A five-thousand-mile drive with my dog through this landscape was suddenly the best idea I had ever had.

Jessica and I lived most of the time in a faded Victorian village outside Saratoga Springs, New York. I had lived there when we met, and Jess lived in New York City. We had been unwilling to fully commit to either place when we got together, so we had managed to inhabit both somehow, and become a scrappy version of the multihomed elites, mainly through the tenacity of not letting go. Saratoga had a fabled racetrack and a strong tourist economy that kept it growing and lifted all the towns around it too, including our little town, and so we lived in a sweet, comfortable bubble in which it was possible to ignore the larger world's troubles, including plenty of addiction and poverty in our midst, hidden in plain sight. Ours was objectively a nice life in a nice place where, in theory, anyone could be happy. It was a boat worth not rocking. When I arrived home from Girls' Week, I flopped on the couch and started rubbing Jessica's feet before she even asked me to. "I figured out how to use my sabbatical," I said.

We were both college professors at small colleges, and I had scored a sabbatical for the coming year during which I was supposed to study social media's impact on journalism. It was something I could do anywhere; I just needed a subject to focus on, something to tweet and blog and whatnot about. I didn't really care to do all that, but what wouldn't I do to take a break from my job? As I rubbed Jessica's feet I told her I was going to take a long drive to as many of the most depressed and unappealing places I could get to, and study them. "All those sad little places that hardly anyone knows a thing about, you know what I mean? Why are those places even there? Like, Indianapolis. Right?" (I searched her eyes; they shot back, "Right, right. Of course: right. Keep rubbing.") "What's the deal with Indianapolis, Cleveland, and also, too, like what about all the little towns that grew up in the thrall of westward expansion and now have no reason to exist? What about those places?" I took a breath. I wanted to go feel their pain, I said. I wanted to know how they might begin to feel alive again. I was thinking maybe I would get a little trailer and take Colby; we would drive off and go away for a really long time.

"Oh, yes! Yes, you should do that," Jessica said enthusiastically. "It's exactly what you should do." She frankly could not believe I had not thought of this sooner.

"You know what I think," I told her. "I think the whole country is in the midst of a midlife crisis."

"Ooh, exactly," she said, and she shifted to offer me the other foot to rub. "That's why you'd be so good at this. You're sympathetic. Get a trailer. Go-go-go."

If I didn't know better, I would have called her enthusiasm suspect. But Jessica understood the need to travel. She was always up for an adventure, though unlike me and my family's midwestern roots, her parents uprooted from Europe and her adventures tended to go in that direction. The journey I was called to take would have felt like death to her, I'm sure, but that was no reason for me not to go. And anyhow, she must have needed a break too. Before the sudden crisis of my unconsummated adulterous affair with someone who could have been my sister (something about which Jessica did not know, except that, really, she did know; she was a smart woman and I was rubbing her feet without being asked), I had already become hard to live with—my hormonal mood swings had been disturbing our peace for at least a year, and Jessica had her own worries, her own work to focus on, and it might have been nice to have some time alone with all the things that were not me that she also cared about.

So I told Jessica I was leaving and she said okay, because maybe she was relieved to be alone for a while, or maybe she wanted a chance to cheat on me too. I hadn't really thought about that. Maybe, though, and this is likely, she just wanted me to be happy. I had not been very happy lately, she knew. I needed to face the middle of things; I needed to go off with my dog and reflect. And, as a result of all this, I also needed a trailer.

The trailer had to be light enough to tow with my Toyota, and small enough to be inconspicuous because I was really not a fan of the whole RV scene; it brought to mind family vacation disasters I had heard tales of, and wheeled "campers" larger than most suburban homes. Good things were happening in the trailer world, though. It was scaling down. My research turned up a sweet little thing called a Scamp, a thirteen-foot-long fiberglass trailer that weighed less than a thousand pounds with a kitchenette inside and a table that flipped into a bed. The model I liked also had a tiny bathroom. A private toilet somehow seemed essential to my safety on the road. I was firm on that.

The perfect secondhand Scamp turned up in Vermont. Jessica, Colby, and I went to check it out. The Scamp owner's name was Warren and he and his wife were both lean and strong and blond and nubile, and they had just had a baby and couldn't imagine ever camping all crammed into a little pod again.

Warren seemed delighted at the idea of selling his beloved trailer to someone with an epic journey in mind and especially to someone whose partner was another woman. Jessica and I stood clumped behind Warren in the trailer's small square interior as he demonstrated how to convert the table into a bed. He did this, yanking out the metal leg with a firm jolt, then dropping the flat tabletop onto the little ledges of the seats it hung between and—voila!—bed. The seat cushions, laid out, became a mattress. Then he said, "It's comfy, you'll see. Go ahead. Both of you get up there. You can bounce all around on that bed and the trailer won't rock or shake or anything. Go ahead. Get on up there." He was standing in the pod with us, hugging himself, rocking on his heels and smiling. We shuffled around in that square space designed for approximately one-and-a-half human beings, not three of them, until finally Jessica and I had navigated around Warren and were able to sit on the edge of the foam bed and look at each other. We bounced a little bit and swayed.

"Go ahead!" Warren said. "Lay down! Bounce away!"

This suggestion was awkward for the obvious reasons. But also it caused us to freeze with what I would call disappointment, though perhaps it was fear, and the awareness of that might even have provoked a fight had we been there alone. My body stiffened in a too-familiar way. There would be no bouncing. We could blame my shifting moods, or my near-fifty body putting on weight; we could say life had gotten busy, but the truth, as usual, was more complicated. The bounce had gone out of our life almost altogether, and the resulting problem was really inconvenient. It kept returning my mind, at least, to what was actually wrong. That day we shifted our weight awkwardly on the Scamp bed as on any other bed we had visited for so long, unable to connect, but promising to work it out; then not working it out; then blaming middle age. I lay there in the Scamp and remembered the friend I had seen in the parking lot in Wisconsin. My body tightened even more.

Had we given it a shot that day we would have found that the trailer was hardly steady at all, that it rocked jauntily with the slightest whiff of any unconventional motion back there in the hollow of the egg. At least, that's what I learned later, in October, when Colby had begun sleeping on the bed with me and was having those dreams where his legs pumped and his withers quivered and little yips escaped his fuzzy, chuffing, rabbit-chasing snout. When that happened at places like the state park in Carbondale, Illinois, or some Kentucky KOA, I could only hope that no one out there in the darkened campground had noticed the rocking or, if they had, that they would not judge me in the morning when I emerged from the trailer with only my dog.

In any case, back in Warren's driveway, Jessica and I had grudgingly lain back on the bed in almost the exact same motionless way in which we had tried out mattresses at chain mattress stores under the creepy gaze of salesmen—a mattress-testing method so stressful that we had not once but twice bought the completely wrong thing and finally just had to live with it.

The instant we lay back on that bed in the trailer, Warren's wife popped the infant-slung upper half of her body through the trailer's door and said to her husband, "Have you cleaned out the fridge?" Jessica and I shot up and she and I and Warren all looked at the wife as if we had been caught playing doctor. "Sure," Warren said, and he opened the little fridge beneath the stovetop to prove that it was clean, releasing a stench of rotten eggs and revealing two energy bars inside. He unwrapped one, bit it, and offered it to me. "Still good, look at that!" he said.

I towed the trailer home and began planning. The map of this country is spread thick with places that sprang up practically all at once in the nineteenth century, then grew old, then had been more or less abandoned, and now had endless causes for worry. It would be absolutely impossible to see them all. I sat staring at the map for hours trying to plan and then I would panic. I could spend an entire year in Mississippi and still not come close to understanding it; forget about seeing the whole country.

In the end I settled on a plan to dash out along the corridors of industrialization—by which I mean, I would begin with the Erie Canal, then I would cross the Rust Belt, reach the Mississippi River, and shout "tag" somewhere in Missouri, which was the middle of the middle, the heart of it all. Then I would turn around; I would dip down to find a mystifying and desperate place or two in Appalachia, grapple with the profound mystique of coal. I would leave for this journey at the end of summer; I planned to return for the holidays.

I knew the models for this kind of adventure. William Least Heat-Moon wandered the country on back roads in a van; John Steinbeck and his dog Charley looped it in a camper. And guess what? Those guys found endless fonts of delight and optimism. Folksy American dreamers, dreaming. They found the country's goodness to be infectious. I admired Steinbeck's ability to wax eloquent about the simplest things—he was moved by the miracle of hot soup dispensers, feeding travelers in the shiny new service plazas of the country's shiny new interstate highway system, all of which he found incredible in 1960. Those were heady and glorious days in America; Steinbeck called the soup machines "the height of some kind of civilization," the peak of a certain beauty we were prone to lose, and he rode the hot-soup vibes like maybe he had been smoking something, except that also I think he was right. That was the moment, the prime of some kind of life for some kinds of people. Since then, things had changed.

The world fifty years after Steinbeck's postwar expansionary romp had turned "postindustrial," a reversal of the momentum that had reached its peak—the vertex of its parabola, as I like to say. The prosperity that was blooming in his day had been played out and the wreckage in its wake was sometimes surreal. We had built a country to last, not to fall apart. One set of bookends: our pop culture in 1962 could barely imagine recreational drug use; by now, addiction is a plague. Illicit drug deaths have become so common they are pulling the average life expectancy down. The drug of the moment as I planned this trip was methamphetamine, all manic and ragey. It started popping up on me everywhere. Researching where I might camp in Missouri, for example, I learned that Missouri led the United States in police seizures of methamphetamine labs. I had been only vaguely aware of the meth epidemic before I started plotting; I had, for example, witnessed a phenomenon around Saratoga known as "meth mouth." Here and there I had seen gaunt-faced young people with mouths full of alarmingly bad teeth. It can come from smoking the drug. I tucked that revelation away and tried not to think about it, or let the subculture of addiction drag me down. But then for some reason meth began inserting itself into all my web searches; it started to haunt me. It would not be ignored. Thousands of meth labs were being scouted out and dismantled in the country at that time, and in the middle of the country it was the worst. This was just a moment before the shift toward heroin, the ultimate pain-numbing high. One scourge passes and another rises up and this seems likely to continue until we heal what's really ailing us. But before heroin, it was methamphetamine in the headlines, and in Missouri it seemed there was a meth lab in a basement on literally every block, and those were just the ones they had found, and that was just Missouri.

"Oh, Lori," Jessica said over my shoulder as I pondered the contours of the Ozarks, strange land of z and k. "Don't camp near any meth labs."

"I'll do my very best," I said sweetly, "to have no contact with meth."

I set a loose course and left the rest to fate, and in late August, I gave Jessica a long hug good-bye. At the end of summer we had always returned together to the city, to our jobs. This time she left and I stayed, and as she hugged me before she left she said, "You're my life," and kissed my cheek. "Come home to me."

"I will do my very best," I said sweetly, "to come home."

I packed my trailer with everything from soap to spaghetti and one great, big cupcake-shaped dog treat for Colby; we would leave the day before his fourteenth birthday.

But of course, on the morning we planned to go, the trailer lights did not work. I cursed the whole world viciously. I won't pretend I didn't. My disappointments in that time would so quickly turn to rage. I felt the weird familiar heat spread out from a place beneath my spine, pearls of sweat rising on my neck; my vision narrowed, and I sat down on the driveway and cried. We hadn't even left and already, I was crying. I dragged the trailer to a U-Haul dealer, using hand signals out my window all the way. I pulled up to the garage and I wept and pleaded and jabbed my finger at the wiring harness on the offending trailer lights as Colby looked on, panting. In half a minute the U-Haul guy fixed what I had done wrong, which was something too simple to admit in writing. The next morning, a day late, Colby and I hit the road.

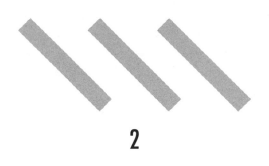

2

The Ditch

We had been on the road for almost ten whole minutes when I slammed on the brakes, cut the wheel hard, and learned really fast how much momentum a small trailer can generate. But there was this amazing long line of old high-voltage electric power towers running alongside us. They gobsmacked me, out in the fields, one steel Herculean skeleton after another strung thick with wild grapevines, raising its fists, holding up cables that ran all the way on to forever.

These were no ordinary power towers. They were art; they were a welding of beauty and industry, the product of exuberant expansion, and they looked old, like the original power towers of our industrial age when it was still new and exciting. This was exactly the sort of thing I wanted to see: artifacts. Points along the way to our difficult, postindustrial now. Our national state of perimenopause. Moments of: "We had such dreams, what happened?" The steel towers stood there in rusted oblivion, as if they mattered just as much now as the day they were built even if the world of today looked right through them.

When I left home moments before, I was singing. A Grateful Dead song had shown up on the radio to see us off. Wind blew through my hair, and Colby was sitting up and smiling as if he were a young pup, graying ears fluttering around his fuzzy black face. He was looking ahead and panting because he was excited, because he thought we were going to the pond for a walk. That's where we usually went on sunny mornings. This time was different; this time we were going far away to find difficult places where we would cling to each other in loneliness and fear. We would cry; god forbid, we might even wet the bed. Or, he might. But he didn't know this yet. He was watching for the pond. Within minutes, I spotted the towers, which had been there long before I was born and had stood along that road near my home for all the years I had lived there, but I had now seen them, really seen them, for the first time. So I stopped.

I left the car engine running to give Colby some air and I walked across the road with my camera. Before I could get closer to the towers, I was distracted yet again, this time by sounds in a barnyard. It sounded like someone was raising randy monkeys. I decided I better document this too, so I whipped out my digital recorder and marched off in search of monkeys but found, instead, big ugly birds. Colby watched from the back seat, nose pressed against the window. The farmer whose land I had pulled over onto, a portly old man in overalls with a walrus mustache and hearing aids in both ears, limped over from the barn. He asked what I was doing.

I said I was on an epic journey with a trailer and my very old dog, exploring American places that had lost their original purpose or were growing worn with age, and I was wondering how all these old, failing, postindustrial places ever came to be and how they might revive themselves now that they were ruined and irrelevant, and also, since I had found one, I was admiring small farms. I did not mention my disastrous brush with adultery in Wisconsin and I passed right over the hot flashes but perhaps he could see all this in my eyes.

"Oh!" he said, louder than necessary. "How far ya been?"

"About seven miles."

The man, whose name was Dick, did not hesitate. He got right into the spirit of the thing, offering up a tale of two cemeteries just down the road. Every place has a story and generally people want their stories to be heard but normally no one asks. Road trippers ask. It's the whole point. Dick said a soldier from the War of 1812 was buried in one graveyard up the road, which I could see from where we stood, and his buddy was buried in the graveyard across the way, and so the soldiers' ghosts crossed back and forth at night to find each other and had been doing that for two hundred years. Beyond that was a spot called Blue Corners that had once been the busiest wagon stop on a north-south road to the Adirondacks. That road was still there and paved now but unlined and really almost didn't exist, certainly not as a well-traveled thoroughfare, and the churches and hotel that had once graced Blue Corners were utterly gone; not even foundations were left, not a trace. A plaque marked where they had once stood. More ghosts. I had the feeling Dick could keep going with historic references step by step up that whole road, across the state, all the way to Canada, even if not a stick of what he could see existed anymore. The birds that sounded like monkeys, by the way, were guinea fowl.

As Dick told me all this, his wife came down from the field on an ATV and joined us. Her name was Mary. She was covered in mud and not as chatty as her husband. In my experience, women encountered on road trips seldom are. Women encountered on road trips always seem busy working at this or that while men, especially older men, seem to spend their days drinking coffee and they will talk at you as if they have saved up this talk all their lives.

Mary wondered who I was and why I had stopped to talk to her husband in the middle of a work day. I told her about my epic journey through America with my trailer and my very old dog as she squinted, perhaps searching for a reason to care, and when I finished, she said, "Where did you start this epic journey?"

"Ballston Spa," I said merrily.

She nodded. Confirmed nut: I had been traveling for about ten minutes.

"You're doing all this with just you?" she asked, sounding as if such a thing was not possible. Maybe it wasn't. I hadn't considered it but she seemed pretty sure.

"Just me, my dog, and a paintball gun," I told her. The woman who cuts my hair had suggested the paintball gun. It was an intimidating but nonlethal self-defense option that I could legally carry across state lines. I didn't bring one but told Mary I had because clearly a lone woman needed something for safety, and I hoped to repair my image with her. I wanted her blessing; it mattered for some reason.

"And how is it you have so much time to travel?" she asked. Which really cut through all the bullshit. The question contained the problem everywhere with everything: some people had time to travel because they still lived in the shrinking world of aspirations, the world of growing bigger and better, not of scarier and worse; they had good jobs, or lots of money. Others had time on their hands because their worlds had fallen apart and they had nothing to do, or nothing to lose; they could not find good jobs in a completely disrupted economy. I felt a bit of all those things but was unarguably privileged when it came to my job. Most people did not have lives or jobs that allowed them time to drive around and consider their plight. Like Mary. Mary's face, while not unkind, said she would be right there working each day until she died and there would be no sabbatical, ever, though she would take my place in that trailer in a heartbeat if she could. Not because she wanted to get out there and see it all so much as she wanted to get out. Her eyes narrowed; she said her daughter wanted to teach kindergarten, had all kinds of college education, but had not found a job so she was living back home, helping on the farm, and indeed, up on the hill behind Dick and Mary's barn, I could see a dark, coat-bundled figure trundling about, doing something with a small cow, also known (Mary reminded me) as a calf. Times were tough even for teachers, she said. "Whoever thought that could happen?" She eyeballed me. "Right . . . professor?" she added.

"Well, professor is kind of just a word we use," I said and looked away from her.

The towers I had stopped to see were like a line of steel ghosts marching across the land, rattling their cables like chains. I suspect they were built in Franklin Roosevelt's rural electrification program in the 1930s, which was in fact the decade that the rural parts of Saratoga County, New York, became electrified. This is all part of the ongoing drama of labor and industry, and the rise and fall of fortunes that echoed through centuries with the result, in this moment, of Mary's daughter being stuck working on her parents' farm. All the parts of the story are connected; the parts march on like the towers, a succession of events along a road that only Dick can still see. I wanted the vision. Here is the story in part.

Electric towers in Charlton, New York

The power-tower drama is related to what is known as the War of the Currents. Choosing AC over DC as this country's dominant type of electrical power set us all on a course that hardly anyone thinks about anymore; what we see is all there ever was, we often think, but everything we see involved choices, and even the light switch has a story. Direct current, or DC, can't be transported far from its generation source but AC can be; Thomas Edison was the DC guy and when DC current dominated, civilization clustered around power generators. DC was anti-sprawl electricity. DC meant building everything around its own big battery, in effect. AC, or alternating current, can travel long distances over cables. AC transmission was developed by Nikola Tesla and backed by George Westinghouse, and it won this battle; around 1890, Westinghouse defeated Edison in the War of the Currents (I picture them slashing at each other with light sabers, like in *Star Wars*), factories and homes were wired accordingly, and AC power was ready to roll out across the land. With AC, industry—factories and mills—could locate anywhere; work didn't have to sit next to a power source like a generator, or a waterfall (nature's generator). Work spread out. Houses sprouted in the hinterlands because creature comforts were no longer tied to cities. Towers holding cables meant spreading the light and gave us the world-shaping power to plug in a lamp nearly anywhere.

By 1930, though, few such cable-strung towers had actually been built. Only one in ten farms had electricity. The countryside was still dark and thinly populated. Power companies couldn't see the profit in stretching lines out into the sticks where no one lived; who would they sell the power *to*?

They had the equation backward. Franklin Roosevelt, as a Depression-era, infrastructure-building president, created the Rural Electrification Agency and with that, the power lines stretched into the country. Suddenly, boom: the population followed. And once everyone out there had power, they wanted so much more than light bulbs. They wanted electrified stuff—refrigerators, radios, waffle irons, washing machines—and so GE and Westinghouse invented new electric stuff and marketed the stuff as modern and luxurious, all for the purpose of selling more power. The stuff itself—electric blankets, electric knives, electric curling irons, electric razors, electric clocks—all these crazy good gadgets that had worked perfectly well before they were electrified were now getting "invented" so that the electric companies could sell more power. The stuff didn't make the real money; the jackpot was in powering the stuff. Generating electricity also meant a fortune for coal miners, whose quarry was suddenly in far greater demand, but that's getting a few months ahead of myself. What I saw on day one of my trip was that AC power and a government infrastructure program enabled a particular type of growth in our country, and so we grew up along those power lines, and now here we are.

Mary and Dick drifted off back to work as I photographed the old steel towers, the guinea fowl, the two abandoned graveyards in the nearby weeds, and also their enormous Brown Swiss cow, Cookie Monster, whose drool resembled clear laundry detergent streaming from a leather purse. Then I got back into my idling car, where Colby welcomed me and set his eyes forward, looking for signs of the pond.

That day's actual destination was a campground in St. Johnsville on the Erie Canal. If I was on a journey to places that sprung up in earnest and then fell apart, I picked the right place to start. Colby and I entered the New York State Thruway in the old dead mill and factory city of Amsterdam. The road through Amsterdam is like a shoreline awash in mill shells. Empty brick buildings with high windows and smokeless stacks stand in weed lots in that city that for generations kept reinventing itself as a place that made stuff, until it stopped. That was in the 1960s, not long before GE shut down most of its manufacturing, in places like Bridgeport and Schenectady. Postwar industrial glory began to wind down all at once in that era, and everywhere you looked, this is what was left behind.

Our route crisscrossed the Mohawk Valley, a place littered with seriously old dead mills that had once run on waterfalls. All along the road to St. Johnsville, this is what there was: hollow industrial mountains, buildings of brick and high windows that had been mined for all they were worth and then left, empty, in Canajoharie, in Gloversville, in old towns that continued to exist but in dreadful disarray. These places, and nearly all of New York State's major cities—Schenectady, Amsterdam, Utica, Syracuse, Rochester, Buffalo—are strung like gritty beads on the long thread of the Erie Canal. It was the canal, a thing I had not thought much about, ever, that caused all this to grow up. Then it had grown old. Then the whole canal age died an unthinkable death when someone thought "trains!" and made that happen. These places held on for a time but had not done much to reinvent themselves as the world changed and they had by now been left, most of them, to return to the dust from which they came. And because the Thruway was built alongside the canal, driving across New York means driving through the canal's 363-mile industrial graveyard.

I took the exit for Canajoharie, where an abandoned Beechnut factory was one of the biggest empty shells in the entire Mohawk Valley. Beechnut arrived on the Erie Canal in 1891. It made candy and coffee and condensed milk and stuff for 120 years. Two years before the day I passed it with Colby and our Scamp, the wave of loss had come and dragged that industrial giant out to sea. Beechnut had moved to Florida.

My god, Florida. Here was a truth of what Walter Mondale, in 1984, became the first to call the Rust Belt—the land of northern industry, collapsing: Manufacturing jobs that had for so long made the Northeast rich had fled south, then overseas, where labor was cheaper. The very car I was driving was assembled in Kentucky, not Detroit; its parts were made in Japan. I drove by the empty Beechnut plant that day as I had many times before, but instead of thinking, "Hey, what's that big old thing?" this time I knew: it was the ruins of a plant that had gone to Florida in a sick evolution that does not mean survival of the fittest so much as it means survival of those most willing to be poor. Ask Mary.

I did better research later and learned that, actually, in 2011 Beechnut had relocated not to *Florida*-Florida, but to Florida, New York, a Mohawk Valley town just twenty miles down the road from its original home. Okay. Not a total abandonment; I'm quick to grief. But still! Change is hard. The new plant in Florida is automated; many once good manufacturing jobs are gone, and the vacant old Canajoharie Beechnut plant sat asbestos-laden and mold-infested with a large, improbable For Lease sign up on its high white wall. Those who see it every day are reminded that something once central to life in this place is gone, and nothing has replaced it.

St. Johnsville is ten miles away from Canajoharie, on the east side of the Mohawk River, which is entwined with the Erie Canal from around

Waterford, very near its start. Colby and I pulled into the St. Johnsville Marina, a small public campground with a handful of RV sites and a dock on the canal. The campground occupies a strip of grass between the canal and some working CSX railroad tracks, and the Thruway hums beyond the trees, so that I had come to camp inside a perfect slice of American transit history: canal, then rail, then interstate, one replacing the other in time. When I shut the car engine, Colby stood up behind me and put his paws on the console between the front seats and he panted right into my ear. He saw the water. Things made sense again.

The marina and campground were run by a guy named Bernie, whose office was decorated in mounted fish and fish heads and photos of men holding up big fish they had caught. A pack of white-haired men joined Bernie daily in the back room, where they played low-stakes poker and mocked each other for sport. There was a Keep Out sign over the door to the back room. It was like a tree fort for old guys.

I've always enjoyed the company of old men, mainly for the reasons I like all kinds of older things—the stories they tell, the history in them— but also because so many have this habit of acting like big grumps and pretending it's funny. They get away with all kinds of bad behavior. Grumpy old age is a tool in the big box of flirting tools for men, one they can put to shameless use just when the box is looking pretty darn empty. But no: The box is never empty. There is no man-opause.

The old men of St. Johnsville were abundant, which was fun if you like flirting with old codgers, but is also a symptom of a dying place: young people leave. Old folks stay. They retire, their nests empty out, they live in their empty nests as long as they can, then they sell the nest and buy as big an RV as they can afford and head to Florida. Actual Florida. In summer, they come home and live at the marina. The old men playing cards or lounging by their trailers had become living shades of the town itself, having been young and vital when the town was younger and more vital. St. Johnsville once had an opera house; it once had neat sidewalks and a place that built pianos and a shop that made cigars and pretty much a shop for everything else you might need but by now there was only a dollar store and a pharmacy. Nearly everything else in St. Johnsville was gone, and the old men were also nearly gone or on their way to leaving. The gas pumps in the center of town bustled, yes, but the diner across the way was no longer serving. Ever. Empty storefronts were boarded up or decorated solely by faded, bent signs that said: "Coming Soon . . ." and named things, but these things were more wishful than true, and "soon" had meant soon a long time ago. The men at the marina recalled working at the Beechnut plant fondly as if its loss had been merely inevitable, not tragic. They grew old; it grew old. We'll all die, one day. All is already lost. Deal the cards. But I had never really looked close enough to understand what was happening. These little towns we all called "dumps" where I come from were not dumps at all; they were old guys playing solitaire. They contained complex stories.

The temperature had nearly reached 90 outside, very hot for September in New York. I chose to camp near the canal, but the sites by the water weren't shaded. Bernie tried to warn me about the heat but he also told me about fish as long as his arm that often clustered near a storm runoff grate near one campsite and if I set up there I could stand right on the shoreline and catch those fish on a worm. This somehow mattered to me more than anything. I had a fishing pole in my car and I had thought of using it as a way of bonding with America as I traveled and there I was on my very first day about to do it. So I camped in the blazing sun and bought worms.

The canal's banks were rocky and steep and Colby ran up to the edge and paced, panting. He wanted a drink of that slow-churning, murky canal but couldn't get at it. I stood alongside him but didn't see a clear path down the bank. I did, however, see a clutch of fish near the surface of the water, each one indeed about as fat and long as Bernie's arm and floating lazy just a foot from shore. I left Colby and dashed to the car to get my pole, baited it with a big nightcrawler, and chucked the tasty mess into the water, creating a splash that instantly scared the huge fish into the darker depths of the canal and ushered in a spell of utter fishlessness that would last me almost until Kentucky.

After neither of us managed to connect with the canal in some meaningful way, Colby and I gave up and turned back to camp. I set up chairs while Colby whined and drained his water bowl, then wandered off to find shade, flopping in despair beneath the unoccupied RV parked next to our site. I did my best to set up the sweet-yet-complicated awning attached to

Erie Canal at St. Johnsburg

the side of the Scamp, giving our spot a finished look and also making
shade for Colby, who watched from his shelter beneath the RV and didn't
move. Distress crept over his milky old eyes. Nothing I was doing was familiar; the canal was not the pond. A puce sunset began scalding the water
and the CSX tracks, which glinted sharply. I faced my camp chair to the
canal and watched.

 Here's the thing about the Erie Canal: it's not just a ditch. It was in its
day an absolutely miraculous 363-mile-long waterway that linked Albany
to Buffalo and thus the Great Lakes with New York Harbor and thus,
frankly, the Midwest (which was known simply as "The West" back in
1825) to Europe. It is also just about the least sexy historical interest one
can cultivate, second only to costumed military reenactments, including
medieval jousting events. Not sexy, no, but bear in mind that many things
become more appealing when given half a chance. People too. I used to

wear clothes two sizes too large for my trim thirty-year-old body and I had gone through a series of unfortunate haircuts over the years, but these things could be seen past; Jessica saw the good in me when we met and took charge of my wardrobe and I was transformed. Likewise, I saw a nearly abandoned preindustrial ditch and, with a mere micro-dose of historical knowledge, understood this masterpiece to be one of the wonders of the world. It was not something I had ever taken seriously, until I really looked. Then I fell in love.

The problem is, we've sort of infantilized what we should understand as a primary driver of America's destiny. Look up the Erie Canal at any library and you will find yourself directed to the children's section. I think it's because of the song. Before my trip with Colby, pretty much my entire canal education consisted of memorizing the lyrics to the Erie Canal song, which I learned one afternoon in third grade. Thomas Allen wrote it in 1905. Pete Seeger sang it a lot, if that rings any bells. Here are the essential lyrics:

> I got a mule and her name is Sal
> Fifteen years on the Erie Canal
> She's a good old worker and a good old pal
> Fifteen years on the Erie Canal
> . . . .
> And you'll always know your neighbor
> And you'll always know your pal
> If you've ever navigated on the Erie Canal

The song—and the fact that canal boats and mules look great in shoebox dioramas—makes the canal ideal for third-grade history lessons. But this mule fixation buries the staggering genius of the thing. It was dreamed up by men who studied the canals in Europe, then came back to New York and eyeballed the Mohawk Valley wilderness, then scratched their whiskers and said, "Well yes, why not." Just clearing 363 miles of vine-choked forests for the towpaths was a feat in 1817, when they started. They didn't have crosscut saws, much less chain saws. They used axes. They pulled whole trees up from the ground, roots and all. This makes my knees weak. It takes me nearly a full day to trim my forsythia bush with hand tools; I can't comprehend building a canal that way.

Making this ditch was memorable enough, but that was just the start of the story. This singular achievement launched our country into its future. Before the canal, anything beyond the Allegheny Mountains was a wilderness. The Alleghenies are a long ridge from Pennsylvania down to Virginia. They are part of the Appalachian range, which runs the length of the East Coast. We barely notice the Alleghenies anymore, but before 1825, they stood between the settled East Coast and everything else, "The West," with no functioning path across. Anyone who wanted to see Ohio (before it was Ohio) had to bushwhack. The most-traveled route over the mountains was a dysfunctional muddy, potholed mess called the National Road on the Pennsylvania-Maryland border. The National Road is a thing I had never even heard of before I took this trip—almost certainly because it had no song attached to it. The whole American project was pinned down to the East Coast until the Erie Canal solved the problem, and then suddenly, in 1825, a smooth passage was opened for business, and the world changed.

The summer before I left for my trip with Colby, after I came home from Girls' Week, I decided to travel the canal by boat. Jessica and I would go to visit my family in Wisconsin in August, but we wanted some other more exciting summer adventure together; while the canal wasn't exactly like two weeks in Prague, it was certainly a venture into my state of mind and Jessica gamely resolved to go there with me. The Erie Canal had for some time been trying to stage a comeback as a boater's paradise. It's more or less a desolate string of dead factory towns, really, but brewpubs had been popping up along it with decks facing the water—the same water along which barges had been dragged by mules, and the mules were whipped by canal men, and the canal men cursed and drank and spat in the dirt. There is, today, family fun to be found in all of this, and a growing number of hotspots on the canal for history-geek tourists and beer connoisseurs. Jessica and I decided we would try it.

I wanted to kayak the canal, but 363 miles was more paddling than a spontaneous adventure allowed. I decided to try it in a motorboat, though that's not so easy either; there are strict speed limits on the canal and thirty-four locks, and so it takes at least a week of focused, all-day, nonstop boating to get from one end to the other. The canal is mostly a straight line of nine-foot-deep, forty-foot-wide, murky water, potentially a bit numbing, really—especially with me as skipper, singing the old canal dirge, shouting out peons to decrepit factories all the way. The canal shuts down in winter, and during the boating season the locks close at 6 p.m., so if you're on a more isolated stretch with nowhere to stop you can get stuck. You have to plan a canal trip. You have to prepare. You have to ask yourself why. Why do this? You have to have a good answer.

I didn't really have one, and anyhow, it turned out that a hundred-year flood had ripped through the Mohawk Valley that June—that very June of Girls' Week and lust and yearning. There had been a terrible storm. As I struggled with my mostly abstract losses, whole stretches of the Mohawk Valley had been actually flattened. The flood breached locks and swept an old woman to her death and leveled many homes in the small canal town of Fort Plain. Consequently, the entire eastern portion of the canal was closed to travel well into the summer. Boaters planning to navigate up to Lake Erie were stranded in marinas. It was a really big mess.

Ultimately, then, my dream ride along the length of the Erie Canal got mashed into one day during which we would take a little motorboat up through two locks and back again. And even for this scaled-back adventure, we were ill-prepared and we got a very late start because we spent the morning drinking coffee at our fancy little inn up in the hills. Still, we launched. And when we reached the gates of our first lock, I wasn't sure what to do. We couldn't seem to properly signal the lockkeeper that we were waiting below to enter; our tiny boat bobbed around in the strong current below the high cliff of this lock, trying not to crash into any rocks, until eventually the lockkeeper up above saw us. Then the enormous gates opened, but Jessica and I couldn't agree on a strategy to move through them into the stone chamber without being tossed around in the big waves and crashing into everything we passed. We argued as we fumbled in, and then we didn't know how to safely grab the ropes hanging from the old stone lock walls to keep us from thrashing around and slamming into those walls as the water rose. Jessica shouted at me. I shouted back that I was the skipper and shouting at me was forbidden. Then the steel gates slammed shut behind us with a resounding clap of mechanical thunder—a sound strikingly final, as if we had been sentenced to die in a dark and watery dungeon. We stopped speaking to each other altogether; a near silence fell briefly around us and we looked up at the top of the lock in terror. Then water started cascading down the rough, cold walls and filling the chamber, and I saw the improbability of our surviving this project. I tried to maneuver the boat into some safe-seeming position but the rising water rocked us, tossed our pretty motorboat against the stones; in my memory, sheets of cascading water spun us in circles and flooded down heavy across our crying faces, and oh how we cried, but the water drowned the echo of our screams, felt cold and mean and deadly, and damn near sunk us as we spun out of control, heading for a drain, feeling ourselves sucked mercilessly into this massive and very deadly infrastructure that was no child's diorama after all.

But of course that can't be right, because the water does not pour in through the walls of the locks on the Erie Canal; it rises gently and gradually from below, and the real sound of it is not the sound of a waterfall but more like a deep hum and some splashing. Still, it seemed like torrents; it felt like hell. Confusion and anger and a desperate sad certainty told me that in this coffin-shaped stone aquarium designed for barges, not motorboats, Jessica and I would die. Our bodies would not be found. Perhaps many had died before us. Sitting in stony silence in that outsized cell, I could not think of one kind thing to say to the person who had loved me for years, if imperfectly, and so my mind began to revise our history, meaning mine and Jessica's, and also the long history and even the very existence of a place called the United States of America: it may have been a good idea once, but in hindsight, probably, it had all been a cruel and often murderous mistake.

Then, at the top of the lock, another gate opened and let us out, and it was a sunny day again. Eternal hope! We motored with renewed curiosity to the next lock, the highest on the whole canal—the forty-foot Lock 17 at

Little Falls—and we rose almost as awkwardly and unhappily as we had in the first lock, though a little less fearful because now we were experienced. A moderately less-sullen silence suggested that Jess and I had reached a truce.

At the top of Lock 17, the day was again still beautiful. We spat out into the long lane of water with just exactly enough time to dock in Little Falls and sprint to the antique store/bakery in a quaintly renovated canal-side neighborhood, one of several spots where tourism had indeed taken hold, spawning spiffy waterfront facades in an otherwise sad little town full of vacant buildings. Jessica and I each got a foam to-go cup of watery coffee, then sprinted back to the boat and down to Lock 17 in time to experience the heinous yet fascinating lock process in reverse, descending, and then, half an hour later, we were very luckily allowed to pass back through the friendlier, smaller Lock 16 even though we had arrived there perilously close to 6 p.m., when the lockkeeper goes home, and then, finally, we returned to the marina dock and put the boat back on its trailer. We returned to our inn beside an eighteenth-century mill on a roaring waterfall and in the morning my car battery died in a place where it was not possible for a tow truck to get through to jump it. I stopped speaking to Jessica altogether, then, as if this were her fault.

But I don't blame her now. The canal exposed a discontent that I didn't want to think about, though it had been jarred loose back at the cabin and had been uncomfortably close to the surface since then. It had been easier to ignore before that summer, but now I saw the failing of everything around me. Nothing worked. My body hurt in places I had not previously noticed. Jessica and I also did not work in a way that mattered to me, and at night at our mill-side inn near the canal, we drank wine until it was time to go to bed, still smarting from our battle for control, I suppose; we went to sleep on our far sides of the mattress and in the isolation I had come to expect. I woke up thinking about discontent in America. As we packed up the car, I thought of how the past gets sanitized, the hard parts ignored, object history transformed, finally, into theme parks. The bowels of American industry and the awesome power that had spawned our nation's unparalleled supremacy were not easy places to be tourists, or certainly not tourists in pleasure boats, navigating canals built for continental transshipment. To see the truth is hard, but then again, nothing else is much worth seeing.

The canal had mattered so greatly for so long that once upon a time, let's say 1843, a kid standing on the lock wall above Little Falls watching the steel gates release a boatload of Amsterdam woolens, or watching those gates shut behind a barge of timber or grain, or watching his own spit drop forty feet and disappear in the foam on the churning green-brown water, must have felt as if he were standing at the height of some kind of civilization. It must have been inconceivable that this water would not forever be a force in the world. For the century of its prime, the canal was as obviously permanent as network television was when I was twelve, something about as likely to stop mattering as the continent itself was likely to break apart and slip out into the bitter ocean, then disappear.

(Note: actually, the continent is going to break apart and slip out into the bitter ocean. Probably in about 220 million years. I saw that in *National Geographic* in June 2013.)

Colby sulked in the shade under the neighboring RV on our first night in St. Johnsville while I hummed the Erie Canal song and thought about Jessica and how rarely we had fought about anything, ever, but something was changing, and on our short trip on the canal, I could not ignore it. In the past I had believed my discontent was all in my head, but what if there was something real that I needed and didn't have? I had to be careful with what I said; certain words might cause our contract to fall apart. Sometimes Jessica's blue eyes told me as much: "Don't say it. Don't leave."

The air cooled as the sun set. The water disappeared into the dark. I fired up the little barbecue I had brought along and cooked some turkey sausage and finally coaxed Colby out of his spot beneath the trailer by holding out his fourteenth birthday treat, which was shaped like a cupcake but felt like a brick. He was interested. He groaned and stretched and walked slowly over, snatched the treat from my hand, flopped on his camp blanket, and got busy chewing.

Colby's old age was showing. I had been dismissing the signs but that was getting harder to do. He had arthritis. His vision was cloudy and he had lost some hearing; sometimes, though, he would raise his head and listen to sounds that were not there. He had a fatty tumor the size of a cantaloupe on his right side that was, the vet promised, benign, but I swore it was growing and it would, I feared, overtake him one day, and that would be my best friend's strange end. At times he acted senile, which is one way to explain his standing in front of his own reflection and staring at it, though in truth I had lately been given to doing that myself. I would see my reflection and wonder who that was. Who knows what Colby wondered. About five times a day he forgot that he had already eaten dinner. He drooled more than ever. The previous spring he had suffered a ruthless bout of incontinence; he had begun letting loose whenever the spirit moved him as if he had forgotten that, in the special time after he barks but before we actually get outside, he is supposed to hold it. Poor Colby. He stood above his puddles on the floor, looking up confused at me. The people passing us as we limped along the sidewalks had no idea what sort of vital, alpha creature he had once been. Dammit. He had really been something once, boy.

That night in the trailer, I curled up with a book on the foam-cushion mattress and Colby did a circle and lay down on the tiny trailer's floor—a space that was about two feet by two feet. He looked around tentatively, then up at me, then must have decided it was okay because he put his head down for sleep. I read two pages of the book; it was a good book. A damn good book. I read another page. It was too good and written by a woman who was, like, thirty. I was nearly fifty. This pissed me off. I chucked the book against the bathroom door and it clattered to the ground near Colby's rump; Colby lifted his head and sniffed. I shut the light and went to sleep.

The next sound I heard was rain pelting fiberglass. It was like music, at first, but then I woke up enough to know. It was not music. The sky was so dark with rain that I had not realized it was morning for some time, but it was 7:20 a.m., and as I lay very still, praying to dear Jesus that the rain would not bring any thunder, a thunder crack loud enough to rattle the coffee pot woke Colby, and he raised his head. He was never deaf when the sound was thunder. He started panting.

Colby was terrified of thunder—and of anything cracking and loud that could be thunder. The once happy hollow where we lay turned

ominous, and I silently prayed it would be a one-boom storm. Then a
second crack of thunder wracked the trailer, which revealed itself all at
once to be a pathetic slip of plastic, and a very dumb place to have brought
an old panicky dog. Very dumb. Colby stood to pace but there was no
room to pace so he rammed his head into the walls, hyperventilating. I
lifted him onto the bed and held him, thinking I could comfort him, but it
was no use. The Scamp rocked and bounced to the rhythm of his panting.
He tore from my comfort-hug and turned frantic circles in my bedding
on the foam mattress. Circles are a warning; I realized what was about to
happen in the exact moment it became too late to stop him. Rain pelted,
thunder rumbled, the trailer shook, and Colby let loose a long stream of
urine on my bed.

I discovered as I tried to push the trailer door open that I had set up the
camper's awning at the wrong angle. The awning was now a big sagging
sack of wet. The sack blocked the door so that I could not open it more
than a couple inches. Colby fit his nose through the small crack I had
managed, and I snaked my arm out to shove the awning up just enough
to dump the water on myself; more water poured on me as I gradually
emerged from the trailer, pressing up, pushing out. As soon as it was physi-
cally possible, Colby squeezed out the door crack into the rain and mud
and ran directly to the car. He wanted, no doubt, to go home. Just, go
home. Just, admit we had made a mistake and return to the good life I had
taken for granted and was about to completely destroy. Please. Lesson
learned. We'll all be good and true and faithful forever if we survive this.
Please let us go home.

The car, at least, felt safe so we got inside it and I played the radio loud,
covering the sound of thunder and rain. We sat in the dark, soaked, shivering, suffused in wet-dog smell and panic. I sang along to classic rock song
after song after song. Singing soothed us. Eventually the storm slowed,
then passed; gradually the sky cleared. Colby calmed. We fell asleep in the
car and stayed there for hours.

A neighbor back home who worked for the National Park Service and was
a canal geek supreme told me that if I was going to St. Johnsville, I should
go see an old lock in a tiny and mainly unvisited park there that turned out

to be almost directly across the water from my campsite. He did not merely suggest this visit; he instructed with calm certainty, a glint in his wizened canal-knowing eyes. The canal had been enlarged and improved twice over two centuries; the stones in the dry weeds of this park, set back far away from any water now, are all that is left of one of the original 1825 canal's locks. In order to truly know the power and majesty of the Erie Canal, this old lock must be seen, for its stones are seminal and constitute a holy relic on the order of the saint's finger Jessica has told me is stored in a gilt box in a shrine in her favorite church in New York City. At the old lock I could lay my hands on the very same rocks once hacked square and stacked into a wall by laboring men determined to do great things—or, men hungry enough to risk malaria for doing brutal work, which may be its own kind of greatness. The stones in that lock—those very stones, not some other stone you might come across in nature—those square stones had opened the continent. They were the foundation of the whole long, sordid, and magnificent American expansion tale. Now they stood like old mares in a pasture, and maybe you could count on your fingers the number of people who knew or cared. My neighbor was right; I had to go there.

The city park and the old lock in it were at the end of a narrow street majestically named Dump Road. This road ran alongside the old towpath that was now a bike trail. There was no one biking on it that day. I found Dump Road and drove on it not quite a mile back along the water past a few tippy two-story houses and one strikingly grand brick house where maybe a barge captain or a Revolutionary War general or a lockkeeper once lived, but it was now shuttered and decayed and of no importance whatsoever.

At the end of the road was a clearing that must have been the park. It was hard to know for sure without anything as formal as a welcome sign and hardly any parklike accoutrements to be found, except for one bench that faced the canal's slow-running water. Off in the weeds to the side of the road was a short row of large rectangular stone blocks near a dry ditch. The stones and ditch were flanked by a historic marker, which Colby and I got out to read. The marker described how improvements to the original canal made it deep enough to carry barges a hundred times larger than the first barges on the first Erie Canal. That's growth. That's gutsy vision. I saw in my mind's eye my neighbor slowly nodding his head, as if to say,

"See? That's no cute little folk song," and I also saw, in my peripheral vision, a large, orange-and-white, early eighties vintage RV parked in the shadows about a hundred feet away. I looked at the RV while trying to pretend I hadn't seen it, which is hard to do. A stocky and distinctly unsmiling young man with a shaved head and a muscle-stretched T-shirt sat on the RV's doorstep holding a leash attached to an even more muscular-looking spike-collared pit bull, who in my judgment was also unsmiling, though with some dogs it's hard to say. A nasty-looking sheet covered the RV's windshield from the inside.

I decided to continue enjoying the old lock despite the presence of the creepy RV, the large man, and the mean-looking dog. This was America, where a woman on an epic journey with a very old dog who wets himself when it thunders should fear nothing. An American woman in this day and age could go see old rocks if she damn well pleased, meth lab or no meth lab parked in the brush back behind it.

Let me note here that most people did not believe me when I told them the RV at the old canal lock was a meth lab because they didn't think meth was actually getting cooked in New York State, even if they acknowledged that there was and is a drug problem in this country, even if they knew, too, that meth was the drug that had lately been ravaging more people than any other, even with Oxycontin use on the rise; they might even acknowledge that crystal meth had long been a popular club drug in New York City, and that the crystal meth supplied to clubbers must have come from somewhere. Still, people believed the meth problem belonged to some place else, like Seattle; or Missouri; or Tulsa County, Oklahoma, where in fact meth labs did frequently turn up. (To their point: the DEA found 979 labs in Tulsa County between 2004 and 2012, the most of any single U.S. county; the highest-ranked meth-making county in New York in that time was Chemung, where thirteen labs were busted over the same eight years. None were reported in Montgomery County, where I was. But I maintain the low rate of meth busts in New York just demonstrates that really, no one was looking. They aren't that hard to find.)

This drug stuff was not something anyone decent wanted to contemplate, and denial of it was as rampant as the drugs themselves. But aside from the really cool electric towers I had photographed in Charlton, the meth lab was one of the most important things I had encountered in my first twenty-four hours of travel, the stones of the old lock notwithstanding. The meth lab was more important to the American story of the era I was living in than even I wanted to know, but I had months ahead of me to learn it.

Anyhow, if there wasn't a meth lab in that camper, I don't want to know what was hiding there because it was surely something. The man with the dog sat on the step of the RV and watched Colby and me taking pictures of the lock. I turned to him and waved a small, tentative, information-seeking wave. He did not wave back. This was perfectly good information. I took eight pictures over the course of about twenty-four seconds before I moved one step too far in the general direction of the meth man, and he and the mean dog rose and started marching toward me. I hustled back to the car, lifted Colby in, and left.

The rain had broken the heat wave and so, after doing my best to wash the dog urine from my bedsheets at the marina laundromat, I decided to go for a jog up the canal towpath. I left Colby in the locked trailer with the fan on and a bowl of water, pulling the trailer's screen door shut and then shutting the big outside door too to be sure no one would take him. Then I ran off. Rain had made the woods misty; steam rose from the earth in a lazy fog. White sunlight streamed through the mist and raked the tangled trees. The path through this was beautiful at first, but then it was lonely. I ran two miles into the woods not far from where the meth gets cooked in St. Johnsville, and then realized what I had done. It was exactly the sort of thing I had promised Jessica I wouldn't do: I had wandered into a deep forest alone but for the company of stealthy drug-slinging murderers who cook meth in seedy trailers. Here bodies of snooping women could be hacked into parts and hidden, unbeknownst to the authorities, who in New York State had turned their heads to meth's reality, apparently. This is what I had done. Of course it was.

I turned right around and sprinted two miles, singing the Erie Canal song loud to shield myself from evil until I made it back at last to the Scamp, and once there, I called out, "Puppy, I'm home. I'm home and I'm alive!" Then I pulled open the outer door to discover ripped-up nylon mesh jutting this way and that from what used to be the screen door. Colby looked up at me from his seat in the shredded ruins, hyperventilating, cloudy eyes bulging, lolling tongue streaming drool. I had left him alone in the evil den of thunder and he had panicked the moment I left. I held the big door open as he bolted through the shredded screen and into his safe spot beneath the neighboring RV, panting hard and looking at me like I was such an asshole.

Colby stayed in hiding all through dinnertime. I went inside the Scamp to unhook the little table for its nightly transformation into my (hastily laundered) bed. I was exhausted from our escapades, from the panic of the morning and the afternoon's death run. Bed would fix it. I pulled the table forward and yanked its hinged leg firmly and ripped the whole thing out of the wall, screws and all, and tumbled backward to land flat out on the floor. The table landed on me. The clatter lured Colby, who stuck his face through the door shreds to see what the trouble was, then backed out with disinterest.

I made my broken bed as best I could. I had to be brave for Colby and act as if all was still normal. I carried him inside for the night, made him a nest on the floor, then read two pages of a new book, not the one I had thrown against the wall the night before but another book by another absurdly young author of such genius that, despite knowing that the universe contains creative success enough for all of us to share, my perimenopausal rage kicked up and filled me with thoughts of my own uselessness and infertility, and finally I stuffed that book in the hatch beneath the sink and shut the light. Colby started panting. Then he stood up and panted, and then he whined, then he started turning circles in the dark. He could not settle down. I buried my head under my blanket and tried to ignore him. Now and then I muttered what seemed like soothing words, but it was useless. He fussed for hours. Hours. For brief periods he would tire himself out and we would both sleep a bit but then he would snap up and start in again, and it went on like that until, at 4 a.m.—desperate and afraid that life would always be just exactly this, a panting dog in a cramped space and no rest to be had, ever—I opened the trailer door to liberate us and he charged to the car like death was behind him. It wasn't raining; there was no thunder, but still, he was terrified and only the car, its familiarity, its promise of home, could soothe him.

And yet it didn't. He panted until his sides were heaving. I crawled in the back seat to lie next to him while he cried. I was wrecked. My dog was going to die because I had had a selfish, senseless pang of desire for a straight woman I had been childhood friends with and somehow that meant I had to drive away and destroy all our lives. What was wrong with me? What kind of fool does that? I started crying too, then, and shut the radio off and decided to accept that I had ruined everything.

Then all at once and for no apparent reason Colby took a big, long panting breath and let it out in a sigh. He stilled himself and then in a moment, he lay his head down on the back seat near mine, snuffled some, and licked his lips. Then he fell asleep. The panic ended for no reason I could see. It had simply run its course. A little after 5 a.m., lights came on at a small plant by the CSX tracks. A truck gassed up at the pump nearby. The morning routine had begun; we had lived to see another day.

Colby's vet told me over the phone that any time he starts to panic, two Benadryl tablets would safely knock him out. People do this with their kids and it's called child abuse. Colby was a dog. So I got the biggest box of Benadryl I could buy at the local pharmacy, where federal law required that any cold medicine containing PSE must be kept behind the counter, because PSE is used to cook methamphetamine, and the meth problem was really that bad. Benadryl does not contain PSE but it was lumped with the other cold medicines behind the cash register, perhaps because it has diphenhydramine in it, and if you eat a handful of those pills you'll hallucinate. (I should add that about two weeks after I bought Colby his Benadryl, New York's governor signed a law forbidding cough syrup sales to minors, who were using it to sedate themselves in alarming numbers.) I gave Colby two Benadryl pills right then, and twelve hours later I gave him two more, and the next morning when we were packed up and ready to leave St. Johnsville, Colby lay across the back seat, drugged, lifting his head a bit with a "Where am I?" look, and I scratched it and said, "Come on, buddy. This will be fun!" And we headed west to Buffalo.

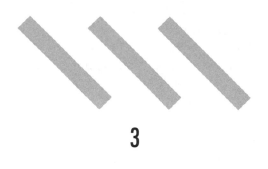

3

Buffalo

Two words often used to describe Buffalo are "cold" and "depressing." Why? Cold, sure. It can't be helped. But then, why is such a large, storied place so depressing? Why would tens of thousands of people choose to live in this gloom? Is it the cold that gets them down? Well if the cold is so awful, then why put a city up there in the first place? How could sentient, warm-blooded human beings have conspired to create such a cold, sad thing? I wanted to understand. So Colby and I drove out across New York on the Thruway, which runs west along the Erie Canal to its terminus: Buffalo.

It was raining. Everything in the trailer was damp. The trailer's screen door was shredded; the dampness drew a pee scent from the bed cushions, and the clever folding table had been yanked from the wall and was useless. My dog was on the verge of a stroke or something and was lying in the back seat of the car, sedated with a strong dose of antihistamine. We had been three days on the road and this was our condition, so it seemed wise to stop someplace where I could regroup and hammer out the whole camping thing. I picked a Motel 6 just east of Buffalo.

I would like to note that this particular motel chain has mastered the art of austerity. Our room was a spare and sterile place, with thin towels and bare floors; bureaus with drawers had been replaced by simple shelves.

This stripped-down design left not one nook or shaggy surface where vermin might loiter, which in a way creates a sense of well-being in a motel but not a drop of comfort. The most astute online review of the specific Motel 6 I stayed in with Colby read simply, "It beats sleeping outside." That was true enough, I thought, but only because it was raining.

I gathered up our wet clothes and towels and the trailer's urine-scented bed cushions and spread them across our motel room to air out and dry as I searched the internet for a suitable camping spot in Buffalo.

For all of my life up to the time I went to Buffalo with Colby, if I knew anything about that city at all it was only that people had been fleeing it for decades. I would see Buffalo's long, flat rows of small houses as I passed it on the Thruway and wonder about the people inside, why they stayed, how they passed the time. Now as I approached, Buffalo's abandonment struck me as terribly sad; the place was not the object of an eye-rolling joke but a real place suffering real pain. Perhaps the people in the houses felt pinned down by something faceless and dark. It's what I felt, at least, contemplating life in all those boxy domiciles far from the center of the known world, and the slim likelihood that anything would soon change for the better. I felt the abandonment in my core. Perhaps they felt it too, I'm sure many did, but really, I did not know anything about Buffalo, or how it felt to live there.

What I imagined of Buffalo before I knew Buffalo was more poetry than fact. It is a place of grand human striving and progressive triumph and political importance that had all run out, leaving an unfillable hole. I saw her lost in her drab rings of sprawl and felt a pain as I approached that must have been my own. The place touched me. Maybe I could learn from Buffalo how to make peace with disappointment, or simply how one came to feel at home in boxes like barracks, or prison cells, bumped up tight to one another, irrelevant and unseen and strapped down by miles and miles of thick electric cable whipping the sky, filled with alternating current, webbed above a city ringed by superhighways. The highways buzzed, six lanes, eight lanes, twelve lanes wide and rolling in a tightening gyre that could choke old Buffalo, choke her to death, and even after death, keep choking and choking and choking that city. Jesus. Then what? What do you do with the corpse of a place? Roll her up in a pee-soaked Scamp blanket and dump her somewhere, never look back, be glad she would no longer beg us for comfort, this Buffalo. This lonely, needy girl. This city who seemed, by plan or neglect, easier to kill than to love.

Well. I had some feelings about Buffalo apparently, none of which really inspired me to go camping. I should have realized much sooner that this would be the case, but truly, I was not blessed with the gift of foresight. Jessica had the foresight; I had courage. These things are largely incompatible. You might think they create balance and sometimes they do, but generally the status was gridlock. I was free to take all kinds of terrible risks when I was alone, though. The camping problem that I had not foreseen occurred to me as I left St. Johnsville. Urban places in general are not big on camping, particularly the sort of distressed urban places I most wanted to see. I had vaguely imagined that no place in America outside the coastal cities could possibly be more than a short drive from a campground, and I had studied RV camping enough to learn that in fact many cities do have RV parks within their boundaries, but my research too often linked those parks to news stories of drug busts, particularly stories of meth labs. (Truly meth kept ambushing me; a quick online search for "RV park meth lab news" will offer some proof of the problems out there.) Reviews of urban, or "residential," RV parks also frequently mentioned vicious dogs, loud parties, and, more often than you might expect, sex offenders of the highest order (who are challenged to find any other place to live). If this bad news wasn't bad enough, the worst news was that Buffalo didn't even have a crummy "residential" RV park; it had nothing. I would need to get creative to find a place to stay.

One part of my Buffalo visit was already settled: I had reserved a spot on a half-day kayak tour up the Buffalo River, which promotional pictures showed to be lined with industrial ruins, old graffiti-covered warehouses, and enormous mystery tanks that looked to me like the world's oldest oil refineries. These tanks turned out to be abandoned grain silos. There were hundreds of them along the river, and the river itself looked much like a sewer in some places, running inky and flat through the sheer, high corrugated walls of these steel and concrete monsters. Paddlers on Buffalo River kayak outings would beach for lunch on an especially grim-looking peninsula known as Silo City, a brownfield scattered with abandoned grain elevators. These ruins were gritty and mysterious and held stories, for sure. I booked my kayak trip months ahead, and when my hunt for an insider's guide to urban camping grew desperate, I called the owner of BFLO Harbor Kayak, Jason, for help. He was at a total loss, really; he suggested Niagara Falls, nearby. But eventually he said, "I don't know how adventurous you are . . . ," which was my cue to draw a deep breath and wait for the best possible weird-in-a-good-way suggestion to follow. Colby let out a long, sorry sigh from his spot on the floor between our beds at Motel 6, where he had been hiding since we arrived. "But if you want," Jason said, "you could camp at Silo City."

Not everyone I met agreed on the proper use of the expression Silo City. Some believe it's an apt nickname for Buffalo as a whole, but Buffalo's official nickname is the City of Light, since the hydroelectric power of nearby Niagara Falls gave Buffalo the first electric street lamps, and also because Buffalo in its day was known as (and designed to be) America's Paris—that other City of Light. The name "Silo City" is a term lately given to the entire region of mostly abandoned grain elevators in the city's First Ward. But it is also used to refer to a specific six-acre property purchased in 2006 by Rick Smith, the third-generation chief of a family-owned metal fabrication company with its headquarters next to the silo "campus" Smith came to own.

To be clear: the individual nine-story-high concrete cylinders that look like million-gallon beer cans in tall-boy six packs sitting on the ground in Buffalo are grain silos; the clusters of those silos with loading machinery attached to them are called grain elevators. This kind of knowledge locates Americans on either side of an experiential divide; my description of grain elevators here is either ridiculously obvious or painfully obscure, depending on your relationship to agriculture. This country produces something like 450 million metric tons of grain each year but it's remarkably easy to know nothing about it.

Smith bought his silo campus thinking he could build an ethanol plant there, fed by corn shipped in from the Midwest and stored in his grain elevators. The ethanol plan fell apart, but the silos are still there looming in

Abandoned silos on the Buffalo River

the rubble, rusting and flaking, clusters of high, hollow concrete edifices
that a bomb wouldn't take down. Not easily. So with no other evident use,
those silos where men had labored for generations loading and unloading
grain had become a kind of grand art installation.

The gate to Silo City was watched over by a man called Swannie Jim.
He lived on the site in a dimly lit, cluttered shack with an iron stove in it,
which he used to burn logs and busted-up pallets. The shack had power to
keep the lights on and the beer cold and to run a ten-inch television during
football season, and I'm not sure what else might have mattered, there;
Smith described Jim as "a modern-day Thoreau, living in his Walden." Jim
had in his day been project engineer at a number of large industrial sites;
he had come to Buffalo to more or less retire, then got involved in Silo
City and the ethanol project, then stuck around when that project failed.

Silo City, bereft of industry, was attracting everything else. Painters had discovered it; poetry readings and music festivals were held there. Films had been shot on the grounds; movies had been projected onto a grain elevator's high white walls. Wedding parties used the barge docks and silos as a postindustrial chic backdrop to their photographs. An arts extravaganza called City of Night brought art installations and performances into the silos, and the brownfields around them, for several years running. Remnants of those art projects mingled with the ruins. I wandered through, and stray art turned up in odd places. Art ghosts. In an abandoned grain elevator or beside an old hops oven I would hear nothing but my own footsteps and then there, a portrait of a white deer, or a large hammock with candles all around, or in one place a painting so real as to nearly stir the air: a painted dancer on her toes who was not alive but not quite dead either. Buffalo hipsters once set up a mustache museum in the silos; flea markets were held there on weekends. University at Buffalo architecture students built an enormous obelisk beehive on the grounds, but after a year the bees abandoned the hive, and it stood on the side of the road after that, tall and shiny but empty.

Jason, the kayak guy, had asked Swannie Jim to watch for me, and when I pulled up to his shack with my trailer, Jim approached my car with his pit bull, Champ. Champ's face was fawn-colored with almond eyes and a licorice-black nose. Jim's face was thin and rough like worn red leather with a stubble of white whiskers; his eyes, squint-thin through square glasses, were deeply creased in the corners. He looked like he had spent a fair amount of time working outside in the sun, or on ships in bad weather, or in Buffalo.

"You think it's safe to camp here?" I asked through my cracked-open car window, like a bear-phobic tourist at the gates of Yellowstone. Most Silo City veterans would have been appalled by this question, but in my defense, it really was an abandoned industrial site, accurately described as a creepy, deserted brownfield at the edge of a poor and sometimes violent city. Later, pictures I posted on the internet drew speedy and satisfyingly worried responses. My father was following my travels via social media, and when I reached Buffalo, he urged me to please stop advertising my location to would-be murderers. My favorite comment came from a friend back home who, upon seeing pictures of my trailer squatting in a field of scrap metal and splintery debris, wrote to say: "Remember, palm to the nose, knee to the groin. Palm to the nose, knee to the groin."

Jessica issued a supportive comment—the kind of thing a partner offers when arguing is pointless. "Be careful, my love," she wrote me as I slipped into this glorious hard and strange place. "Don't get hurt," she said.

In my idling car, I craned my neck to size up the silo clusters rising from the dirt, near and far. The ground was barren, and the wind blew endlessly. Silo City seemed to be an unreconstructed warzone. Swannie Jim, a man I had known less than a minute who apparently lived in a shack, assured me I would be safe there.

"We don't get a lot of trespassers," he said. Champ snapped at the end of her rope. Colby was whining to get out of the car, which could have meant grave danger was imminent or that he had to pee. Odds were on pee. I told Jim that I would stay.

In Buffalo's First Ward, people know the names of the old grain elevators the way Coloradans know mountain peaks and New Yorkers know tall buildings. The Perot Towers, the Great Northern, the Nesbitt, Cargill, Marine A. The property Rick Smith bought, which contained about a half-dozen grain elevators and related buildings, was special among the many miles of industrial ruins in the First Ward; it was, for one thing, home to the oldest solid concrete grain silo on the planet. In fact, the slip-form process of silo construction was invented there, so that the millions of concrete silos all over the world have this spot in Buffalo to thank for their existence. It is a distinction that might matter to approximately seventeen living humans, including me, and mean nothing to most of the other six or seven billion, unless you are moved to consider that there, among the weeds and rubble of Silo City, hard proof exists of how fast glory fades, and how a truly transformative idea can, in short time, cease to matter whatsoever.

The Scamp was parked next to the Marine A grain elevator. The reflection of the setting sun turned the top third of the Marine A silos dark orange, a wide ribbon of color rolling high up along the cylinders like a gigantic ululating flag. It was beautiful. I made a ring of rocks around my campsite like a fence, bringing pioneer order to the wilderness, then set out chairs and my barbecue, made a campfire, and sat alone in an abandoned place and felt curiously at home there.

In the morning, waking to bird song alive and unmolested, I went out to rouse Colby from the back of the car, where he had insisted on sleeping since our disaster that first night on the canal. Swannie Jim had left out a key to the men's washhouse at the Lake and Rail—one of Buffalo's last active grain elevators, a small one. Jim said I could use the men's room if I got there early, before work started. In the Lake and Rail bathroom, hard hats lined a shelf near the communal showers and a copy of Playboy was slipped into the crack of the fourth toilet stall's door, which seemed as quaint and lost in the era of internet porn as any other lost thing in Silo City. Colby and I washed up in there, then sat outside our trailer with coffee and watched as a handful of Lake and Rail workers rolled up in their trucks, heading for the elevator. After that, young guys in battered cars showed up with their tools and got busy working on a yoga studio/climbing wall that was being installed in Marine A. This was the current vision for revival: climbing holds had been attached all the way up the outside wall of the Marine A elevator; it was going to be the world's tallest man-made outdoor climbing surface, when it was done, topping a 165-foot Reno wall that held the current record.

Jason, the kayak guy, was involved in the rock climbing project and described himself as a businessman more than an outdoorsman, but it happened that kayaks and climbing and yoga were the businesses where money could be made in a place like Buffalo. He came by in the afternoon to show me around Silo City. We entered the Marine A elevator through an opening at the base of one concrete silo where huge decorative metal doors would soon be installed. Inside, all was cool and damp.

An empty grain elevator is like a dark, spare cathedral. The silos are vertical tunnels traveling down from the sky. About fifteen feet above the dirt, massive steel hoppers—ten-ton funnels with spouts that open and close—were once built into the base of each cylinder to stop the tons of grain they held from pouring down to the floor. At ground level, in a loose maze of concrete walls and steel girders, carts once pulled up on rails beneath the hoppers so that when the steel spouts opened and grain poured out, the carts could haul it to the trains. The dudes who pulled up in battered cars with their tools had removed most of the old steel hoppers from Marine A with torches and tractors, so that when I looked up from the ground inside, nothing blocked the full view of each empty silo. Thin light pierced the darkness through holes at their tops. Shouts and coughs and whistles echoed up into that vacant space, out into infinity.

The banks of the Buffalo River are lined for miles with hundreds, if not thousands, of similar towers of windowless concrete, attached to dark mechanical structures and funnels and rails. The vast industry that thrummed there a century ago molders now in silence, in brownfields veined with railroad tracks. Grain silos stand like the poet Shelley's Ozymandias. They are trunkless legs of stone in the desert, ancient and petrified, bright ribbons of graffiti at their feet. Up on top of the silos, nine stories high, silt has piled up so deep that trees have taken root; ducks and geese paddle along the barge docks on the shoreline and deer sometimes wander by, but there are hardly any people; on thousands of acres along the river, all that was built was abandoned a generation ago, so there is no reason to be there. It is exquisitely lonely.

Jason explained the rise and fall of the grain industry to me and showed me where the new yoga studio would go, and then he left me and Colby to enjoy our dinner of salad and kibble on a riverside loading dock. University at Buffalo crew sculls shot up the river through Elevator Alley in their evening workout, then disappeared beyond a bend. I was walking Colby back to the trailer in the dimming light when Swannie Jim, who was standing outside his shack smoking a cigarette, called me over. "You've been talking to the wrong people," he said.

This worried me. Jason had seemed so nice, and so excited about Silo City and its history and "the responsibility good people have to the ghosts of this place"—which, actually, he did not say; I said this thing about responsibility and ghosts and I swooned and he nodded profoundly. But Swannie Jim said if I really wanted to know about the silos, I had better follow him. He chained up his dog, then Colby and I entered the shack and there, sitting around the stove on a collection of broken chairs in the bad light, were Rick Smith, Bob the Builder, and Kevin the Horse Thief, whose nickname had a witty anecdote behind it that Kevin liked to tell but that I never quite understood. Didn't matter. The names gave their gatherings a kind of tribal feeling. Someone handed me a beer and offered me a chair and then Bob leaned way back on the busted springs of his seat and said, "So you've come here to learn. What do you want to know?" All eyes watched carefully, as if this were a sacred riddle.

I wasn't sure how to put it. What had I come to learn, really? I could have said: Why are these big things empty, guys? When did they cease to matter? But all my life when faced with this question, this "what do you want to know" moment, I always somehow went right to this: "Teach me to love, wise ones. Why are we all so alone? And who do we trust with these questions? Who do we trust with our hearts?" Once I took a trip with a girlfriend to a writing workshop in a small and, as it turned out, haunted village in France, where another woman in our group drew a Ouija board on a sheet of handmade paper. We apparently channeled a spirit in that haunted café with that Ouija board and a tipped-over glass. It actually worked: the glass flew around the letters making words. It was really quite bizarre. This was several years before I met Jessica, and my girlfriend and I were a tough match; we fought constantly, and it all felt like a trap I might never bust out of. But then, the Ouija board. It offered a chance to resolve mysteries. The glass moved so fast and uncannily that I mistook its animating force for god. I asked: "What should I do to be happy?"

The entity answered, "Date Men." Asshole.

I had since been more careful in oracular moments. In Jim's shack, my eyes moved across all those waiting eyes. A board in the fire popped. I cleared my throat. "What the hell happened to Buffalo?" I said.

They sized me up and then looked at each other. Then they started talking.

This group I had stumbled upon in fact was none other than the— *the*—secret society of the Buffalo Brain Trust, though if you ask them they will surely deny it. They first started meeting at the old Swannie Inn nearby, the pub from which Jim takes his nickname and where, before moving to the shack, he could be found most evenings grousing about the 32-foot wooden boat he was building. The brain trust guys had spent their lives living and working in Buffalo and they knew a thing or two about it and that meant they knew about a lot of things. It seems that once you understand Buffalo, by simply adjusting names and locations and substituting commodities once made or exchanged, you could understand most cities in most places. You would know why the Rust Belt was rusty and how the general state of chaos in the world was in most ways utterly predictable. They could have told me themselves if I had asked them ten, twenty, thirty years ago that what rises will fall, and the ones with the real power were always ten steps ahead of it, having already gotten rich off the ruins the rest of us were living in.

This is true not only in postindustrial Rust Belt America but all over; understand Buffalo and you could see with complete clarity the future of places that were presently booming, like China, which had boomed once already but that was centuries before; like North Dakota, which was at that exact moment booming with gas and oil, not rusting at all. Check back with North Dakota in twenty years, they assured me, and I would find a new Silo City; I would find Derrick City; I would find decay. None of this was hard to grasp if properly explained.

Kevin, a retired state employee, started the process of my enlightenment by tipping his head back and entering a kind of dream state. "The key to all this is the War of 1812," he told the hushed room. Kevin's seat, a broken desk chair on a wheeled pedestal, squeaked beneath him. In all my life, as far as I knew, no one had ever suggested that the War of 1812 had any lasting importance. I believe it was taught to my third-grade class the day after we learned about the Erie Canal and two days before I was stricken with some sort of vomiting flu, because I remember both the canal and the war equally well, which is to say not at all, and without a song like "Fifteen Years on the Erie Canal" to sketch the outlines of it for me, there is little chance I would retain much detail of this event anyhow. No song? No war.

"Actually, the song most associated with the War of 1812 would be 'The Star-Spangled Banner,'" Kevin said, correcting the fallacy that the war was songless. Kevin was a stout, silver-haired man with a trim beard and a mustache twisted up into points. He wore rumpled khakis, a white shirt, and boat shoes; he had a professorial air about him—erudite and rich with fascinating lectures filed away in his mind; he had been waiting for my audience all his life, I supposed.

"You see, most people think 'The Star-Spangled Banner' was written during the Civil War but they're wrong," he added, and in this case most people did include me. Everyone in the room nodded or pressed his lips together or made some other solemn gesture of grief over the depth of human ignorance, which is limitless.

Facts matter. Turns out I had arrived in Silo City two hundred years to the day—seriously, to the day—after the start of the Battle of Lake Erie, a turning point in the War of 1812; this apparently linked me inextricably, if unimportantly, with my new favorite city. I had been called there. No one, it seems, ever ends up in Buffalo by accident. Something brings you. Usually the water or the Thruway but perhaps also fate. The battle's bicentennial explained the presence of the tall ships I had seen out in Buffalo Harbor, which looked as if they had sailed in from a preindustrial dream. It was a commemoration; fireworks were planned for later in the week. I made a mental note to sedate Colby.

The Battle of Lake Erie mattered so much because the lake was a gateway. Controlling Lake Erie meant controlling the gateway to the West, to all the land on the continent that in 1812 was still unsettled by western newcomers. Sailing the Great Lakes out to what we call Ohio and Michigan and Wisconsin was the easiest way to get to those places. If the British had gained control of Lake Erie, they would of course have had a base from which to attack the former colonies down the East Coast; they would also, and possibly more importantly, have possessed the key to western expansion. Lose the lake, and England would have a claim to all the land it led to. Keep the lake, and soon, settlers from the states would begin pouring west across the water, expanding the country, and Buffalo would become the second-largest port in North America.

"We realized how important it was to control the water," Kevin said. "That's what the Battle of Lake Erie showed us."

Kevin sat with his legs crossed and his head tipped thoughtfully, scratching his beard. Jim leaped from his stool and made for the fridge. He passed out beer to Kevin and to Bob the Builder, who waved his empty bottle in the air. Then Bob leaned in to tell me something privately.

"I'm not supposed to be here," he said.

Bob was a restoration contractor and a roughly handsome man who wore sunglasses, a bushy mustache, and clean, neat work clothes. He told me that his girlfriend was twenty years younger than him and that they sometimes had troubles, possibly exacerbated by the difference in their ages, and apparently one trouble was that she didn't appreciate the importance of his stopping by Swannie Jim's to take stock of life and drink beer every day. He sighed and fell back in his seat and we gave each other an affirming nod; clearly Bob knew I was sympathetic. Clearly he had sniffed out some sense of my having undertaken a long road trip to run from my fear of turning fifty and to deny the potential ruin of a once historically significant love affair. I raised my empty bottle and Jim tossed me a full one. Colby began making rounds of the room, trying to hump all the men's legs and, failing that, licking their knees incessantly.

Meanwhile, Kevin's lesson on the War of 1812 had progressed to an intellectual climax. He tipped way back as if watching his lecture on a PowerPoint projected on the shack's low ceiling, and Bob swiveled in his chair, now and then checking the time. Rick Smith presided silently beneath his cowboy hat, wiping beer off his mustache.

Kevin said it was only four years after the Battle of Lake Erie was won against the Brits that work was started on the Erie Canal. That logical connection isn't typically made, not as a true cause and effect, but the idea is hard to resist—a Buffalo Brain Trust interpretation of history, a light conspiracy theory in which the ol' military-industrial complex comes into play a full century and a half before President Dwight Eisenhower warned us against it. Yet so many pieces of our world began as military projects: microwave ovens, space travel, interstate highways. Transportation infrastructure means national security as much as it means economic growth; Lake Erie was essential to America's naval defense. Once the country figured that out, boom: the canal that had until then seemed impossible—too expensive, too difficult, a pipe dream—suddenly got the government backing it needed, because a canal would get men and material up to that crucial lake quickly. Just like Eisenhower's highways 130 years later: a defense plan that, once established, would be used mainly by commercial truckers and vacationing families.

To this, everyone tossed back a good slug of beer. The water made Buffalo. A major city in that spot where the canal meets the lakes was inevitable. It doesn't matter if that city gets an average of 93.6 inches of snow in the winter. It doesn't matter if a place that touches Canada appears, from the perspective of the Boston-to-Washington corridor below, to be floating off the map of the world. The water made Buffalo utterly essential. Greatness was its destiny.

This journey I took with Colby occurred at what in hindsight might be seen as the part of a sleeping dream just before it shifts into a nightmare. The situation is strange, yes, but not dangerous yet. That was the mood of the time as I experienced it. A deep seething anger had taken hold and was starting to cripple our national body, as anger will do. Barack Obama was president. A government shutdown was looming. On right-wing talk radio in my car, Michelle Obama was being flayed for encouraging Americans to drink water. It was as if she had searched for the most benign cause to champion and found this: the human body is made of water and needs water to stay healthy. Her detractors accused her of evangelizing fake science. Every granted truth could be flipped over. Every good idea could be made to look wrong. Americans could not agree on anything.

I drove downtown to see Buffalo from a new direction. From the viewing platform atop Buffalo City Hall—a thirty-two-story art deco beauty—Lake Erie seems to run off the edge of the world. Buffalo sits lapping at this water. In another direction I looked out across the ruins of old warehouses and factories, and all the towers downtown and the rooftops of hotels and hospitals and churches strung along green parks and paved parkways, and I saw the houses that had lost more than half their occupants in a handful of decades, and from the air I could not really see how empty the buildings and the sidewalks were and it was all still beautiful.

By 1860, when the Erie Canal peaked in its importance and trains had not yet taken that importance away, Buffalo was one of the largest cities in the country. Frederick Law Olmsted designed it to match or, better yet, exceed the elegance of Paris in the Second Empire, to outshine the renovations the French architect Baron Haussmann was just then wrapping up for Napoleon. Buffalo was an American prodigy, wildly surpassing normal expectations for a place like a four-year-old chess master, or the stringy kid who becomes the star of her soccer team. When you are seven and your coach says you'll do great things, you believe you are headed to the Olympics, not to asthma and credit card debt and bad knees. Work hard, and your eminence is guaranteed. So it was for Buffalo. Two American presidents lived in Buffalo, and another, William McKinley, was murdered there; Teddy Roosevelt took the oath of office on Delaware Avenue. This is the sort of stuff that only happens in important places. Places you respect. Presidents get killed in Washington, D.C.; Dallas; and Buffalo. That's it. And thank goodness too, but anyhow: Buffalo. Great men had lived and died there.

Majestic as it still appeared from the observation deck, by the early twenty-first century Buffalo contained twenty-three thousand vacant houses and empty lots. Its economic decline had not been subtle; the cleanout had been swift and thorough. They say the St. Lawrence Seaway is what killed it, because after 1960 when the Seaway was opened, no one needed the port in Buffalo anymore; ships could head straight out to sea and skip it, so the once second-largest U.S. port died fast just as, long before, trains killed the canal—no matter how miraculous its creation had been, in no time at all it was useless. Creative disruption: Facebook's Mark Zuckerberg once said, "Move fast and break things," but the only truly new part of that twenty-first century idea is the definition of fast. It's getting ever faster. After 1960, manufacturers along Buffalo's waterfront were declining for their own economic reasons, and combined with the port's shift toward obsolescence, the unraveling was complete. Warehouses emptied. Industrial-sized bakeries and breweries no longer stuck to Buffalo for its grain; the grain was gone. And it was so cold, way up there.

I had left Colby at a pet shop for a bath while I explored the neighborhoods of Buffalo, partly because he needed it but mostly because he had to be somewhere; I couldn't leave him in the car all the time. When I picked him up in the afternoon, he trotted out in a dinosaur bandana and a big, toothy grin. He was a handsome guy and he knew it. I said to the groomer that it seemed to be getting cold out, to which the groomer, a slim girl with white spikey hair, laughed nervously and said, "Well yeah . . . ," like my observation was both dumb and somehow upsetting. But it was still only September, and had been above 90 only days ago, where I had come from. Later, in a shop in the city's hip Elmwood neighborhood, where I was hunting down souvenirs, I told an insanely chipper gift store clerk, "It's cold out. Guess it's true what they say about Buffalo."

The young woman looked up from what she was doing and dropped her smile as she eyed me sternly. She shook her head slowly and said, "You have no idea how cold it is here. It is a cold place. You should thank god every day that you don't live in Buffalo. Every single day. As soon as I can, I'm leaving."

On Sunday in the silos, I watched football inside Swannie Jim's shack on what might have been a twelve-inch TV, maybe smaller; three quarters of the Brain Trust and a couple of architects from the University at Buffalo were there. Jim's shack was irresistible to all kinds of strays; he spent a good part of each day vetting curious visitors who wandered into Silo City, some of whom he welcomed into his circle. For a hermit living in a shack, his world was full of people. I was less lonely in the company of all the others who had been drawn to sit in that astonishing loss, and after a few days, I felt as if I had found a home in their creative, misfit community. It occurred to me that my whole road trip could just stop right there; mission accomplished. Wandering soul finds home in spooky, broken place of kindred spirits. Sorrow understood as our prerequisite. Nothing left about that to say. I loved those guys.

It was week two in the NFL season and it was a beautiful crisp day and for that moment at least it seemed like anything was possible, even for the Buffalo Bills, whose recent losing streaks were noteworthy. Rust Belt teams had lately stopped dreaming of winning championships; some had given up on even winning games. Continuing to exist was enough. That day, though, the Bills won a heartbreaker in the final second and our cheers shook the shack. After that, optimism brightened the cool evening. We ate buffalo hot wings and pizza around a fire outside, and I passed out cigars to the Brain Trust. Rick Smith pocketed his. Kevin unwrapped his and held it in his teeth. Swannie Jim and I smoked ours, and when Bob the Builder didn't show up, I gave his cigar to Jim too. The silos felt blissful, then, filled as they were with fast friends, cold beer, and—over in Marine A—a pack of hipsters making music.

A woman named Jax Deluca was playing her ukulele in Marine A for a recording called "The Silo Sessions." The ukulele music was slow and haunting and rang out from the tubular cathedral. Kevin and I walked over to watch Jax play. She was perched in the dim light on a bed frame, which had been part of an art installation and left there a year or two before. When her song was done, I wandered back out into the night with Kevin. Swannie Jim had turned his light out.

Kevin, at maybe sixty, was built soft and comfortable, and he had a nice way of talking long. One night we had tried to find the right image, some vivid way to explain Buffalo. Prosperity seemed to be a force without end; it only moves. It's like weather. Buffalo was a city with its face turned to the sky, waiting for the rain to come. Lately it had begun to seem possible that Buffalo would find its happiness again; people were saying something felt different, even hopeful. The hipsters had started coming home. The moment might pass; the silos might never be anything again. The yoga studio and climbing wall never did open, I know that now, but I've heard there's an excellent restaurant in the space instead. It doesn't matter. The new feeling of hope was a feeling worth sticking around for.

That night when the Bills won and music echoed in Marine A, when Kevin and I wandered back to Jim's shack and found the door shut and the lights out, Kevin dared to ask, carefully, if I might like to close the night with one more drink, somewhere out there, beyond the gates of Silo City. I know well this wish to make the good feeling last a little longer, but also I couldn't risk leaving the silos that way, heading out to regular drunkenness with Kevin, the Horse Thief. Swannie Jim would lock the gate across the road, and I might get separated from what safety I had found in this chaos.

That's not all that scared me. My own loneliness, and the way the love feeling mixed with drink makes anything seem plausible, had been scaring me for months, or even years, or even forever if I let myself see it. I longed for something I did not have and had no words for, and I didn't know where I could find it, and for a deluded moment I imagined a rowdy tussle with Kevin in my trailer might soothe for a moment, at least, that deep longing to connect. Was this the answer? But then I floated out of myself and saw us standing in the gravel looking up at the stars, two pale, graying stumps of humanity, each nursing an all-day beer buzz. How beautiful. How strange.

"I guess I better not," I said, and Kevin smiled. "Okay," he said. "Okay." And I went back to my place beneath the silos, stone walls empty as church bells.

4

Allegheny Mountains

Wait. Did I actually just suggest I was about to fool around with a sixty-five-year-old married man who wears Top-Siders without socks? Is that what I said? Did I think this kind, gentle, very married man had any intentions beyond striking out into the night to find more beer? Of course he had no such intentions. What was I thinking?

Cold light of day: Sun rising in gray, postindustrial waterfront gloom, birds winging through concrete detritus, steel skeletons rising in the murk, I had become dangerous. I had to go. I hitched up the trailer and avoided saying good-bye to Swannie Jim; I hate saying good-bye. In fact, I really didn't want to leave at all, so I pretended that I wasn't. I slipped off when Jim was out building pallets down the road at the metal plant. I left without sharing my plans with anyone, even Colby, until we had logged some miles. Then I checked the rearview mirror and caught Colby's eyes, the dismay. We were driving again. When I said I loved Buffalo, I guess he thought I had meant forever. I guess I had meant forever any time I had ever said I loved anything. Or anyone. But in the long shadows cast by Silo City, the concept of "forever" was not so comforting.

I called Jessica and told her there was a great jazz bar and at least three coffee shops in Buffalo that I knew she would love once she got to know them, and then I started talking about the abandoned house I had seen with "good bones" that I was sure I could "do something with." I described the old-school bowling alley on a downtown corner, white brick and neon and an old, green BOWLING sign above the door. It was a sweet nowhere I would belong to if I could just be born again into something new and strange; I could carve a path there, unburdened by my own history. Jessica listened to me describe these places for a good, long time. Then, right after I told her I was leaving and that I was "so scared" that I would "never see any of this again," she said in a voice that did not belong to the silos but came, instead, from a living room, "Sweetie. We are not moving to Buffalo."

"We aren't?"

"No."

"But why not?"

"First off, it's . . . Buffalo."

I answered this with silence. Perhaps she could hear me breathe.

"It's the middle of nowhere," she said.

Jessica was humoring me, because of course Buffalo was impossible and of course my suggesting even indirectly that we might move there was a joke. She was correct, except she could not see the pain at work even inside this joke we shared—the one where I would want to move to whatever place I saw; the one where she would take me seriously for a moment, then laugh, and hope that I would laugh too. She must have had longings of her own, but she did not let on if they pained her. She said she was fine. She never told me she was unsatisfied, but if she was she had managed to laugh it off, because that's just what you do, maybe, and what had come off for years as general grumpiness in me was easy to laugh off too until that summer, when all my moods were magnified and swinging like monkeys. We had driven around Little Falls, New York, on our short summertime Erie Canal adventure; Little Falls is a faint shade of Buffalo two hundred miles downstream, and in it an emptiness kicked up in me like a warning. What had I gone there to see? Evidence? An equal in my grief? I would not have called the feeling that: grief. I did not think that's what it was. But when I hold it in the light of hindsight, the word fits well. We drove along the edge of Little Falls on a road above the water and stopped to stare for a while at the empty *Evening Times* newspaper building on Second Street. For a moment I mourned newspapers, the whole earnest and hardscrabble good-versus-evil Clark Kent determination of them. I had once loved that culture and devoted myself to it at the start of my working life, but that time was also gone now. Left behind. Newspapers would never again be what they had once been. Later, on a street of shuttered storefronts, we passed a very goth-looking girl walking down a sidewalk, full speed. This girl looked like she was heading somewhere in a big hurry but it seemed to me there was nowhere to hurry off to in Little Falls. Perhaps a funeral? She was dressed head to toe in black, with dyed black hair and dark eyeliner, with pale skin and a scowl on her face, and as she walked she smoked a cigarette. It was late in the day and any life that remained in the buildings on the street had gone dark except for a corner bar. I didn't understand. I wanted to follow her.

"Where on earth could she be going?" I wondered aloud.

"She is having an affair with her English teacher," Jessica said. My heart ached for the girl. I wanted someone to tell me she would be okay, that we would all be okay somehow.

"They sneak their visits at night and on Sundays," Jessica said. "They read each other poetry."

"Really?" I said, watching the girl.

"Yes," Jessica said. "Then they fuck."

"I bet you're right," I told her. It did feel right. I get that. In a moment I added, "It's sad."

"Why?" Jessica asked. "Why is that sad?"

At this point, we had driven past the girl but I was watching her in the mirror, and driving so slowly that this might have been obvious. Jessica was getting frustrated.

"She must be so lonely." My eyes shifted onto Jess; she was watching the road. Then she turned to me and her eyes were so big and flat and blue, like a painting. I looked into them and saw her, and an emptiness opened up between us. She said, "She'll be fine."

Of course she was right. Jessica was steady on her feet and knew others would be too, if you let them. Or maybe she just figured it was none of her business, which is a sane and necessary way to look at the world, and she was right in her approach. Nonetheless, I didn't believe her. We drove off and the girl became a speck, then disappeared.

Now she said into the phone, "Lori. We are not moving to Buffalo," with the same authority. Again, this was right and rational, and yanked me back to reality. But she was missing the point. Buffalo gave form to something in me that I did not understand, but I recognized. Jessica and I had gone to Mexico once and a shaman in a sweat lodge made a figure from dripped candle wax that he called "your sadness." We thought we had gone to see the shaman to heal Jessica's cold. But no. He took the wax of my sadness and told me to leave it somewhere; I put it beneath a statue of the Virgin Mary at our inn and walked away but then there it was, again and again, and on this day its seed had grown up into a cluster of silos in Buffalo. There. Imposing containers walled with concrete and empty, and dark, inside. As lonely an object as you could ever see.

It's not that I really thought we would ever live in Buffalo, but for the moment, it felt like I belonged there. And Jessica was in New York City and I could not find words to explain this to her. Blocks of houses painted in murals. Etchings of angels on the doors to a furnace. Beauty that exists with hardly a witness. Abandonment. Something I had felt, perhaps from birth.

"It's cold as fuck in Buffalo," Jessica finally said. She was right about that.

Colby and I headed south to camp in the Allegheny Mountains by way of the "Gateway to the Alleghenies," a small New York town called Salamanca. So many places claim to be the gateway to something in this country—St. Louis calls itself the Gateway to the West and doubled down on that claim in 1963 by building an arch to prove it. But in 1829 when the canal opened, Buffalo was the gateway to the West. Then in turn Pittsburgh claimed to be, with its knot of rivers that led deeper into the country, long before roads did, and then when Cincinnati grew up downstream from Pittsburgh, it claimed western gateway status. Louisville, Kentucky, is the Gateway to the South but so is Cairo, Illinois, a really important ruined city very few of us have ever heard of; it's the southernmost point in Illinois, and was, in fact, the gateway where trains stopped in the era of Jim Crow to move black passengers back into the filthy rear train cars, separate from white folks,

before the trains continued south across the Ohio River to Kentucky. Anyhow, all these gateways prove that Americans have always been leaving one
place for another, trying to get somewhere. I entered the Alleghenies through
the gateway of Salamanca, which is at this point more or less a portal from
nothing to nowhere.

Let's note that New York is a really big state. People seem to forget this
when they focus on the twenty-three-square-mile island of Manhattan.
New York, in truth, is fifty-five thousand surprisingly desolate square miles,
and Salamanca is a small city in its least-traveled quadrant, on Seneca Nation
lands; it is the only U.S. city located entirely on an Indian reservation. For
this reason, I would have guessed Salamanca was a Seneca word. The Seneca
word for "Bucktooth" would be a reasonable guess; when it was still just a
wild, piney, unsettled spot on the Allegheny River, white travelers called
the place "Bucktooth" after a Seneca tribesman who lived there and traded
fish and game with them.

In fact, Salamanca doesn't mean Bucktooth or anything else in the
Seneca language; Salamanca is a Spanish surname. In the mid-nineteenth
century, José de Salamanca, a one-time minister of finance for Spain, was
sinking his money into trains. The "New World" was hot for investors, and
railroads were a budding technology in which staggering fortunes could be
made. José de Salamanca invested in the Atlantic and Great Western Rail-
way, which connected to a bigger line, the Erie Railroad, right on that spot
once known as Bucktooth. The junction spawned a town, and the town
was named Salamanca in José's honor. His speculative fortunes rose and
fell; over time, they mostly fell, so that in the end, José de Salamanca was a
broken man, perhaps a dubious namesake for anything.

Railroads that passed through Salamanca really boomed when the
nearby Pennsylvania oil fields opened and all that crude had to find a way
to market. Pennsylvania oil spawned the Standard Oil Company and with
it the world's first billionaire, John D. Rockefeller, who made his fortune
by combining oil with trains. I thought about this and felt a tingling sensation in my brain, psychic pins and needles like a sleeping foot waking up;
something utterly vital about oil in Pennsylvania was drifting out of my
amnesia. It was something enormous that, as I stood in Salamanca, could
be forgotten and never matter at all. So strange. What I knew then was

that, with the force of a half-dozen railroads meeting in one place, many of them shipping Rockefeller's oil, Salamanca grew into a small world of brick-fronted stores and houses and train depots; a 1901 history describes Salamanca as a "manufacturing and railroad center" with seven churches, five schools, three newspapers, twelve hotels, two banks, a hospital, and a gymnasium.

In September of the year I traveled everywhere and nowhere with my dog, Salamanca, for all its charms, had lost most of that. The oil dried up. The trains did too. A *Pittsburgh Tribune-Review* columnist called Salamanca in 2011 a "failed American city." But it seemed to me to be a place stuck in grief, where something was missing that was not coming back; it was no more failed than so many other American cities, large and small, with its abandoned buildings and razed homes and a new casino buzzing just across the highway.

Failed or not, it was still a sweet spot with a river at its center. The Allegheny River sparkled up from beneath a bridge. I stopped to let Colby out to pee and we walked across the bridge and watched the water. It was a pretty place, really. I found myself thinking that Salamanca should open a lodge and a few hiking trails, turn itself into a fishing and hunting paradise. Which is of course exactly what it had been two hundred years ago, before industrial glory, back when Bucktooth lived there and was perhaps a happy man.

Passing through this gateway into Pennsylvania, I stopped in Bradford to buy groceries and ice at the Save-A-Lot; I splurged and bought myself and Colby a big hunk of beef tenderloin for dinner, and then I drove off and got lost for a good twenty minutes in the approximately six-square-block, brick-faced, mostly empty commercial district of Bradford, Pennsylvania, looking for the one road that came out of that knot of roads and led up to Willow Bay Campground on the Allegheny Reservoir, about fourteen miles away. I found the right road after a long search and drove it up a mountain and deep into the woods.

Of all of the hundreds of campsites in the vast, woody Willow Bay Campground, only three were occupied that particular September Monday afternoon. It was hard to imagine the place awash in peak summertime car-camping humanity. The hush at Willow Bay enhanced the sensation that Colby and I had found a true wilderness—one that just happened to have paved roads and flush toilets. We were dangling off the edge of civilization, where a central problem of remote lonely spaces quickly occurred to me: If we died there, who would know? I caught a glimpse of a large, shirtless man slipping into a shuttered old Chevy van at the far end of the campground; he was never seen by me again. The campsites were carved back deep in the trees along an empty paved loop; the only other campers I came across—a couple—were walking along the pavement, holding hands. This pair looked so young that it was possible they were away from home for the first time, and they wandered along, holding hands, watching raptors circle the reservoir, two sweethearts surveying a vast, abandoned civilization—a thoroughly organized, paved, parceled, numbered, and yet now empty world that sat in baffled stillness.

The hand-holders were sweet and young and I wondered if they were in love. I wondered what would happen for them in the future, and whether this moment was the past they would one day mourn for, and if they would cling to each other in the dark, when they were scared. Clinging can feel like passion. Passion is not exactly love; it's a gateway. Clinging is definitely something else. I think. Perhaps I should have warned them. But of what? That I was afraid? The couple were beautiful, and they were in an objectively strange, deserted land, and it seemed to me they would know, eventually, if their happiness was a dream or something real passing between them. I sat and breathed the clean air and I watched them as I had watched the girl in Little Falls, though this time with a bit of envy, because they had each other.

And then I realized I had been staring at them from my perch in the woods way too long, in a creepy way that surely lumped me right in there with the big perv in the shuttered Chevy van, and I snapped out of that haze and got back to business.

I chose a campsite far enough from the couple to stay out of sight, yet near enough that they might hear my screams, should I be attacked in the night by wolves, and while those screams surely would only drive the couple deeper into each other's arms, it was still comforting to think someone would know if I died there, alone with Colby, in my trailer. This is about exactly the right definition of "neighbor" to me, in a make-believe wilderness. It is just one tick to the left of total desolation; there is yet a thread to connect us.

I set up camp and pulled out my folding chair and Colby's folding chair and we sat side-by-side by the fire pit, watching the lake across the road as the day faded. It was tranquil, so tranquil that it turned out, of course, to be one of those rare and precious remaining places on Earth without cell phone service, which I discovered as soon as I tried to call Jessica, holding my cell phone at four or five different angles with no luck. This isolation had to be the whole point of working so hard to find a vacant campground deep in the Allegheny Mountains. But I still had to let her know where I was, in case I died, or if perhaps she simply wondered; it's a basic right of partnership to always know each other's physical coordinates. It kind of annoyed me but also it was nice to know someone cared.

So I ripped the needle off my vinyl record of serenity, "rrrip," sprang up from my chair, loaded Colby into the car, unhitched the trailer, and drove back down to Bradford to call home. The twenty-five-minute drive was fast devouring what daylight remained, and I truly feared I might never find my campsite again if I returned after dark. Therefore, I could stay in Bradford only long enough to make a call and state my location. Not a moment longer. No time to mess around: I shot out of the campground and back down the steep Allegheny hill that hid Willow Bay inside it, and Colby stood on the back seat with his front paws on the console beside me, swaying to the S curves, watching the road, panting and smiling, alert to signs of home. The car descended into the thickening clutch of houses near Bradford, the log cabin–style bars and convenience store huts at the edge of the cellular stratosphere. The sun was setting behind us. I called Jessica but she did not answer. Voicemail. I disconnected. The edge of town appeared; I tagged it and turned to head back up the mountain, back into the trees and across that line where the twenty-first-century stops and all the rest of time remains in effect—but first I tried Jessica again. This time she answered. I managed to say this: "I'm camped at Willow Bay and it's a wild, beautiful place where I am vulnerable to bears and criminals. I've seen no staff there and have no way to call for help if anything bad happens so write this down. If I disappear, the last place you knew where I was for sure was Willow Bay, near Bradford. The light is fading."

"Okay, sweetie," she said, above the sound of water running over dishes in the sink (and I saw her in my mind, familiar: the kitchen is small, yellow; through the window is a view of a brick wall, and Jessica might stand there to mix a salad, pour a glass of wine, take out a book of poetry to read while even there in New York City the sun would be setting, the night drawing down), "have fu—"and that was where I lost her.

I raced the falling sun back to camp so that I could hurry up and relax. I found my campsite and rushed out of the car, helped Colby up into his chair, and then plopped into my own. At last settled in, we watched the sky and the water join across their evening shades, and the fantastic show of three bald eagles, one heron, a batch of kingfishers, and a flock of geese passing the sky's great stage, and then a huge full moon rose and shined bright and changed everything. Again. Things change and change. All of this happened easily; all I had to do was sit there as the splendor of the world outdid itself. And then finally, the moon settled down into a simpler shape, smaller, and the sky darkened, and the night arrived.

Alone in the dark, I prepared to be scared. I had camped alone in a tent once so I knew what to expect. I would panic. And because I would panic, I gave Colby a strong dose of Benadryl; it was the least I could do. I made a large campfire. I put my steak from Save-A-Lot on the grill but then it got too dark to see if the meat was cooked right, and then, above the hiss of meat on fire, far out on the edge of night, teams of coyotes began to howl. Coyotes don't howl, actually, but sing in a yipping whine that sometimes sounds like an evil laugh, like they know something terrible. It's something humans avoid but, in our quiet depths, we know; the coyotes' laugh is cruel and ugly and it has to do with death. The lovers in the nearby tent probably liked this terrible sound. It would be music to make love to; the man in the Chevy would endure the howls alone, as I too must endure them. Only the very young are free from the fear of death but their youth is hubris, and obviously (it seemed to me, caught up in fear) what's far worse than the hubris of youth is the hubris of women nearly fifty who still cling to youth, who come up into the hills to be alone with themselves when they know perfectly well that being so alone is terrifying. Such folly;

it all ends in death. The wolves—I mean, the coyotes—laughed and laughed. Colby held his fluffy head up to listen, far more alert than he should have been on Benadryl. He knew we were going to die. Weren't we? Yes; of course we were. Everyone would die. Dammit.

I fed the tenderloin to Colby and doused the fire; I lifted my old dog into the trailer ahead of me and shut the little door, and lay down in my pod and closed my eyes and waited for the coyotes to come eat us.

The Alleghenies achieved mythic status to me when I was a child, driving across them with my family each summer from New Jersey to Wisconsin, then back again. So much was carried inside that car: my tiny mortal tribe, a dog who bit people and a big brother who bullied me, and all my dreams of summer at the cabin, all my dreams of lives lived behind those mountains that I saw, where I imagined small-town American blonde-haired kids, slim as string beans, spending days riding dirt bikes and skipping stones with big brothers who, in their case, were all really nice. It took us six hours to cross Pennsylvania, home to the Allegheny National Forest. Gateway to our summer vacation, and, as seen from my backseat window, a mysterious world of people and children like me hidden deep in the trees. How could there be so many lives that I would never even see, much less know? This bothered me.

Our station wagon breezed across the Allegheny range almost effortlessly, quick and smooth, as if those rugged rolling hills had never been an obstacle so confounding that, instead of pushing through them, it had once been easier to build a 363-mile canal and go around. Crossing was simple by the time we got there, but the mountains wedged between the East Coast and the Midwest remained curiously desolate. Western Pennsylvania didn't even have a service plaza to visit; it was beautiful and out of reach, which is undoubtedly what attracted me. I valued all that was remote as if what it withheld would somehow complete me.

Curiosity turned to longing over time. I was a teenager when I first saw the movie *The Deer Hunter*. The story takes place around 1970. It's about three young men from the Pennsylvania steel town of Clairton who work in a mill, but they are about to leave home to go fight in the Vietnam War.

They start out pretty psyched about it but then everything goes terribly wrong. The story becomes their struggle to return home, to Clairton, to 1970 and all of its regular worries and pain: work, and family, and hunting, and things they believed in easily before they learned something new about suffering, about how thoroughly destructive fear and pain can be. After seeing that movie, when I passed through Pennsylvania I imagined a world back beyond the rocks and trees so desperate for healing that I hurt just to think of it. Mill workers. Veterans. Pockets of life so well tucked away. I would stare out at the hills rolling by and ache for that darkness. I wanted to say, "I know you." I imagined I did. I was eighteen, a young, closeted lesbian with an abusive boyfriend, harboring a land mine or a pit hole or an open-pit mine of hurt, all those images come to mind now; I could not wait to leave home but I could not imagine a place for myself in the world. Perhaps back in those hills, I would find what I needed; maybe that place would know me too.

The Deer Hunter is most remembered for its steel mill furnace sequence, its long, unscripted wedding sequence, and its Vietnamese torture scenes, but it also has scenes of hunting in the Alleghenies. In those mountains in that movie the young men, or at least one young man, played by Robert De Niro, grasped something elemental about suffering, and about pain that changes people. It breaks them open. And then, love: it can transcend cruelty, but what it demands of us often seems cruel too. De Niro saw the friends he loved destroyed by grief, and he wanted to bring them home.

See enough of that kind of pain and you'll wish for some fast, efficient way to end suffering forever. In *The Deer Hunter*, relief comes from De Niro, who rock-hops through the mountains with a high-powered rifle and takes aim on a deer: "One shot," he says. "Two is pussy." BANG! End the suffering fast. Neat and clean.

Of course, I would have just let the deer run off, and end its suffering by not shooting it at all, but it wasn't my movie. And anyhow, the point is taken: to knowingly prolong any creature's suffering is cruel.

The Allegheny Mountain scenes in *The Deer Hunter* were filmed in Washington; most scenes of Clairton were shot in West Virginia; the cathedral in the movie's famed wedding sequence is actually in Cleveland. But that doesn't matter. It wasn't what the mountains or the town looked like that moved me; it was the values they held. I had a feeling of longing for home too, and it seems that journey must always pass through hell, and sometimes we get stuck there.

In the morning at Willow Bay, I woke in a sweaty knot on my vaguely pee-scented Scamp mattress and I was immediately aware that both Colby and I were, yet again, alive. What *was* this obsession I had with dying? It occurred to me for an instant that forty-nine was not yet fifty and fifty wasn't exactly one hundred and I really should try to stop rushing toward death. And then came the most significant observation: Colby had finally slept through an entire night with me inside the Scamp. He had not awakened shaking at 3 a.m.; he had not made me move him out to the car. It was the first time he had slept in the Scamp since our first night and the storm in St. Johnsville. He stayed, I imagined, because I needed him, and he knew it. Or, it was the Benadryl. Either way, he was now stretched out on his bed on our small square floor and when I sat up, he lifted his head and thumped his tail against the bathroom door and smiled, then dropped his head back down with a groan and waited for breakfast.

Later, when I walked to the edge of the reservoir to drink my coffee, not three but four bald eagles circled the water—two adult, two juvenile— and with that sight alone, the Alleghenies surpassed their promise. The terror and the joy are all in it together. The day was of that quiet time between seasons, the leaves a faded green and not yet fully dry, but rattling. It was very windy.

The campground manager appeared. He was a retired guy in a ball cap making his rounds in a golf cart, and he hooked me up with a canoe. Later that day I paddled off with Colby to explore the reservoir. Outside the placid shelter of Willow Bay, the reservoir was a vast, gray riot of tossing chop and white caps. Colby had been sitting like a hood ornament up on the seat in the bow until we hit open water, where the wind was serious, and when it struck the canoe he slipped down onto the floor and looked up at me, watching as if I had gone mad. I love boats and I paddled this one as hard as I could, but the wind beat me. It took my bow and turned it as if the wind and the canoe wanted me to land on one shore and one shore only, no matter what I did or thought. Eventually, I gave up and drifted to where the wind took me.

This was magic, of course. The story of the world keeps wanting to be told. The beach we landed on was covered in shale—flat rocks that piled on each other like giant gray cornflakes and were, it turned out, completely riddled with fossils. I helped Colby onto the rocky shore and he stood at the edge of the water and drank it as I turned over flat shale rock after rock from their piles on the beach, and found each one imprinted with the fans and spirals of ancient shells. Hard little critters had lived here eons ago, then died, then sunk into the still-soft shale of their graves and disappeared, leaving only impressions of the world as they had known it. Many, many millions of years later those creatures were not even dust, they were gone as gone could be, but still, here were their traces. That the world in my palm existed when this land was the floor of an ocean was an idea so large it left me speechless and staring at a rock, as Colby wandered about peeing on everything.

This is the story of those rocks: Four hundred million years ago, two huge land masses drifted through prehistoric oceans in immeasurably slow motion until they smacked up into each other and pressed hard. The seam where the two masses met became the Appalachian Mountains. The Alleghenies are a part of the Appalachians. Note for perspective: our earliest evolutionary ancestors in the genus Homo only showed up on the planet about two million years ago, and most of that two million years passed before one arrived in North America, and even once the humans got here maybe fourteen thousand years ago, they were in no apparent rush to modernize this place. Homo sapiens lived here almost that whole time before finally, in 1959, one Homo sapien named Eisenhower commanded "Highways!" and humans started blasting out a swath through the Alleghenies. By 1970 the interstate highway across Pennsylvania was finished, and my family rode in our woody station wagon along that crusty prehistoric zipper line, shale stone crushing beneath our tires, bad country music banging through the AM radio, bored parents and bickering kids unconcerned with the eternity that had preceded us. We were less than nothing in the googolplex of time; our car was a tiny flea trotting down the spiny back of prehistory. And yet, every moment of those rides is caught in its own amber,

Willow Bay Reservoir, Pennsylvania

preserved memories that remain vivid and remind me that for all this enormity, who I am is really all I have.

Geologists call the age in which the clashing landmasses created the Appalachian Mountains the Devonian Period. Here is a nice description of it I found in some marketing material written for a sandstone countertop manufacturer. I suggest reading this aloud in a deep voice, like a movie trailer:

> The Devonian Period . . .
> A violent collision of continents . . .
> The creation of an inland sea . . .
> The formation of an ancient delta
> 5,000 feet thick on the edge of the Catskill Mountains . . .
> The end result is . . .

exquisite, richly colored
Glacier Blue® Devonian Sandstone . . .

. . . countertops. The shifting of the earth created countertops. You can buy the stuff in slabs or in square tiles, use it as flooring or even build it into custom furniture, you name it. It's pretty neat.

In the fossils of this era, so many new plant forms were found that geologists named this fecund moment the Devonian Explosion. It was a happy time for fish too, and all manner of sea critters that made their homes in shells—shells trapped in the murk that became rocks; rocks that a few tens of millions of years later, Colby and I walked on.

To celebrate our stumble upon eternity, I took a swim. I love the water; if, as Darwin tells us but many Americans refuse to believe, humans evolved from apes, then I must be a freak exception to the ape thing. I might be the beast who links at least one line of humans to otters. I often keep lists of each place I've swum over any given summer, noting specially the first and last swims, hoping to expand the dates as far into spring and fall as possible each year. It is my constant wish that summer will start early and last long. Water is summer, and summer is youth, and youth is possibility, and I have been known to swim in November. This day by the Allegheny Reservoir was September 20, a respectably late date to swim. Colby had wandered into the water up to his knees and was trying to drain the whole reservoir with his tongue. I skipped past him and belly-flopped onto the surface of the frigid waves, then burst up through the surface face-to-face with my dog, who stood in the water barking at me because, if he himself did not like to swim, he most certainly did not like for me to do it. I dove back under a few times as Colby worked himself into a frenzy, and then, when I felt I had soaked up enough of this water to have officially swum in it, I scrambled back across the rocky lake bottom to the shore like a Devonian arthropod. (Think, flea. Think, scorpion.) I was invigorated with cold. The water was a clear stew of ancient minerals. The wind dried me quickly and blew Colby's black ears back over his head. I loaded us into the canoe and shoved off, and the wind caught our backs and blew us to camp easily.

5

Oil City

Ultimately, fossils in shale mean one thing to humanity: oil. But I had never thought of oil as an essential part of the American story. I had never thought a bit, not even a little, about an American place called Oil City.

Oil City is a name on a map that can be ignored for a long time—until one time it pops out and grabs you and begs for your attention. That's how it happened for me. I'm embarrassed to say I wasn't much more careful than that in choosing my route, or really, in choosing practically anything in my life; what appears usually looks right so I go there. Without really trying, I had managed to follow a kind of "how we met" story about America and its history as if it couldn't be missed, which I suspect is actually true; the way America grew up, you almost can't move without stepping on something that mattered.

We were on our way to Oil City, then, because apparently there was oil in Pennsylvania, but who knew what kind of oil; I imagined a deck above the Allegheny River where diners dunked crusty bread into dishes of Oil City olive oil. I stopped in Warren, Pennsylvania, to walk Colby in a park around a Civil War memorial, where he vomited. He had eaten nearly a whole beef tenderloin the night before, so I wasn't shocked. We walked for an hour in Warren. It was a county seat, which often means relative prosperity; a river ran through it and well-kept Victorian houses lined its streets. Colby vomited again, and I bought a cup of coffee at a coffee shop run by a Christian youth center. Christian-run coffee shops were becoming a trend, I noticed; they were cropping up particularly in small places where teenagers don't have much to do. I was happy for all that. There are worse things than luring teens to Jesus with coffee and anyhow, Jesus himself would like coffee, I'm sure. It's that good.

Partly because of this break for a little vomiting and coffee, it was dark by the time we reached the Oil City Family Campground out in the countryside between Oil City and Titusville.

Titusville, Pennsylvania. Land of Devonian fossils. I learned immediately (because it is announced in one way or another all over town) that this was the site of the world's first drilled oil well. Not Iraq. Not even Texas. The first oil well was drilled in Pennsylvania. It later became the source of John D. Rockefeller's fortune. Here was one of the most important regions in the history of industry, and I had somehow never heard of it, not in third grade, not ever. Complete blank. This spot had boomed beyond hysteria in the late nineteenth century. Drilling rigs and oil barrels were invented in Titusville. The Standard Oil Company sprouted from the dirt upon which I had parked my Toyota. All I had known about any of this was related to Standard Oil, and my general awareness that Rockefeller ran it and that his business practices were hated by many, but to me, that could have been said of anyone so wealthy.

The small library in my Scamp included a very famous book that I always seemed to travel with but had never actually read—written by the muckraking journalist Ida M. Tarbell and unsexily titled *The History of the Standard Oil Company*. My god, if Ida had wanted future people to read this book, she should have named it *Fat Bastards Rule the World!* We have come so far with book marketing. I had carried this particular book around with me through the years because it was a journalism classic. It was something I had always known I should read, but I didn't really think it still mattered, and in truth, I feared it would be painfully dull. Then there I was, in the land of Ida Tarbell and John D. Rockefeller and Standard Oil, a place I had stopped mainly because it was located conveniently between Buffalo and Pittsburgh. But it turns out that everything is connected in a kind of grand cosmic chain, and once you begin to look you can't miss it. You will literally step on the pieces of this story as you pass. It was truly strange, what happened that evening: I set up camp by flashlight at the Oil City campground and, looking for something to read among my eclectic portable library, I happened to pull out *The History of the Standard Oil Company* and examined it. When I realized what it was about—that it was about the place where I was, in that moment, sitting—the connection I felt to the cosmos gave me chills, but also, I may have been shivering because both Colby and I were apparently coming down with something. He was still vomiting and had not wanted any dinner. I read Ida Tarbell's book by the dim light inside the Scamp and it was not boring, and her mind was still sharp across all the years, and I devoured what she was still telling us as Colby slept and filled our tiny enclosed space with his noxious stomach gases.

Here is what most of us don't think about as our country fights endless wars in the Middle East, building resentments that spawn terrorists, doing nefarious and dastardly things to control the world's oil: We started it. Here. In Titusville. All those Allegheny Reservoir fossils were left by critters who decomposed and turned into oil. The oil leeched into the creeks and soil of western Pennsylvania. Native Americans tried to make medicine of it; white farmers thought it was a nuisance, mucking up the water. Salt miners dredged up annoying bucketloads of crude that they ditched in search of the salt below. They could get rich on salt. Oil was just messy. Then in the mid-1800s, oil gained value. It could burn in lamps, and it was good for machine lubrication (think: industrial age gaining momentum in the new world, many new machines, much need for lubricating oil). A few visionary businessmen saw this. In the Pennsylvania wilderness, they began bottling oil instead of tossing it out.

Speculating geologists hired a guy named Edwin Drake to design a well to bring the oil up more efficiently. Drake had no special resume. He was not an engineer. There was no reason to expect him to succeed. Some thought he was nuts and his financial backers had written him off already when, in 1859, he struck a gusher in Titusville, and when he did, the world changed.

With Drake's well, the mystic orb of prosperity that had rushed up the Erie Canal to Buffalo suddenly veered west to hover above an outpost of small farms that, overnight, transformed into a hive of oil boom towns. The Allegheny oil region lit up a wilderness; Pittsburgh to the south was not yet Pittsburgh as we know it; the other close-by city was Erie. (My Erie! She *did* matter! I knew it must be true.) Neither Pittsburgh nor Erie was exactly a metropolis in 1859, but both were on major waterways. Titusville was an unknown dry-land outpost stranded between those cities; the crush of fortune seekers that followed Drake's gusher had to bushwhack to get there. Historians compare the Titusville oil rush to the California gold rush of 1849; they say the rush to Titusville was bigger because Pennsylvania was not so far from the settled world. Still, it never came up in school. Maybe that's because no one stuck around when the oil rush ended. San Francisco without gold is still San Francisco. Beautiful. Waterfront. The gateway to the East. The oil industry moved overseas, and Titusville became a footnote.

In the morning at the campground, Colby kept vomiting and I started to wonder if he had swallowed a bone back in Buffalo the night we ate hot wings after the football game. It was either a bone, or a bout of the Thousand-Dollar Flu—a mysterious illness Colby managed to contract every few years. This wracking illness would drive him out to the sidewalk clenching and heaving, his brown eyes tearing up; the process always reached its puking and shuddering zenith at about 3 a.m. on a Sunday, when the only option for dog doctoring was the emergency vet. After a long wait at the 3 a.m. vet followed by X-rays, blood tests, and various probing examinations, the 3 a.m. vet would invariably determine that my dog had what is commonly known as a tummy ache. Then, I would pay a thousand dollars and go home with some pills. But the thing is, I had to do it; I had to take him to the vet time and again for a thousand dollars because the alternative seemed to be watching him die and that was unthinkable.

I sat eating a bowl of cereal in the pleasant, mowed RV lot of the Oil City Family Campground and after a little food, my own sour stomach began to settle down. Colby, though, turned his nose up at his bowl, which was very strange indeed. Half an hour later he was sitting in the grass, above a small batch of vomit, looking up at me with his cloudy old eyes, tail weakly sweeping the ground, drooling.

I brought Colby to the Titusville Veterinary Clinic, a pet hospital cleverly disguised as an old split-level house: a low, white-shingled, friendly looking thing perched at the top of a wide driveway that also served as a parking lot. Colby was not fooled by this architectural camouflage. He sat mulish in the driveway. I dragged him up the asphalt, alternately begging and cursing as I pulled on his leash. In the reception area, I added our names to a list that included Ally Shade and Moondance, Linda Boone with Alice and Harry, Gizmo, Tippy, Lizzy, Smokey, Wallace, Stella, and Gertie. I'm not sure which of those were pets and which were people; the room held a roughly equal number of each. Colby and I took our seats. Whenever the receptionist barked out a name on the list, the room erupted in protesting yelps, then one by one the humans dragged their shaking, crying dogs off to be examined in rooms hidden behind a pair of flapping doors. Occasionally, muffled whimpers passed back through. When his name was called, Colby shook himself into a convulsion. I pulled his leash and he slid across the floor. In the exam room, the apparently teenaged doctor complimented him on his stunning good looks, gave him an anti-vomit shot, drew his blood, then sent us sprinting back down the driveway. Colby was feeling much better already.

His blood, I learned later, was not only free of major diseases but also gave us proof that Colby was "in far better shape than most dogs his age," which I had suspected but was glad to know for sure and which made me feel glad we had gone for the visit, just to hear that good news. The other news was that there was no particular reason Colby had been vomiting.

"Seriously?" I asked. "Why would he vomit for no reason?"

"Probably carsick," the vet said, and gave me pills for this nausea, then handed me a bill for $170. For this reason alone I could have fallen in love and settled down in the place once known as "Oilderado." What a fair price to learn there was no reason for Colby to vomit, and he was cured after that.

I went off to explore Titusville as Colby moped in the back seat. What I found, seeing it for the first time in the daylight, was nothing at all like my imagination had guessed the home to the world's first oil boom should look like. Titusville is near a little spittle of a river that is definitely not the

Persian Gulf; its streets are lined with old buildings that are empty and flaking apart. I did not expect to find Dubai, but I did think I would find a place that was a little more . . . wealthy. When I think of oil I think of rich sultans and palaces and that sort of thing, or at least Texas. At least a little bit of gaudy outsized everything. This being America, I would not have been surprised to find a tourist district in Titusville, maybe a theme park, "The Place Where Oil Started" land. I wasn't expecting to find another tired old American city of vacant brick buildings, all these overland shells of human endeavors that will perhaps one day disappear into fossils themselves. I did not think Titusville would be so sad, but it's possible the place looked a little sadder because my dog and I were nauseous before we even got there.

Still, consider: John D. Rockefeller birthed an empire in this forgotten town, took its oil for himself as if the fossils brewing oil for eons in this earth had done so for one man's personal enrichment. It made me think Ida M. Tarbell was clearly right in what she saw coming: a new, relentless style of business—a force that would enrich a powerful few, and change the world for all of us whether we welcomed the change or not.

In the boom years, the oil fields of Western Pennsylvania drew thousands of fortune seekers who bought land and then slapped up scores of wells in a fast and lawless way, drills inside scaffolding like origami birds, fully intricate and still fragile. Men poked around for gushers even before anyone figured out how to barrel the stuff properly. It just gushed. It's almost embarrassing now to think of those early wildcats striking oil and not being able to catch it. So much was wasted. Stockmen tried to cart the stuff away on roads so muddy that exhausted horses were known to drop dead in the muck. Yes, it's true that our country has changed; today we would not tolerate horses drowning in muck in the interest of exploiting natural resources. Would we? Was low tolerance for horse death a sign of a weakening nation? I know I would have chosen horses over glory, just as I find the best way to avoid causing deer to suffer is to stop shooting them. I wonder what a soft world would actually look like. Perhaps we would be living in caves; perhaps we would be happy. We'll never know.

In any case, our forebearers hardened their hearts to horse death and other tragedies and the oil boom messily progressed. Ida Tarbell's own father got rich by inventing oil barrels—the unit by which oil is still measured, thanks to him. Horses hauling oil barrels made their deadly slog through the muck to shipping points on Oil Creek, which connected to the Allegheny River, which led to Pittsburgh, which connected to two more rivers and thus brought oil to the world.

Except, only half the oil sent by barge down Oil Creek ever got anywhere. Oil Creek was hardly a river; it's more rocks than water. It was not deep enough to actually float a boat, so oil drillers created "pond freshets" to move their goods—a technique developed by sawmill owners to move logs downstream. They would dam the creek, build up a good burst of water, then release the water to create a deluge strong enough to move tons of cargo. This pond freshet method of water transport might be called a flume today and would be a great ride in the Titusville theme park that didn't actually exist. Again, we've changed; 150 years ago, men did not look at water and think about amusement. They thought about utility. They took the world much more seriously, but amusement is where the money is today.

Titusville drillers figured freshets worked for logs so they would work fine for oil too. Only, not really. When logs jam in a river they don't spew out flammable slicks of toxic goo. The Oil City Pond Freshet Disaster of 1864 left dozens of skiffs piled against the footings of a bridge on Oil Creek south of Titusville. Oil gushed. Fires flared up. It was a major disaster, but not the only one: other times, even without the aid of these freshets, heavy rain caused floods too dire for hastily built boomtown infrastructure to handle, and flooded messes and raging oil-fed fires flared up regularly. You can see it all for yourself in miniature, at the Drake Well Museum in Titusville. Clearly, there had to be a better way to exploit the continent's natural resources than to rely on the caprice of small rivers. Actually, there was; the railroads were coming, and John D. Rockefeller too.

Ida M. Tarbell was born to a farm family that rode the American wave away from agriculture into industry. Like so many families, they left a small farm that had sustained them in what was still a wild country in Western New York and Eastern Pennsylvania and they took up life in what was, in that time, a more cosmopolitan Titusville. When her father invented his oil barrels and became a self-made man, Ida saw what a boom looked like and what enterprising Americans could do with opportunity. All boats would rise, metaphorically, if people worked hard and many small fortunes were made in oil even before the car had been invented. Then Ida saw how other American inventions—monopolies, huge corporations—could crush smaller rivals and their smaller ambitions. She became a journalist, traveled to Paris, landed in New York City, and then wrote about what happened to her all-American, enterprising hometown, Titusville, when John D. Rockefeller took over the oil. The other aspirants were left behind, many of them ruined, their hopes drowned in muck.

Rockefeller got his start as a young man in Cleveland, a city that was growing up on the shores of Lake Erie; Cleveland was the main point at which midwestern goods—like all that heartland grain bound for Silo City—was loaded onto ships and sent east, to Buffalo. Rockefeller clerked at a shipping company, and when he got into the oil game, he shipped oil from Titusville back to Cleveland, where he built refineries. He negotiated a transportation monopoly from the railroads that saved him big money in shipping costs and crushed nearly every rival oil driller; he either bought out or crushed his rival refineries too, and soon he controlled the whole oil industry. Those he had crushed despised him. So did Ida Tarbell.

I fell in love with Ida. I spent time with her in my mind, in my trailer, and imagined us to be soul sisters. Practically twins. Doppelgangers. So uncanny:

Ida: Raised by educated parents who never tried to stop her from living her somewhat risky (for her day) and eccentric dreams.

Me: Yes. My risky and eccentric dreams: thanks, Mom and Dad.

Ida: A diligent student in an era when not everyone believed women could or should be so smart; she blew away expectations, reveled in intellectual achievement, was fascinated by biology and the natural sciences, was a whiz at math.

Me: I have a master's degree in creative writing.

Ida: Worked at Chautauqua Magazine, where she discovered she could write.

Me: I've always wondered how to spell Chautauqua.

Ida: Scraped and saved and worked her way to Paris, where she lived in the 1890s with three friends she had convinced to go with her, and there established herself as a freelance journalist.

Me: Colby and I wanted to visit every town called Paris in America, like Paris, Illinois. There's a Paris, Texas. There's a Paris, Tennessee.

Ida: Was fascinated with biology in the era when Darwin's *On the Origin of Species* had just been published, upsetting the world's notion of God and science; she had nearly gone on to graduate studies in the field because she understood that the concept of evolution would change everything, and it did. Evolution is a defining characteristic of life, and now that we understand it we know that we are all, always, evolving. It's a concept so disturbing that even now, 42 percent of Americans reject it.

Me: I had a fossil in my pocket.

Ida: Swore at a young age that she would never marry and she never did; biographers speculate on her dalliances, mainly but not exclusively with men.

Me: Can't explain my romantic life in a bullet point.

Ida: Embraced temperance and sober living.

Me: I was thinking I should probably quit drinking.

Ida: Wrote an exposé of the Standard Oil Company that was serialized in *McClure's*, the boldest and edgiest publication of its day.

Me: I started a blog about my travels with Colby.

I can't say for sure after learning all about Ida whether I wanted to marry her or to be her, though it hardly matters; she died, inconveniently to me, sixty-nine years before I was born so there was no trace of her when I arrived on the planet, except for her books, which are full of conviction and passion. I can at least say that Ida M. Tarbell was the embodiment of my imagined Better Self—someone fascinating and independent, whose most important work had something to do with unwanted change. Stranger still was that the best available biography of Ida Tarbell was written by Steve Weinberg, a journalist I was going to meet at a dinner party in Columbia, Missouri, in a couple of weeks. Columbia was to be my pivot point, the place I would reach and then turn around, and now I knew why: Ida Tarbell had something to say from her side of the grave.

When Ida M. Tarbell returned to visit Titusville in 1894 after living three years in Paris, she found the world of her childhood had changed radically in a short time. Nothing had changed quite so much as Pithole, an oil town that shot up from the weeds, becoming a city even larger than Titusville in the years before Ida left for Paris. Only five years later, the boom had halted and Pithole had been completely abandoned. All fifteen thousand people who briefly lived there were gone and the buildings they left were stripped to their foundations. Ida and her brother spent a day on her visit home walking through the scant remains of Pithole, then left feeling sick over what she called in later writings "the impermanence of human undertakings."

Pithole is gone. I mean, I have never seen a place so gone. It is a grassy field. Having visited plenty of old boomtowns fallen into seedy grief, I have to say, I was impressed with Pithole, Pennsylvania, for having had the decency to disappear so thoroughly. Colby and I walked through Pithole 119 years after Ida's visit, which is to say, we traipsed through a field of historic markers stuck in the grass. I stood on a hill and looked down at a field and read a sign asserting the site had once been a large town with a grid of densely populated streets. Crickets sang. Butterflies wandered the weeds.

All these ghosts seemed to make Colby nervous. He walked behind me, panting, and any time I stopped he barked. He wanted to go. This made me wonder about the things a dog can sense but a person cannot. Or maybe after two bad carsick days he was suddenly hungry. Still, had it not been for my dog's apparent foreboding, or for the testimony left by Ida M. Tarbell, whose judgment I trust entirely, I would have thought Pithole was actually a joke concocted by locals to mess with nosy tourists, like me.

At a certain point in Western Pennsylvania, possibly right there in Pithole, I came for the first time to doubt my belief that storied old things really should be saved. When buildings stand empty and untended in the center of a place, they become constant reminders of our failings, or, as Ida wrote, of our "impermanence." Once-grand places whose grandeur has long passed become monuments to futility. The silos in Buffalo, Rick Smith said, can't be preserved simply because they are old; they need to find a use.

Colby and I packed up and left the Oil City Family Campground and drove south through Oil City proper—the place where Oil Creek meets the Allegheny River, where oil skiffs in their day turned south for Pittsburgh (or sometimes just turned over). We walked in the rain through the old "Victorian business district," as places I would simply call "downtown" are often referred to these days. It was empty, nothing like what it had been. People don't build cities as temporary things, like camps; most cities exist for particular reasons, come alive with communities drawn to that reason, and grow into complex organisms that suffer as they die. I can say the same thing for marriages, and families, when they fall apart; what we invest our hope in we expect will last, yet so much of what we make does not turn out as planned. And we suffer.

Sometimes distance aids perspective, and my search for this perspective led me to Alistair Cooke, the British luminary who in the 1970s hosted *Masterpiece Theater* on PBS. Britain is a good deal distant from Titusville and Cooke had a unique view of the American colonies that long ago evolved their way away from the Empire. In 1973, anticipating our bicentennial celebration, he authored a picture-loaded coffee-table book alongside a documentary series that tells America's story very neatly. Clearly it took a Brit to explain our nation's wounds of separation with such ease. Of Titusville, Cooke said that after the first oil well was drilled, "Oil towns sprouted like weeds"; on a nearby page he pointed out that in the postwar 1870s, "America began to spawn small cities like rabbits." Places just kept happening, as if Americans were a collective bunch of exuberant newlyweds, going forth to multiply unselfconsciously and, hopefully, to prosper.

So now, we are a country of empty nesters, trying to stay in a long marriage despite the pain and reckoning of middle age.

The center of Oil City contains a block of buildings clumped into a mall named Drake Square. It was entirely empty when I saw it, and the vacant storefronts there and throughout the town had For Sale signs in the windows; there were For Sale signs on cars, and on things that were dragged out to the sidewalks in front of old houses. I couldn't imagine who might buy all of this. Oil City, like so many cities, is pretty but shrinking; its life seemed to me to be over, though the rain probably made it feel especially grim that day.

The rain was coming down hard. It was the day of the Oil City Cranberry Festival, which lasts one day and one day only each year; no rain date. Anyone who had decided to attend it was far braver than I, because I was not going to go eat funnel cake in a downpour. Instead, I found a coffee shop that sold me a cup of watery brown coffee and I walked Colby in the deluge, staying long enough in Oil City to witness it: the old buildings, the churches. Teetering wood steps scaled up the backside of brick apartment blocks; I wandered along a row of homes with doors left open for the air, exposing their insides. Overstuffed couches, mantels full of photos and figurines. If I had crossed my eyes, each home might have been an antique shop, a kind of shop I had come to see not as galleries of valuable objects but as resting spots for unwanted junk. It is the same with most places; a person could peer into my windows and see the parts of me I am unwilling to give up. I felt a mix of admiration and despair on that walk, the way I have felt at nursing homes, visiting old folks who have lost the ability to tell me who they once were and why they mattered, even though I do know they mattered, very much and very dearly, in their day. And they still matter; I do know that, just the way I know how once, not so long ago, Oil City was booming, boy. It was really something.

6

Pittsburgh

As I drove south toward Pittsburgh, the rain did not let up. It took the heat away and the heat never really came back after that, or when it did it came only in flashes that seemed like mistakes. Hot flashes. Bursts of wet heat from beneath my skin. Cruel reminders of change, and I missed summer already and I wanted it back.

While driving, I listened to Jessica tell me over the phone about something at work that was making her way too busy. This disrupted my focus. It's hard to be with the plight of humanity and my dog and my soul-searching self when I'm on the phone with Jessica and she has had her morning coffee and she is chattering without stopping for breath. Note that I did love this about her. Just not right then. News from home had a palpability that wrenched me from my private Pithole. The world of work and general busyness was out of place on the Great American Midlife Crisis road trip, on which I had gone off to study places more troubled than even I was over what they had lost, or appeared to be losing, or had wanted so much but had never quite managed to get their hands around, all of which left them (and me) afraid for what lay ahead, if indeed anything did lay ahead—other than slow decline and ruin and, of course, eventually death. I wanted to drive and drive until I could know for certain that something good was right straight ahead of us and that I knew at last how to find it.

That's when Pittsburgh flashed up in front of me and I nearly hit it.

Jessica was saying, "Words, words, words, sigh, words, sigh, words," and I said, "Ummm, yeah. Uh huh, mmm," and the highway led without fanfare to a bridge, and I drove onto the bridge, and then all at once there was Pittsburgh like a bobbing jack-in-the-box, cranked up tight till it popped: Bang! I'm Pittsburgh! Glass towers above a river, a bright and shiny mural I was about to smash into.

"Whoa!" I told Jessica. "I'll call you back." I disconnected.

Then the road curved down and the car did not strike Pittsburgh but instead was ushered safely around to the right. At the edge of the city down along the river were old waterfront office buildings squatting beneath a modern sky-scraping metropolis like quaint, musty shadows, and then around another bend, the whole mirage was gone. There were tunnels, and all forms of bridges—bridges over water and bridges over roads, bridges carrying cars, bridges carrying trains, and the trains were full of slag and oar and ingots all tugged by diesel engines, muscling in and out of Pittsburgh. The city was pitched at its edges, heavy with the fruit of superhuman labors. I wanted to go back to see all this again, but first I had to ditch the trailer.

Colby and I made camp at a KOA in Washington, Pennsylvania, about twenty miles outside Pittsburgh. The KOA was essentially a large, muddy parking lot on top of a steep hill. Our presence instantly brought down the real estate value in that KOA, by which I mean my Scamp was a slum in a fabulous collection of high-end luxury RVs and trailers, all of them decked out in patios with gas grills and flat-screen TVs. Outdoor television on a camper, imagine that. I set up the Scamp awning to shelter Colby and me from the rain, and later when the rain finally stopped, I strung my damp socks and Colby's wet leashes on the awning to dry.

Next to us in the campground's low-rent corner was a retired couple in a van who had been traveling all summer to see baseball games in the hometown parks of every baseball team they had never seen play before. It was a great project. They had logged thousands of miles doing this, gone to so many places they never would have seen if not for baseball. They had come to Pittsburgh to see the Pirates in a playoff game. I told them my own project involved traveling with my dog on an epic tour of depressed, ruined, and seemingly hopeless places whose best days were behind them and whose futures, sadly, looked bleak indeed. The couple stood very still, smiling, waiting for me to say I was kidding. I didn't say it. We were in a standoff. "Well, have fun!" the woman finally said, and we all went about our business.

We were damp and cold, and I did laundry at the KOA mainly so that I could sit on the clothes dryer and warm myself as it rolled. The Scamp had a gas-powered furnace, but I hadn't yet read the manual to learn how to ignite it, which was a daunting and potentially dangerous project. I also had not once used the bathroom I had insisted that my trailer have as a safety feature. I couldn't quite accept the idea of peeing into a sub-trailer bin and storing my urine, etcetera, down under where I slept only to pour it out into a sewer later. Public restrooms so far worked fine.

I put a blanket on the floor in the laundry room for Colby and he lay down by my feet as the dryer tumbled and I read a magazine about people who travel the world in their boats. In it was a profile of the woman who had played the part of a cruise ship activities director named Julie in *The Love Boat*, a TV show on the ABC network from 1977 to 1987 that I watched faithfully as a kid, spending Saturday nights on the couch with a snack, usually sitting with my mother and her needlepoint. Life was so easy, then, when even bad TV seemed wonderful. These pleasures were quaint. Sometimes I want these pleasures back. In hindsight I see that this show began in the decade of Watergate and gas rationing and long lines at gas stations and stagflation and post–Vietnam War social disorder and un-employment and polyester leisure suits and all kinds of ominous signs of impending doom but, see, *Love Boat* helped us heal from all that, like we could go back to a life that was simple again, and I felt safer watching TV with my mom than going out into my painful teenaged Saturday night misadventures. It was all okay, with *Love Boat*. In the magazine article that I read at the KOA near Pittsburgh, I learned that in real life, Julie had been a raging coke addict.

Wait. How had I not known this? The fresh-faced lady on that boat where folks found love when it was least expected, *that* Julie, the blonde in the blazer, had been coked out the whole time? Pop culture tricked me. Reading this article, which tried but failed to draw my attention to her recovery, somehow robbed me of many innocent years. And yet I was also richly fascinated, as I often am when I discover the world is a much darker and more dangerous place than I had once imagined. There is a relief in knowing the truth, however dark, and also a relief in accepting that life is not TV.

The next morning, the baseball couple left and a truck pulled up and a sixty-something couple sprung from it and began opening a pop-up trailer into a groovy A-frame-shaped triangle thing, and then they pulled out some patio furniture and opened the windows and in about forty-five seconds, wow, they were right at home. Their truck's North Carolina license plate rim said U.S. Navy Retired.

The man who drove the truck was wearing a U.S. Navy Retired baseball cap and greeted me with a handshake so vigorous it felt like part of a training exercise. "Hello there, young lady!" he said, nearly saluting, and I loved him for judging my perimenopausal self young, though I couldn't decide if he was saying it the wrong way, as in, the way I've heard cops or deli clerks call quite elderly and easily confused old women "young lady" with jovial kindness. This usually comes just as the old bag nearly drops something heavy or damn near trips on a rug and breaks a hip. "Ho ho," the jovial cop might say, coming to the rescue. "Watch it there young lady, looks like you've had a little tumble!" Was I that kind of young lady? The old kind? I was not sure. How old was forty-nine? Older than I wanted it to be, but beyond that, I had lost my bearings.

Pat and Richard were in their late sixties. They told me they had met after they had both been widowed; they had been married to each other for four years—"As of next Thursday," Richard said, smiling. Pat pulled a thread off his shoulder and fixed his collar in a way that somehow said, "We'll be having sex tonight."

"We met on Christian mingle," she said.

"Darn right," he said. "We never would have met without the internet."

Suddenly I felt as if I had missed the sexual revolution not once but twice—first it was the whole birth control pill/liberation/dopey-hippie orgy of the 1960s that passed while I was still in diapers; then while I was busy looking back at that bawdy time with confused envy, this whole internet dating situation developed, and people were not only dating but also hooking up casually with hot strangers. It was all just click, boom, sex. I had paired off in time to miss the whole thing, and while it did occur to me that a road trip might be a place to give it a go and not get caught, I also remembered I was on that road to begin with because I had caught myself straying. There I was, doing it again in my mind. Why? What did I want so badly? It was more than sex. According to The Girls, married people were generally better off without sex, though I watched Richard and Pat and knew better. I needed something that was sex but not sex, and I didn't know why I didn't have it or how I could get it, and I could not safely ask anyone about it. Anyone I talked to would either judge me, I was sure, or would end up realizing how fucked up her own private life was, how much of a loveless desert she had agreed to endure. This is why "private lives" are private. They're too godawful to reveal. We all know. You raise this shit with a friend, you may as well go write a book about it, tell everyone. No one's that dumb. Listen, it's never just sex you're talking about when you talk about sex in a marriage, or a long relationship; it's a confluence of many things we're afraid of, among the scariest of which is the likelihood we will wreck the relationship we're secretly unhappy with if all this difficult truth gets out of its box. Jess and I tried, but long ago had reached an impasse, and folded our impasse up and put it in a box in service to a greater happiness, we thought. I would have liked to have kept all this business in its box and I really did try, but all the fear that had flowed through me since the generally happy Jess era began and much more from long before then had been stuffed into that box and it was too much and time passed and I changed and I could no longer contain it. Bang. This stuff was springing up like a big scary clown. Surprise! Like Pittsburgh.

"You traveling all alone?" Pat asked me at the campground as she stroked Richard's cheek.

"No," I said. "I have my dog."

Colby lay on his blanket chewing a stick. I watched Pat's eyes move to Colby and back to me as she worked the puzzle of my relationship status. "Well, that's sweet," she said. Apparently to some, a woman without another human is alone, dog or no dog.

Let me say here that I really did love Colby. Let me be careful to add that I did not actually have a "romantic" love for my dog, and though I can admit that it had crossed my mind as I drove around Pennsylvania that I almost loved Colby enough to marry him, I was only thinking that because Western Pennsylvania is Rick Santorum country. In 2003, when he was a U.S. senator, Rick Santorum famously gave an interview to Lara Jakes Jordan, an Associated Press reporter, in which he said gay marriage would open a door to all kinds of nontraditional and ungodly relationships, and next thing you know, people would be marrying their dogs. Did he have a point? I think Colby would have agreed to marry me before Jessica ever did; Jessica was no fan of marriage. She had made that clear and it was one of the few things we had ever really fought about, because I liked the idea of marrying. It symbolized connection, as deep as it could be, and that is what I wanted. To stay with Jess meant giving up that desire. But I hadn't, really. Anyhow: Santorum's position was that such a shocking cultural evolution must be stopped before it starts, maybe even before anyone gives it a passing thought. I had therefore given much passing thought to marrying my dog because Rick Santorum brought it up.

"In every society," Rick Santorum told Jordan, "the definition of marriage has not ever to my knowledge included homosexuality. That's not to pick on homosexuality. It's not, you know, man on child, man on dog, or whatever the case may be."

At this point, Jordan perked up.

"I'm sorry," she interjected. "I didn't think I was going to talk about 'man on dog' with a United States senator."

I've always wondered about the tone of her "I'm sorry" in that moment. I had known Lara as a young reporter at her first job, back in Albany, where for a time during my newspaper years I had been one of her editors, so I can kind of see her in this exchange—her very blonde head, her very straight back, her very seriously perplexed face. Lara Jakes Jordan is a sharp woman. By the time she met Senator Santorum, she had interviewed some heavy hitters, including Hilary Clinton when Clinton was a senator. But man-on-dog can throw anyone. Judging only by the transcript of this interview, my guess is that she sat there perplexed, unblinking, as the senator reeled off examples of unholy relationships, and then she snapped out of it and said "I'm sorry," as in, "I'm sorry, I froze there for a moment. Did I actually hear you say what I thought I heard you say?"

"There are consequences to letting people live out whatever wants or passions they desire," said Rick Santorum.

"Sorry," Jordan said. "I just never expected to talk about that when I came here to interview you."

Pat and Richard did not judge my love for Colby as Rick Santorum would have, or at least not outwardly. I petted Colby and Pat petted Richard and then they launched into a story about taking a cross-country trip in their other RV, their thirty-two-footer, back when they were first married. They took Richard's eight-seven-year-old mother along with them, and they told me about how each night as newlyweds they couldn't wait till everyone went to bed and they heard old mom snoring and it was such a relief when they finally heard that snoring because it meant they could finally . . . you know. You know.

I'm sorry. This astonished me. I had been three or four days in Pennsylvania where I had found hardly anyone wanting to talk to me about anything and now I got randy Christians talking fornication within ten minutes of our shaking hands. I backed away to my chaste little trailer. I felt glad to know how lustily life does go on even after, you know. You know. The change, that god awful, inevitable midlife fucking change that changes everything. No one wants to change. Yet all that change goes on and on and then look: Pat is still alive and Richard loves her and she loves him, and as they neared seventy they had been married such a short time and had probably fornicated more than half the people I knew had for years. I was clearly being given the sign I had been asking for: something good was right ahead, I was not too old; there was time and love waiting. Yet I did not know how to get to it, and this troubled me, and also I did not want to get stuck with a mental image of Pat and Richard and you know, you know. So I excused myself to go fix Colby's breakfast.

Sunday was football day and the Steelers were playing the night game down in their home stadium on the Ohio River. I dressed Colby up in his blue dinosaur scarf and we went downtown to mix with a herd of sports fans who were either leaving the baseball park after that afternoon's Pirates game or going to the football stadium to watch the Steelers. Pittsburgh's waterfront was teeming with pedestrians, possibly none of whom would be there if not for major league sports.

Lately, cities had been on a binge of building stadiums and arenas as a way of drawing humans back to the inner cities, and just about every city I visited on my journey had a new one—even Erie, even Utica. Even Brooklyn, come to think of it, had opened Barclays Center just a year before. Pittsburgh was ahead of the curve on the arena concept because it had a stadium on its waterfront as early as 1909; ninety-two years later, the city imploded its old football stadium and built a new one nearby and opened a separate stadium for baseball next to it, because if one stadium was good, dear lord, two would be fantastic. Now Pittsburgh's riverfront stadium zone hums on weekends when it might otherwise be dead. I visited the waterfront on game night as a matter of economic research but was also doing a very serious study to assess how many Pittsburgh Steelers tailgaters would walk up to Colby and say, "Aw, he's so cute!" and/or "What kind of dog is he?" and/or lavish love and admiration on him with happy sounds that aren't really words. This important study of my dog produced no surprises; the rain had let up and the beer was flowing and the number of Colby fans turned out to be too high to count. Colby soaked it up.

Later, when the Steelers game started and the party moved into the stadium, Colby and I walked back across the Ohio River on the Roberto Clemente Bridge, named after a famous Pirates right fielder. The bridges of Pittsburgh, I should note, are not frilly gaudy things but strong and silent types—Bridges in the Hands of an Angry God, Calvinist work-worshiping expanses of industry, lined up one after another down the straight lines of the three rivers that meet in Pittsburgh: the Allegheny, the Monongahela, and the Ohio. When they are lit and you look downstream at the lot of them, the bridges seem to go on forever. One morning, riding on a riverboat full of ladies on a field trip, I studied these bridges and I thought of Italy and of the Ponte Vecchio—the "old bridge"—one of five bridges that cross the Arno River in Florence; the Ponte Vecchio dates to AD 996, except that it got destroyed a couple times so really, the bridge I saw was not the original old bridge but a new one, built in 1345. The original Ponte Vecchio stood only 350 years, a paltry blip and yet a blip far longer than the life of the United States and three times the age of any bridge in Pittsburgh.

The bridge that replaced the first Ponte Vecchio is plain and boxy, a work-ing bridge with commercial stalls on it; the butchers whose shops were on that bridge in the fourteenth century maybe never thought, as they worked, that one day, someone like me would buy postcards instead of tripe in those stalls, or stand on the shore beneath the old bridge thinking in that moment, which would pass, that the old bridge was the most curious, lovely sight in all the world.

Looking up at the steel spans of Pittsburgh I imagined I was seeing the Florence of some future age, so beautiful and unappreciated for now, but given a few more centuries, who knows. The city had already reclaimed it-self from the mess of its industrial glory days, when it was full of hard labor. Yet for now at least, Pittsburgh can't so easily be separated from the story of American industry, as if sweat still runs in those rivers. The first oil barges from Oil City landed there, and for a century the valleys around Pittsburgh were one long, steel-making furnace, fueled by coal dug from those Allegheny Mountains that had been so hard to cross. What were mountains after all but huge mounds of rock and ore piled up by god and waiting to be taken, waiting for humans to alchemize wealth. What Ameri-cans most valued was really very ugly: we stripped and wrung and battered riches from the ground we raged across. Americans had been like Vikings sacking their own declared home, and Pittsburgh was a poster child for that sacking. Andrew Carnegie and Henry Clay Frick smelted their coke-and-steel fortunes here, even as they smote unions with iron fists. Tug-boats ferried Pinkerton guards across the water one night in 1892, landing upstream in a city called Homestead where they shot and killed striking steelworkers. Walking out on billionaires is a crime just that bad, it seems.

Lots of nasty stuff went down in Pittsburgh. People mocked its grit from the start. H. L. Mencken described its "agonizing ugliness" in a 1927 essay: "Here was the very heart of industrial America . . . the boast and pride of the richest and grandest nation ever seen on earth—and here was a scene so dreadfully hideous, so intolerably bleak and forlorn that it re-duced the whole aspiration of man to a macabre and depressing joke."

Nice! The whole aspiration of man. Twisted up into hell. I get that. I've been disappointed too. I found it hard to explain, but places that can be described as "dreadfully hideous" begged me to see them. The "dread" part most of all. How can you heal what you can't even see? But then, bang: Pittsburgh. There you are, darling. I feel you now.

On football night, boats ranging in stature from runabouts to yachts with dining rooms were moored on the rivers around Pittsburgh and fans were partying and all the grief could be erased; there were no oil skiffs around, no tugboats. I wanted to watch the Steelers game, by which I mean football and not some kind of war between striking workers and armed guards. I dreamed of finding the quintessential football-watching spot in or around rugged, honest, blue-collar Pittsburgh, but that dreamed-of spot must be in some basement man cave because Colby and I drove around looking but we did not find a watering hole in a mill town where neighbors gather in the dim, warm light and quaff tulip pints of lager, and where, when something good happens on the field (which always would happen because this vision is of the great world, the perfect world, the world in which the Steelers always win) the whole room erupts into cheers. I had this image of American working towns, and of steel workers especially: muscled men in plaid work shirts, sleeves rolled up to their triceps, telephone pole legs slathered in blue jeans. I was thinking of a mural by Diego Rivera; I was thinking of Bruce Springsteen. And why wouldn't I? Who doesn't want their old, run-down industrial city streets to be lined with bars all full of Bruce Springsteen? It's our collective myth; it is the northern industrial city version of a rural country music fantasy. Cowboy towns and steel towns are places, we are given to believe, where hunky man-singers work very hard and hold their liquor and love women with pure hearts. The world is tough but these men can take it and they deserve your sweet love, lady, so jump on up into that enormous twin-cab pickup truck and give your love up. Or Else.

This fantasy appreciates nothing of how dire things had become for that working-class dude, how badly the myth had failed him by the second decade of the twenty-first century, when he didn't even have a fighting chance in a labor war because there was hardly any labor anymore; whatever working-class nirvana I imagined was out there waiting for me in Pittsburgh I had missed by at least a generation, and I ended up watching the Steelers game at a chain restaurant bar next to a motel in a fast-food zone in Monroeville.

If Monroeville wasn't my ideal industrial city football neighborhood, it was the model early twenty-first-century American town. It is a first-ring suburb of a big old city cluttered up with strip malls and a few University of Pittsburgh medical buildings. It is full of people in cars, waiting for the light to change. The original downtown Monroeville is just one block long and buried in sprawl, and I never saw it.

Inside the chain restaurant, a drunken man stood near me at the bar, where I had parked myself across from the TV. He saw that I was writing in a notebook during commercials and he asked me about it. He was a sullen, unhappy drunken man; the Steelers were losing to the Bears, which he observed with an occasional grimace and a goddamnit look, then drowned his pain in long slurps of beer. Steelers losing? Yep, they suck, Ben Roethlisberger sucks, coach sucks. Watching the game at a chain restaurant on a motel strip outside Pittsburgh? Yeah well, the situation sucks. Had more to drink than you just told your wife on your phone? Yeah well, she sucks, and by the way, mind your own business, you suck.

He said, "I'm not trying to be a total dick or anything, I just want to know what you're writing." It is a funny thing about drunken men who insist they are not being total dicks; saying this almost automatically proves they are, in fact, being total dicks and they know it but on some level they wish it weren't true.

I told him I was keeping a journal of my travels. He asked me why I had "traveled" to Pittsburgh (and the quotation marks here indicate his emphasis, suggesting that no one "travels" to Pittsburgh if they can help it). I looked into his red-ringed eyes as he faced me, weaving, and I told him I was interested in cities that were struggling to remake themselves. That's a simple way I had found to explain what I was doing. I had not understood, before I looked, how much loss was around us—but loss of what? Did Pittsburgh really mourn for its mills and slums? The sorrow seemed to me to be more abstract, like a loss of faith in ourselves, or maybe even a sick, sad revelation that we had never really been happy at all. Or was I imagining my own life again? I worked this puzzle in my notebook.

I should have just told the drunken man that I was attending a really boring conference on medical appliances. But I didn't. I said "cities," "struggling," "remaking themselves," and "me interested." The drunken

man let out a snort before I finished the word "struggling." Possibly his
snort would have been a laugh but he had caught it in time, choked it,
avoided all signs of joy—even the unparalleled joy of mocking something
someone else was into. He squelched this dangerous mirth with beer. I
plugged my yap with pinot noir. He said I should come see the cesspool
where he lived, which I learned was Harrisburg. He was in Pittsburgh because he worked for the railroad, a job that seemed to piss him off. He told
me that the way the steel mills and freight trains have gone all to hell is
criminal and mainly the fault of liberal ignorance and government incom-
petence that has destroyed the whole country.

Of course, nothing screams "liberal ignorance" louder than a lone
woman at a restaurant bar drinking wine and writing in a notebook. But
I was determined to reach across this divide. So I told him that I had gone
to college in Bethlehem, Pennsylvania, back in the 1980s not long before
the steel mills there closed. I told him that one of the only things I missed
about my time in college was the way every night around three in the morning, if I happened to step outside—and for whatever reason in those days I
often did step outside at three in the morning—I could hear the trains
going in and out of the steel mills, and from that hillside campus, I could
see below me in the darkness all the hundreds of small lights that always
burned at the mill; they looked like stars scattered down there, hanging
in air scented thick with sulfur and burnt rubber. Bethlehem had been a
mighty city, an engine of empire, the very place that had milled the steel
that made the Golden Gate Bridge, but all I knew of it at eighteen, nineteen, twenty years old, was that its steel mills were curiously beautiful and
I took comfort in their presence late at night. The industrial hum soothed
me when I was lonely. There was life down there. Even the acrid smell,
which at first seemed offensive, became something I loved because it revealed a depth to life I had been sheltered from.

"It was the smell of people working," I said.

Well, that did it. Even I knew that I had gone too far when I said the
thing about the work smell. Really, I had hoped to say things the trainman
might enjoy. He was such a sourpuss. But I knew there was no pleasing
angry drunks, generally, and my words showed no genuine appreciation of

rough, tough American guys like him with almost nowhere left to use their brawn these days. Those guys didn't fit into the modern economy of strip malls and medical billing centers; their hands were too thick to make lattes at Starbucks and even if they could, they would only make ten bucks an hour, so fuck it.

The trainman focused on the middle space just above the rim of his glass and sucked down some beer and then he said that if I wanted to understand what had happened to America, I should start by learning this: there is so much coal in this country, so goddamn much coal. If we could mine and haul and burn the stuff it would be like the good old days, when people worked, but our government is too goddamn stupid. We can't burn the coal because of the EPA's fucked up antipollution rules. And what we do dig up we sell to China and then they burn it to power their own genera- tors and then they make stuff and they rise to glory. See that? They burn the coal, the air is just as fouled as if we had burned it, but we don't get to make steel and our power plants get shut down. And some guy in Asia has a job that we don't. We get it coming and going, right up the ass. Pardon the French. He sipped his beer.

He kept trying to excuse himself for being a dickhead but I under- stood. The trainman was unhappy, and he had a point about the air get- ting fouled regardless of who burned the coal. But I couldn't really see why it was necessary for anyone to burn it, when solar and wind power is abundant and practically free. I would take that question down to West Virginia in November. I went back to watching the ballgame and making notes.

"What is that, Arabic? Are you writing in like, fucking, Arabic?"

"No," I said. "I just write small."

"So that's English?"

"Yeah."

"That's English. Seriously? Jesus. I don't mean to be a dick."

My notebook was part travel log and part diary, and in it I wondered why I was so unhappy in the middle of my life when on the surface it seemed fine. I could make a list of unhappy people I knew, of failed mar- riages and lost jobs, of addicts, of worse. And then I began to make notes about the angry train man, and about Pittsburgh, which had pulled itself out of darkness and should have been a happier place to visit. Mr. Mencken ought to come back from the dead to take a look today, the way the universities have grown up and have great art museums and theater schools, the way the light shines on those glass towers and reflects off three rivers. People water ski there. All of this, and yet so many are still so unhappy. In the nineteenth century, rivers meant work; immigrants settled in the slums of Pittsburgh and they all went to work, even the children, in terrible conditions and for little in return. That's how great we once were: jobs for everyone, even your kids. Was that better? Was going backward ever a very good idea?

Andrew Carnegie's first job was as a bobbin boy at a Pittsburgh knitting mill, twelve-hour days, six days a week, earning less than five dollars a month. He hustled his way into a train job, invested in all the hot commodities of the day: first the railroads, then the ironworks that were building the railroads. He had a lock on the iron right at the moment when the world learned to turn iron into steel. He made a fortune in the Pennsylvania oil fields when he was only twenty-nine years old; he pumped that fortune into steel technology. In 1888 he bought the Homestead Steel Works, on the Monongahela River near Pittsburgh, and created Carnegie Steel.

Meanwhile, Henry Clay Frick was getting rich making coke—a condensed, intensely hot-burning form of the coal dug from the nearby mountains. Burning coke releases the smell of sulfur that I found so touching in college, and it makes furnaces hotter than hell, and that heat is what turns iron ore into steel. Frick and Carnegie got together and made an empire.

What I love about these stories is understanding how it's all connected. One line connects Rockefeller to oil and oil to Carnegie, and the rivers and lakes connect all the cities and all of it grew up nearly at once, not so long ago. To know of this and see Pittsburgh makes sense of Pittsburgh. To know about Cleveland and Rockefeller, and then visit the refineries in New Jersey, where I grew up, and to know that Rockefeller built those too, is like reaching through space-time to refocus the picture, discovering my own life inside the web. I went not long ago to see the refineries in Elizabeth, New Jersey, in the shadows of the Goethals Bridge; I wandered through a neighborhood beneath the bridge at the edges of a modern industrial badland, an incomprehensible jungle of tanks and ducts and many-storied stacks that grew from a seed John Rockefeller planted. I had never thought of the mess of New Jersey as part of a grand story; it always very simply seemed to me, passing in a car up on the Turnpike viaduct, that New Jersey was an ugly place, and required no further explanation. I was wrong. Down below the web of elevated roadways there was a little world, and in that world are stories, and in one story, in a neighborhood known to locals as "down under," the old houses and bars had been marked for demolition because the Goethals Bridge was soon to be expanded. There was a cul de sac in that near-abandoned maw called Rockefeller Street. It had a strip club on the corner, also empty when I saw it and marked to be destroyed. That a street in this place had ever been meant to honor Rockefeller is itself a strange idea, connecting him to that space in a way I'm sure few imagine anymore, and perhaps few but me have lately considered that Rockefeller, a staunch Baptist, would have been sickened by the dance club on the corner of his street. Whether the oil workers at that club drinking beer after their shift was over ever thought of this or not, they were there because of John D. Rockefeller, because of Titusville. To know this connects me to a kind of secret life, the story of how what we see arrived as it did, and how it was lost, and how this fate awaits everything.

Rockefeller, Frick, Carnegie. Great men, yes, but it was so much easier to make a fortune when all this land's resources were up for grabs. The land itself was up for grabs. It was free to take. We would call that welfare now. We would despise the homesteaders and call them freeloaders. Andrew Carnegie was a truly impressive rags-to-riches guy, and I'm sure he would be a hero to the drunken trainman at the bar, in theory. But a hundred years or more ago, the trainman would have found himself on the business end of Carnegie's union-busting guns and would not have liked him. Guys like Frick and Carnegie started as poor urchins and became self-made men. True. Also true: they had opportunities that Mr. Trainman never had, and never will. Whatever comes next in this country, we can't just grab land and resources anymore, and the future can't possibly look like the past, so it's pointless to want to go back there.

My drunken dickhead friend and I watched the Steelers lose. The Packers and the Bills also lost that day. It was a massacre for the Rust Belt but the Sun Belt did okay. Miami won, the bastards. Fucking Florida. So goddamn unfair. So goddamn disrespectful. The drunken man had a look in his eye like he wanted to kill something. I thought of De Niro, and I thought of my old favorite movie, *The Deer Hunter*, I thought about that group of young men from steel country, and the movie's golden rule: kill clean. Don't add to any creature's misery. "One shot," De Niro said. "Two is pussy." Drunken Dick's lip curled a little, and he slowly slid to the side of his bar stool, then straightened up. His dinner arrived in a to-go bag, and he left.

The Deer Hunter is set in the Pennsylvania steel city of Clairton, a few miles south of Pittsburgh. Clairton was once home to the world's largest steel mill, built by the behemoth U.S. Steel Corporation. J. P. Morgan made U.S. Steel after buying out Andrew Carnegie. Mills and mines and coke plants spawned for miles along Pittsburgh's rivers, and small steel-making cities grew around them: McKeesport and Braddock and Rankin and Monessen, Homestead, Duquesne. All cities built by steel. All distressed cities now.

Monday morning, Colby and I headed down into the Monongahela Valley on narrow roads spotted with dollar stores and pharmacies; here and there were bars and liquor stores, though a fair amount of those were boarded up like most everything else. That's always the last thing to go, I've noticed. We raced along a narrow road into the valley and crossed at last beneath a low concrete underpass, then into its long shadow angled over the road. When we emerged from that darkness, we were facing a sign that said, "Welcome to Clairton, City of Prayer." I took Colby's picture in front of the sign and then pushed on like a touring fan into the heart of the Deer Hunter's hometown.

Perhaps it seems I chose to visit this place because I loved a movie about it. It didn't happen exactly that way. I was following a call, but not quite deliberately, and in hindsight I'm not surprised that I kept arriving at places I needed to see, just as I was carrying Ida Tarbell's book about Standard Oil. Rolling into Clairton, I had a sense of finally arriving in a hidden world I had imagined as a child was some empathetic, kindred spirit home of mine. I had stared into the hills as my family drove by and had longed to see what was hidden back there, and now at last I had arrived. But I had not deliberately gone off to find *The Deer Hunter*. I understood what I had done only as I moved through it, and knew it was exactly right.

The movie, of course, is about loss and sorrow, so I couldn't have expected to find anything uplifting in Clairton, except that it was, in my mind, a *good* place, one that nurtured those young men—those steel workers, beer drinkers, deer hunters; those certain Americans who grew up in a hard-working hometown that they loved. Clairton was home to those friends, thus in my mind it harbored values I perhaps romanticized, but also, I expected something much deeper from it; this place as I understood it had survived a deep trauma. I imagined it to be a wise and strong place as a result. I must have imagined someone there knew how to navigate fear and sorrow and the crisis at the center of a life, and surely someone did. But the only person I would meet or even see in Clairton was a homeless man on a lonely street who asked me for money. I see now the mistake of my imaginings; no longed-for cinematic resolution had arrived. The trauma had come, and then the wound deepened, but the place had not yet survived.

I drove up the hill into the center of Clairton and began searching for a place to park. By searching for a place to park, I don't mean to suggest there was competition for a few open spaces. Cars had raced me on the rain-slick streets down by the river, but up in the old center of Clairton there were exactly zero cars besides mine; the wide streets on the hilltop and the sidewalks along them were empty. Everything was empty but for one tiny bar, lit by a red beer sign, its door a thin crack in a long, hard wall of abandonment. No one actually "needs" to park on a street where buildings are boarded up and gutted, so parking spaces were abundant. What I was searching for, then, was not a parking place so much as a safe place to park the car with my beloved old Colby inside.

Colby, a sensitive and highly emotional dog, must have had his nerves stretched already by the dark mood we had entered. The space around us was overcast and misty and generally unfriendly. In his old age my dog, who once shattered records for speed laps at his dog run, preferred standing and sniffing things to walking, mostly; he could not be counted on to

Storefronts in downtown Clairton, Pennsylvania

run from danger if he had to. It is hard to actually run away from persistent, generalized anxiety under any conditions, but running from it while literally dragging an old dog is a special kind of foolishness, so in the end, for lack of a safer option, I parked on the street and kept moving the car to keep him near me. It was not people I feared, but more the lack of them, as if some malevolent force had left this place not quite alive, but not dead either. A creosote plant remains in Clairton, turning coal tar into wood preservative and other chemicals; the sharp smell of sulfur and tar, and a soft mechanical hum underneath it, hinted at a menacing force that was toying with that place and might toy with our lives if we let it. I conjured a vision of Satan disguised as my Buffalo friend Bob the Builder, in his blue jeans and work shirt, a contractor of doom taking measurements on the sidewalk. "Almost finished," he says. "Won't be long." I see the expression on his face, a wary smile behind a clipboard.

The city was still. It felt as if a plague had swept through. Houses climb steep hillsides in Clairton and there must have been people in some of them, but their curtains were drawn and because of the rain as much as any underlying sadness, the people were not coming out that day. Plague is an accurate analogy, actually, because in the fourteenth century when the Black Death arrived in Europe, something like a third to one-half of the population of that entire continent died; imagine sitting with your two best friends and one or both disappearing in a blink. The Deer Hunter on patrol in Vietnam, his buddies snuffed by sniper fire. Dead. Between 1960 and 1990 in Clairton, Pennsylvania, half the population disappeared. By 2013, four out of five bodies were gone.

Meanwhile, consider the ones left behind: nearly every kid at Clairton High School qualifies as economically disadvantaged. Only about 64 percent will graduate. The proficiency rate for high school science hovers around 5 percent. One year not long before my visit, the number of eleventh-grade Clairton girls who reached science proficiency was exactly zero. Not one of them could grasp it; not one of their minds could hold a thought as critical as, say, evolution. How would they survive in a world they couldn't even understand?

I don't mean to pick on Clairton. It just happens to be the town a movie I love was set in. The Pennsylvania Distressed Cities Act was passed in 1987 to turn the ruined steel economies around. Clairton joined the distressed cities list in 1988. Twenty-seven Pennsylvania cities have been designated distressed over the life of the program; only six ever "recovered." Legislators fixed this problem in 2014. The solution, simply put, was to limit the time cities are allowed to remain distressed. Set a deadline. After that, you can't be poor anymore. You're off the list. You've graduated.

I returned to my car, where Colby lifted his head to sniff the fear, and we rolled through Clairton as if it were a Hollywood soundstage whose last scene was shot a long time before then. "One shot," De Niro tells his friend. "Two is pussy." A shot deer who isn't killed is suffering, and if you let that happen, the grief belongs to you.

7

Rockford

It's not like it's new, it's been happening forever," Ron, my impromptu Rockford, Illinois, tour guide told me, trying to demystify the collapse of American industry while simultaneously weaving a white rented van through traffic. We were racing down East State Street in Rockford, trying to catch up with the Society of Industrial Archaeology tour bus. Ron had organized the tour and I was an inexperienced stray requiring special treatment whom he had been foolish enough to be kind to, and look where that leads: to crazy, lurching rides in a van bound by chaos. But on the ride to catch up with the bus I learned so much.

"Sure," he said, "travel kismet for you. A nightmare for me. I won't do this next time."

Since Pittsburgh I had been traipsing a bit, maybe trying to lose the sting of the monstrous, desolate trail left by steel. It had been much harder to look at this than I had imagined it might be. Maybe everyone should see it, to understand the country better. And luckily, they can: the unabashedly wrecked steel towns around Pittsburgh have been assembled into the Rivers of Steel National Heritage Area; the long-forgotten Erie Canal manufacturing corridor has been similarly designated. People might want to visit these places on vacation, like they visit national parks. It's a great idea, really, if people will go. The drama of fortune's sharp rises and falls is exciting to see, and also perhaps healing, like going to a memorial service—which, as I think of it, is what we all may need to move on from a past that still holds us. But implicit in that healing is our loss, and many who remember a kind of greatness in this past are not ready to talk about losses, or acknowledge their trauma. It is not as easy as I would like to make it seem; it wasn't easy for me to feel such pain, but I had my trailer and car and my unfettered right to run away.

Fifty miles away from Clairton, people had no idea what darkness was back there. The story had not been well told. I had spent a night near Akron, where I sat at a wine bar past closing and described Clairton to a young woman who knew absolutely nothing about Pittsburgh, including why the Steelers are called Steelers, or what the geometric design on their helmets might mean (it is undoubtedly the most complex uniform design story in professional sports); in fact, the wine bartender had never even been to downtown Akron—the city she had lived ten miles from all her life. I made her promise me she would go to Akron and she did promise, but probably because it was past closing time, and the promise was the best way to get me to pay for my drink and go away.

I spent another night in Angola, Indiana, where I followed a maze of signs assuring me I would find apples to pick, which I thought might comfort me. Jessica and I picked apples at home most years, and apples always led to pie. The apple signs in Indiana led to a long, paved driveway next to a faint-yellow, one-story house and a big yard of dead grass with one apple tree in it. A bucket sat on a table to collect money, should I pick an apple. In ordinary times I might have laughed, but just then, I felt desolate.

I spent an hour at the RV Hall of Fame and Museum in Elkhart, Indiana, talking to the two old men in trucker hats who volunteered as greeters there, which is something I might normally have spent the whole day doing—talking to the old dudes, hanging out at the RV museum just because it was there—but I was running out of time. I had this tour thing to get to in Rockford. Eventually, after a few more irresistible short breaks for tourism, I rolled into Rockford for the Society of Industrial Architecture's kickoff dinner at the Midway Village Museum. Midway Village turned out to be a sweet little replica Victorian town with a hardware store, print shop, police and fire stations, plumbing supply store, and lawyer's office.

In short, it was a replica of an actual American town, before commercial sprawl and economic decline gutted many such places; downtown Rockford was such a place, once, and it was just a few miles down the road from Midway Village and you didn't have to pay seven dollars to stroll through it. Still, no one did. People preferred the museum. I parked at Midway Village and strolled into the dinner there road-weary and distracted and just in time to have missed all but ten minutes of the tour orientation. The itinerary was on a sheet of paper; it said the tour bus I was supposed to be on the next morning would leave at seven thirty. I had to drop Colby off at the local doggie daycare half an hour later, at eight. The math didn't work.

I had had several appointments in the days between Pittsburgh and Rockford and had been late for them all so that by the time I saw the words "Bus leaves promptly at 7:30 a.m." on the next day's itinerary, I felt like an utter failure in my examination of total failure. Ron was heroically accommodating. He offered to help me by taking me in his van to catch up with the bus.

But in the morning as we rode in the van, I supposed he was regretting it; he weaved madly through inexplicable traffic in Rockford, a small city with a terribly dead downtown—where did these people in their cars suddenly come from? Where could they possibly be going? There was nothing in Rockford—and as he was chasing down the tour bus he was explaining simple economic history.

"It's all obvious in hindsight, oh dammit!" he said, and he juiced the accelerator and the van lurched rather violently.

Ron was a brilliant, vigorous, and perhaps tiny bit fussy man, on the small side, with small, hard eyes and gray hair cut close and receding. His smile was tightly closed, like he was holding back his best ideas in there. He was a focused guy, a former banker and economics professor who was driving fast and had a tendency to make impulsive decisions about when to turn.

"Places like Cleveland shot up back when the robber barons . . . ," he started to say, then lost the thought while passing a slow-moving Honda. "Well just, shit," he said. The bridge he had been trying to cross was closed for construction, so he circled back and took a different road and at last we did cross the Rock River, but then we were in the wrong lane and were quickly swept by traffic back across the river to the side we had come from.

Robber barons in the nineteenth century, Ron reminded me, included guys like John D. Rockefeller (oil) and Andrew Carnegie (steel) and Cornelius Vanderbilt (trains) and all the big rich names in the country who, back in the days of seemingly endless expansion, had used political power and ruthless business tactics to build huge industries and get massively rich. Cities formed around these industries. The cities rode their lucrative tide for a good long time, into the middle of the twentieth century, but really, nothing lasts forever. Industrialization had come and gone, a phase followed by other phases in the long trajectory of phases; the present was a mystery we would see better in hindsight. And so here we are: not on the right side of the river, no, and not in a land of endless prosperity where we thought we would be or thought we would stay forever but in the midst, instead, of a national identity crisis. And also chasing a bus.

Of course, history is recorded and available for all of us to study. This story has been amply told. Still, everything's new again the moment a person begins to wonder about it. All I had to do was say I didn't understand why things seemed so ruined in the greatest country the world had ever known. (And it is that, isn't it? The greatest? Ever?) The answer came rushing out of Ron like I had rubbed the genie's bottle.

Ron's fingers clutched and released the van's steering wheel. He was an astute perfectionist who in casual situations, I noticed later, seemed to avoid looking at anyone he didn't feel like seeing. Perhaps this is because, for him, seeing was either an all-out and total investigation or it was just not worth the effort. When listening, he would lock on to whatever or whoever had his attention as if his eyes might shoot lasers. He lived in Cleveland, where his job in the financial industry had involved scoping out investment possibilities for banks. What he had always liked most, he said, was getting access to businesses and factories to see how they worked, what made them go, learning whether or not they were likely to thrive. In retirement, working with the Society of Industrial Archeology, he engaged the process in reverse: visiting places that had once thrived but had died, and wondering how that happened, like a geologist examining Devonian fossils.

The tour bus was supposed to be at the old Barber-Colman plant, a factory loft in Rockford that produced knitting machines at first and then made a universe of electronics and machines that it sold all over the world.

All that remained of Barber-Colman was an empty six-story block covered in large, shuttered windows rising from a field of dirt and crabgrass. The abandoned plant had been on the National Registry of Historic Places since 2006 and the city of Rockford planned to use it somehow as a center-piece to its coming revitalization, whenever that happened, as surely it one day must happen, though a variety of plans had not worked out quite yet; life would come around again, as it always does, though sometimes that takes years and sometimes millennia, and I was certain neither Ron nor I would live to know what the Barber-Colman plant would ever turn into, or if Rockford would give up and tear it down and move on.

Ron flew along Rockford's arteries, trying to get to Barber-Colman despite numerous unforeseen roadblocks. He mixed profanities with a rollicking narrative overview of what the hell happened to places like Detroit (yeah, of course Detroit, people always focused on Detroit), but also Cleveland and Rockford and Akron and St. Louis and Little Rock and Memphis and just about any American place, large or small. There are reasons for everything.

Rockford was settled on the Rock River and grew as fast as nearby Chicago, for a time, and in fact Rockford was the second-largest city in Illinois for fifty years, until the city of Aurora opened a casino in 1993 and soon doubled its own size, taking over the number 2 spot. Casinos will do that—gambling being at least a bit to the future what manufacturing was to the past. "Rockford had water—water power," Ron said. That was es-sential a century before the electric cables and AC current came along. And since Rockford sat in the midst of the continent's most fertile farm coun-try, its factories specialized in building farm equipment. And then because new equipment made farms more productive, the farmers began cutting down acre upon acre of trees in order to plant on larger plots of land. And what do you do with all those trees they had cut down?

You make furniture. That's what Rockford became famous for.

"Shit!" Ron said.

He had finally returned us to the west side of the Rock River but we were stopped at a train crossing. A train was passing. The clock was tick-ing. The tour bus would not wait. Ron tapped the steering wheel and stretched his neck to see if the train's end was near, possibly wondering if he could shoot around it. Anyhow, as he was saying, everything makes sense, in hindsight. Very few things just fall from the sky.

I said, "Right! It's not like aliens just swooped in and built all this industry. Not like when they came down and built all the pyramids."

Ron said "right" without missing a beat, agreement being easier than engaging an unbidden pyramid-alien-conspiracy non sequitur. I had aliens on the mind because the night before, when I should have been hustling to attend the tour's orientation dinner, I had taken a quick detour to Tinley Park, Illinois, the site of a famous alien visitation known as the Tinley Park Lights. Before I started my trip, I had made a list of "weird Americana" to watch for, including ball-shaped water towers that have been painted bright yellow with big, black smiley faces on them; towns that claim to be the original "home of the albino squirrel," of which there are about a dozen; and places where aliens, UFOs, and other unexplained extraterrestrial phenomena have been widely reported. One night in 2004 in Tinley Park, a thickly settled suburb of Chicago, a UFO or possibly several UFOs were seen hovering over the local twenty-eight-thousand-seat amphitheater just as crowds were leaving a heavy-metal music event known as Ozzfest. I didn't mean to be late to the orientation dinner, but I couldn't rush past a place to which aliens had traveled light years to see. Was my time so much more valuable than theirs?

Right. Anyhow, when Ron started working for banks in Cleveland in the 1960s, he told me, he paid close attention to the classified advertisements in the daily newspapers. Newspapers used to make tons of money off of classified ads (before the internet made everything from cars to love so easy to find, thus drying up classified ad revenue and sending newspapers into a death spiral). The most lucrative sort of classifieds were known as legal notices, or "tombstones," ads that announced public legal actions, everything from foreclosures to divorce decrees to—and here's our key— announcements of initial public offerings, or IPOs. What Ron noticed in the newspapers in Cleveland in the 1960s was that there were tons of tombstone ads for IPOs, meaning that scores of private manufacturers who had done very well in the post–World War II boom were suddenly taking their firms public. That is to say, the soul of industrial America was for sale. It was right there in the papers.

Why? Why, suddenly, at the height of a gangbuster postwar economy, would those manufacturing firms turn their ownership over to the public? Today that might seem like the obvious next step for growing companies; they get big, then sell stock and get even bigger. It's a common business model to grow big, go public, then cash out these days. But in the 1960s, businesses from knitting mills to newspapers were likely to have been owned and run by families for generations. The factories and businesses were place-bound local institutions around which whole cities often grew. To Ron, the shift from local ownership to ownership by distant interests was a sign. The owners suddenly wanted to ditch what they had built. Selling a family business to the public, or to a huge corporation, was a form of bailing out. When it started happening so often, it telegraphed a big change.

"Smart money in the 1960s was sending their kids to law school because U.S. manufacturing was over." That's what Ron said.

If the pattern was there to see, somehow the shift still caught the rest of the country by surprise. By the 1980s, when Ronald Reagan was president, manufacturing plants all over the country were being shuttered by their new owners, who were not local and not families, and who instead made decisions in distant cities without having to live amid the local impact. Jobs disappeared. The vast northern manufacturing infrastructure—the site of our industrial revolution, so profound to our history that its rise was arguably the cause of our Civil War, because the competing economic model of the south was slavery—all this was disintegrating, and the jobs tied to it were being sent south or overseas.

Communities that had risen around these companies began, in turn, to fail. Detroit. Cleveland. Rockford. This was the story at the Barber-Colman plant Ron and I were looking for. That company started in 1894. It grew large making specialty textile machines. It remained privately owned through the post–World War II boom and expanded to make other things—electronic controls, motors, X-ray machines, all kinds of mechanical stuff. Barber-Colman grew for ninety years, until 1984. Then, the company started spinning off its various divisions. By 2001, one small part of the original company remained in a suburb of Rockford; the rest had been sold and gone south, and the big old factory building on Rock Street was abandoned, left squatting in the weeds above the Rock River.

An intersection in Rockford, Illinois

That's the time-lapsed photography version of America's industrial rise and fall and of Barber-Colman; the same story is told over and over again in Rockford, in the part of the city that roared to life when the Rock River was dammed and all this production became possible. Dozens of businesses once hummed here: Manny Reaper, Eagle Foundry, Rockford Iron Works, and bakeries, fastener companies, furniture makers, mills of all kinds. Few remain. The old Water Power District next to the Rock River is a near-vacant industrial zone, a concentration of what the Environmental Protection Agency calls "industrial brownfields," also known as empty, polluted places, and is soon to be . . . what? A tourist park? There was talk of a new brewpub and loft apartments when I was there. Rockford already had a hockey arena downtown. The city was trying all the things it knew to try and it still was not working, really.

I still didn't understand exactly why all those manufacturers all over the country saw the end coming in the 1960s, before the bottom really did fall out. People shrug and say manufacturing died in this country "because the economy went bad" but that is a tautology, like saying Colby is adorable because he is cute. I asked Ron. Here's what he said: "Well, that's fairly obvious too."

Okay; duh. The steam of the postwar boom could only run so far, he told me. And what a godsend that boom had been! The country had been in a depression and the old drivers of our growth had been played out. The robber baron era was done—they had found and amply exploited the continent's vast deposits of coal, gold, oil, iron, and other natural resources ; the country was developed well enough, so that the resource-demanding, job-creating work of building railroads and infrastructure and cities that popped up like rabbits had cooled from roar to hum; all the original economic drivers in this country had been played out or outlawed; a slump had taken hold; and by 1930 the next phase of economic growth was a dreadful unknown. Something drives economic growth. It doesn't just happen. Then along comes 1939, 1940, and a huge war to fight; a world to rebuild. We went bonkers churning out steel again, building stuff again, getting rich again like this time, boy, we really meant it.

"After the war," Ron reminded me, "Europe and Asia had all been bombed to bits." Few countries on the planet were in a strong enough position to rebuild them—and by rebuilding, we don't just mean sweeping the streets and putting houses back up; truly rebuilding a nation's economy means resupplying it with everything from socks to bricks to Barber-Colman knitting machines. The only countries who could do this rebuilding were the industrialized ones that had not been bombed. That basically left us, and Sweden. Adding to its unbombed infrastructure, the U.S. had a solid workforce, having lost relatively few able-bodied workers in the war, compared to, say, Russia. (Soviet Union total killed: twenty million, or nearly 10 percent of everyone. U.S. total killed: four hundred thousand, which, godawful as it was, amounted to one-third of 1 percent of the country.)

Growth came hard and fast, then, and our strength felt familiar; it was easy to keep believing America had always been superior in every way, as if it was God's plan and not the benefit of being geographically far from the bombers that made us rich. Any talk to the contrary was downright subversive, the commie talk of freedom haters. Especially the part about how the government financed all this growth. The cost of the wars? The

$100 billion Marshall Plan to rebuild Europe? No, you communist, this was not corporate welfare. The cash spent on these things was not a hand-out to industry. It was absolute moral necessity. If people happened to get rich, so be it.

Ron animated for me the tired expression "postwar boom," as in "baby boom," as in "economic boom," as in "housing boom." All that bright, booming expansion in the twentieth century when America felt great now seemed to me, as Ron reeled through it, like a government-financed meth-amphetamine rush. We had escaped a depression by spending on war and reconstruction; we had binged for decades on those government-funded efforts with no interest in pacing ourselves. It couldn't last, and smart money knew it.

"Anyhow," Ron was saying as we swerved, lurching over a pothole, "we were intact and we were providing for the world. For a time, we could build total crap and charge twice its worth if we wanted. We were the only ones with anything to sell." Americans grabbed the contracts and we worked at good jobs with pensions and built ourselves cozy suburbs and convinced ourselves that this was our birthright; it was all normal. And yet, while we were churning out the stuff and having mad, crazy, 1950s cocktail-swilling Playboy Club economic good times, the next generation of manufacturing was being rebuilt to far higher standards in the countries we had helped ruin. Germany and Japan were stronger than ever. Industrialists saw this too, well before most everyone; the rest of us lived that American century as if, once arrived, it would never leave us.

There was no tour bus waiting at the Barber-Colman plant when we finally found the old building across a vacant weed lot. It had apparently left. Ron asked a cop parked nearby if she had seen a bus go through and she sort of dreamily said, "Um . . . yeah. I think maybe I did."

"Shit," Ron said. "We missed them." So we hustled off to Taylor Freezer, a shiny new factory that makes ice cream equipment for fast food restaurants.

At the freezer joint, Ron dismissed me and I joined up with the other members of the SIA, who were for the most part—I will gently say—really, really nerdy. A few were there for academic study; most were retired folks on an extraordinarily geeky vacation. Many were either trained or amateur engineers, scientists too well versed in technical phenomena for me to make intelligent conversation with them. They were good at noticing the kinds of things most people never think about, and they spoke in mysterious equations and acronyms. They taught me the meaning of the words "aluminum extrusion," which I will fight the geek-supreme urge to share here. Many were dressed as if going on safari—hiking boots, multipocketed vests—hunting down our industrial heritage and its powerful mythology. They all had their own hard hats, something Ron admonished that I must one day have too, then he loaned me a very large one. It swallowed my head. Until I caught a reflection of myself wearing the oversized hard hat, I felt secretly sexy among this bunch, and also hipper than I had ever felt in a large group. For one thing, my brain space held more song lyrics than obscure manufacturing vocabulary words by a rate of about six million to zero. Also, for once, at forty-nine I was still the kid in the room.

Yet even as I reassured myself that I was at least marginally cooler than industrial history fanatics, the SIA nerds were in a way the coolest people I had ever known. At a furnace plant, my fellow tourists came up with questions like, "So you (unintelligible verb—boil? stir?) propane down so that it has the same BTU as methane, which is natural gas, correct?" My own questions were more along the lines of, "Why is it so clean in here?" The furnace factory, Eclipse Inc., sends burners around the world, notably to the proliferate factories of Brazil, where those factories in turn manufacture other sorts of things, like spoons, whose creation requires the intense heat American furnaces provide. The United States, it turns out, remains especially good at making furnaces, generators, and turbines that enable developing economies to grow and join the global economy. One of my neighbors in upstate New York worked thirty years at GE making turbines that were sold to China, so that China could generate enough electricity to power their own nascent factories, then make boatloads of plastic Christmas ornaments, dog toys, and coffee mugs to send back to us, and in this way grow into their own power. This is what makes us, now, one big economic organism and what hurts part hurts all. Finally I was ready to go back to college and take my final exam in economics, which in 1983 I had basically failed. I had not caught on to the beauty in this web, which to me gets lost in theorems and equations.

Fascinating as all of this was, the freezer place and the furnace place were nothing—nothing—compared to where we ended the day: Specialty Screw.

It is difficult to express my enthusiasm for Specialty Screw. This was no sanitized, white-jumpsuit, brightly lit chip fab plant, no delicate incubator of delicate things, but a gritty, oily place of machines that make tiny parts for other machines fed by enormous spools of steel wire, which are called spools as if they were little sewing machine bobbins but really, one steel spool would easily crush you flat. Big, heavy, pale-green machines bolted down all across a sprawling workshop floor grind away, pulling cords of steel off their spools and into the machine guts, where each machine in its own (specialized) way takes that steel and stamps it, cuts it, spins it, chops it, fixes it, chisels it, makes some shit, spits it out, spits it out, spits it out splat. Into bins. In that order. Sort of.

The factory does all this in a clanking metronomic repetition of steel parts cracking against other steel parts, stamping, cranking, hoisting, chinking, while everywhere the scent of lubricating oil and husky, sweating workers wafts deliciously. Workers hover over machines stamped with labels indicating that these machines too were manufactured by other machines, somewhere in America, decades ago.

Manufacturing is like any ecosystem. Every step in making something requires other steps; machines make parts for other machines that make parts for other machines that are used to make parts for machines elsewhere; one thing supports the next until one part falters, and then the whole delicate organism falls over in a chain of destruction. Everything depends on everything, which is wonderful until it's tragic.

This is not as complicated as the formula for methane but the notion of so much interconnectedness soothed me deeply; to see it in the machine world of all places meant as much to me as seeing it in the webs of nature, or in the webs of humanity. It was as if life opened up its chest and showed me its heart, how it works, why it matters; how it is an image of a heart just like my own. It exists in connection. It made me feel less lonely to see the web.

Specialized Screw's major market is the auto industry, so when American car makers took a dive in the Great Recession around 2008, the screw folks' livelihood was in danger. Yet they pulled through; this business of making small essential things that hardly anyone else ever thinks about, even for a second, lived through the crash largely because the business was owned by a local family, committed to surviving. Shutting down was not part of the business model. None of the still-operating plants we visited over three days in Rockford were publicly held; they were family owned, locally owned. Rockford businesses that had gone public had mostly been shut down, long ago. That is essential to the change we were so unhappily, most of us, experiencing.

Down on the plant floor, we donned our hard hats and wandered freely in manufacturing glory. The workers wore goggles and earplugs, sported elaborate tattoos on their laboring arms, pushed and pulled levers and buttons and dollies and cranks and kept the machinery rolling. If you want to try to understand the splendor of it all, read the following collection of words aloud while tipping your head left on the first word, right on the second, left on the third, right on the fourth, and so on, back and forth like a gear wheel moving one measured click at a time. Ready? Go: "feed wire, stamp wire, cut wire, spin wire, make shit, wire shit, spit on it, fancy trick, steely stick . . ." If you can do this while huffing over a can of 3-in-1 oil and dropping nails into a coffee can, you may possibly begin to understand what the screw factory was like. Glorious, trust me.

For one breathtaking moment in the center of all this, a woman in a thin, tight white T-shirt came into focus. She lifted a tray of screws out of a machine and turned to take it somewhere, her ponytail lashing the air, and in what seemed like slow motion she then turned her head to look back at me, strands of hair plastered by sweat to her cheek and neck, a pack of cigarettes showing in the tight pocket of her jeans. I stood in my factory safari outfit with my big hard hat perched awkwardly on my head and my goggles askew, a camera around my neck, and when she saw me looking at her, she smiled. I lifted my hand (also in slow motion) to wave. And then I felt it: dear god. There was what I had ached for, right there in that sweaty oily factory in Rockford: love, and sex, and machines that made parts for machines that made parts for machines, and the beautiful humans who made the machines work, and maybe one human here or there who would look up and smile at me from the heart of the chaos. All this need and energy exists in a web that is both fierce and fragile, and I felt for an instant that I too was a part of it, truly, and I was for a moment deeply satisfied.

On the bus, tired but happy, I wondered if Colby was okay in daycare and if he would have been interested in the factory tour. Probably not. I tried to think of someone who would be excited to discuss what I had witnessed. I drew a blank. Then my phone spat out cathedral bells. Jessica's special ringtone.

"I went to a factory! They make screws!" I said.

"Oh!" she replied.

"I know it's not very interesting."

"No, no. Of course it's interesting." I heard the sounds of her looking for something in a drawer. I described the screw plant—the steel wire, the potentially body-crushing spools stacked in an enormous storage room, the clanging and grinding of those oily green machines and screw after screw after screw after SCREW dropping into buckets—filling in every gritty detail I could think of until I realized I had been put on speakerphone and left on the counter of what I imagined must be an empty kitchen. I heard a dish drop into the sink and a distant "uh huh."

I searched the eyes of the geeks on the bus for a moment of connection but found my compatriots all dozing or reading the next day's itinerary. After a while, Jessica came back to the phone and I continued talking as if I had not felt her distance, and had never stopped trying to reach her.

"It was such an amazing day," I continued. "We not only saw cool empty ruined places but also places with people still working in them, which caught me off guard."

"Oh, that's so great. Really. I'm so happy for you." She said this as if I had won an award, or better yet, as if I had finally, finally won a prize I had deserved since third grade, which was an accomplishment, sure, but also a little pathetic.

"These factories, Jessica. They were so interesting."

"Can you say why, exactly? I mean, if you were going to write it. What would you say?" It was hard to say. What I saw resonated again with a need I had best expressed to Jessica in the anger and frustration of this need not being met. It was my fault in this drama that I could not find a way to tell her what I wanted; it was also wrong to believe that I wanted something any human could easily provide. Like sending flowers. I needed something so hard to identify, but I somehow knew it when I saw it.

"Well it's so interesting because there are these places where jobs are, and the places are *interesting*," I explained.

"Sweetie, you know what we've said about adding emphasis."

"It doesn't actually make something more interesting."

"Not really. No."

"Like lame exclamation points!"

"Exactly, my love. Exactly."

"I will try to be more specific."

"Yes. That would be good."

"I'm going to really try."

"Go on."

I took a breath, and started a few sentences that went nowhere special, something like: "It's all connected. Do you see? Everything is connected to everything and machines make more machines, and people are a part of it, all the whole, together, yes, and economics, also necessary. Parts. You see? Very many parts and all the whole, together, and it's, well, it's interesting."

"Maybe you could talk about something that you saw?"

A wave of hopelessness came over me.

"The screw factory girl was wearing a white T-shirt. She was ridiculously hot."

"Ah ha," Jessica answered. "Now you're on to something."

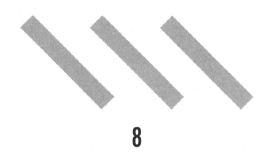

8

The Akron Side of Rockford

What made all this so compelling to me? The power of human effort, the stark aesthetic beauty of abandonment, all that is unseen in the ruins of a thing; a way of really seeing that connects history directly to us. An enormous abandoned factory sitting lonely in a field was made to bustle and hum, to thrive, and like many others who saw such a thing and cared, I wished I could love what was lost back to life somehow. What I saw touched me, and I wanted to be touched, but maybe what I meant by that is that I, too, wanted to be seen. These strange and storied places are not merely artifacts; they are mirrors. I circled back to Barber-Colman before I left Rockford and made my cry for help: me, standing before an empty building, knowing the total void inside, hoping that this building might recognize the hurt inside of me.

It had been this way forever between me and the world. Small towns buried in the Alleghenies, small houses in rows on the edge of Buffalo, an old farmhouse in a Wisconsin cornfield: I always looked, and what truth I saw in these places was always, also, a version of myself. I once imagined in distant places a kind of life I hoped for; then I saw loneliness in them instead, and struggle; now, I had looked closer and I could see near total loss, and a reckoning coming if what was broken did not heal. The world I saw was as alluring to me as it had ever been, just as worthy of seeing, but also foreboding. That I was pushing Jessica away just as I confronted this hurt was frightening in the extreme; she was my best friend, and a comfort, and her constant presence had kept me safe for years from the darkness I knew was there, waiting. I understood, in the middle of my life, that I could not wait any longer to confront it.

But what was it? Depression? Disease? Where did this darkness come from? There are theories. There is a shopping list: family dysfunction, a brother who died young, the eccentricities that made me a lonely girl, desperate to be loved. There are stories in those things but they get told and still explain very little. The grief I felt seemed rooted to a place beyond that, as if the hard parts of life simply inflamed a hurt I brought with me. Maybe the pain of abandonment is part of every human, mixed into our DNA the way plastic pollutes oceans; disintegrated bits have entered every single cell. There is a pain that might consume any of us, a condition we are born with, and some heal it early and others heal it late and some never do. Ask an addict why she uses drugs and she'll rationalize endlessly. Loneliness. Stress. Acne. The rain, the sun. The presence of weather. But this deeper hurt must be what moves her, what aches to be numbed. I think of addicts not to say that this is now a story of addiction, though perhaps in the end it could be; addiction is all around us now, an epidemic, and its cause is one of my concerns. What I want to say is simply that I know a darkness that defies pat explanations, and that such hurt, unhealed, leads to harm. I have the authority to say this in part because it is so obvious. It is happening everywhere we look; we see the awful hurting every day, but seeing such a wound in ourselves is harder. What I have called longing in my own life might simply be myself begging for that darkness, that wound, to heal.

And then sometimes, in these very same mirrors, there it was: all the love, all the beauty. An ecstasy lived in the same depth as that longing and I wanted to share that feeling, too. I wanted to see it and be seen, I wanted to live in that connection. The sweet urge to be near a ponytailed screw girl, yes. To say yes. You are fantastic and I see that. I see all the goodness that exists without pause in the world. I had not thought of the change that brings loss as any kind of friend, but it is a good friend; it promises that everything we know and see changes. Endlessly. Even the worst of it will pass.

Rock Cut State Park outside Rockford is big and really beautiful and Colby and I could have camped there, but we didn't. The park held a very particular danger for me. Back in June, I had stopped in Rock Cut to make a phone call on the drive home from Girls Week in Wisconsin, and as I sat in my car in a deserted parking lot, surrounded by empty green fields and tall old trees, the sky darkened suddenly. The phone call was not important; maybe I was making a reservation for a motel room. What I know is that as I did this, a thunderstorm rolled in and I sat there watching the sky change and hoping that Colby, who was sleeping in the back seat, would not wake up while this happened because he was terrified of thunder. I watched those gathering black clouds and somehow knew I would not get away clean from what had happened, or not happened, at the cabin. Then the rain came, very fast and very heavy, and soon I was overwhelmed all over again by the feelings I had thought I left behind. A vague, omnipresent longing quickened into need, and I thought of my old friend, of her being in my arms and how it would feel to hold her, and the sky closed in and the trees swayed, then swirled, as if a force had risen from nowhere that might destroy me.

On the phone in my car in Rock Cut State Park, I said to the motel chain operator something breathy, like, "Oh, my," and then felt so, so, sorry to want what I did not have.

"Are you still there, ma'am?" a voice on the phone must have said.

"I don't know," is what I should have answered.

So I didn't dare camp in Rock Cut State Park. Very bad idea for me. Plus, I needed a good shower and I felt like watching TV. Colby and I found a room in a Rockford motel with the word "comfort" in its name. It was a cheaply made boxy commercial chain motel and its name tickled me darkly; the word "comfort," and other nice words like "love" and "home," are used so cynically to market this impersonal world we have made. The marketing slogan says "love" makes a Subaru, but we all know it's made of Specialty Screws. In my "comforting" motel, the "reception" area was a fluorescent-lit, drop-ceilinged room where a clerk labored behind a heavy plastic (bulletproof?) shield, just like the liquor store in the slummy New York neighborhood I had lived in years ago, where a burly man exchanged booze for cash through a small revolving portal. The motel clerk plugged me into the travel-sleep matrix, sucking seventy-five dollars and a pet fee from my digital bank account nightly until I unplugged and moved on. "Sign here, please." She passed a sheet of paper under the plastic. A portly white-haired man in plaid shorts and a desperately stretched light-blue golf shirt arrived behind me. He had a stiff little bounce in his knees, wiggling around like he was happy to be there, and was especially taken by the motel literature that promised his room had a comfortable chair in it.

"Will the room have one of these comfortable chairs?" he asked, stooping to put his ruddy face near the speaking holes in the bullet guard, pointing at words in his brochure.

"Uh huh," the woman said. "Sign here."

Had we arrived in Rockford seventy-five years earlier we could have stayed in one of about twenty-four hotels downtown, privately owned, one or two restaurants in each of their lobbies, but at the moment, only one of those old buildings still standing was also still a hotel and apparently it had not been cleaned since the war—and I mean, the Great War. I thought of going there, but then I found an online review by someone who stayed in the place by mistake and wrote, "Don't. Just don't."

The evolution of hotels in our country is hard not to think about when traveling and, in its own microcosmic way, explains the last two hundred years pretty neatly. I had made a thirty-six-hour detour to Akron, Ohio, on my way to Rockford solely to visit a grain elevator that had been famously transformed into a Hilton. That was not on my original road trip itinerary, but I had learned about this hotel while I was camped at the silos in Buffalo. The grain elevator in the center of Akron became a hotel with round rooms in its old cement silo tubes. Miracles do happen. Ideas come along to save what we love, sometimes. I decided to go see the thing.

But then, when I tried to make a reservation at the Hilton that had been built into the grain elevator in Akron, it turned out that after nearly forty years the hotel had shut down. The Hilton in the grain elevator had become a dormitory for the University of Akron just months before my visit. I took this personally. The magic red carpet of American awesomeness had been rolling up just two steps ahead of me most of my life. It's the curse of tail-end baby boomers generally; the world rusts and recedes before our eyes, just beyond our grasp, over and over. Social Security experts project the fund will run out right around my retirement date, and likewise, the silo hotel saw me coming and shut down.

Disappointed but not defeated, I arranged to at least get a tour of the old transformed grain elevator that is now a dormitory. Even better, the university public relations office got me an appointment with none other than Dr. Ted Curtis, the architect who had designed the hotel in the silos in the first place and who was now a University of Akron vice president.

The night before I met Dr. Curtis to learn how he saved an iconic grain elevator by turning it into something it was never meant to be, I had to sleep not in a room in a grain elevator but in a plain old motel in the city's big box wastelands. This was a night in the stretch of time between Pittsburgh and Rockford, and the motel provided the first real bed Colby and I had slept in for some time. The bed was king-sized, Colby's favorite; he rolled his fuzzy sixty-pound self around on the big bed lavishly, panting and smiling and at last falling deeply asleep sprawled across the mattress. I curled carefully in a corner, trying not to wake him. At some point in the night Colby had a really big twitching dream and convulsed himself all the way to the edge of the bed until he slipped, hind end first, into the narrow space between the bed and the wall. His backside sank and his front paws clung to the sheets; I met his sleepy and bewildered eyes in the red glowing light of the motel alarm clock. He was sinking slowly and did not have the strength to pull himself back up so I reached over and pushed him farther down, instead, which seemed to suit him fine, and he stayed on the floor between the wall and the bed until morning.

In this disorienting nest, Colby overslept. I always relied on him to wake me and most mornings he did at seven thirty sharp, but not that morning in Akron. That's why I was a bit tragically late for my grain elevator/hotel/dormitory tour and my meeting with Dr. Ted Curtis. As I raced into the city in a panic with a trailer in tow, I noticed that I was on a spookily empty highway, a road that seemed to come from nowhere and go nowhere, and I was alone. This highway was so lonely that I wondered if it was closed and I had driven onto it accidentally, and was perhaps fast heading for a cliff. It turned out that I was on the Innerbelt, a six-lane,

2.24-mile-long freeway that was planned to be about ten times longer than that but was never finished. The Innerbelt was built with noble intentions in the days of bonkers urban "renewal" projects that typically involved urban wrecking balls in the 1960s; it was to give the masses, who had fled to the suburbs, a swift and easy route back to Akron for visits. Instead, it gave the fleeing masses a more direct route out. Now hardly anyone visits downtown Akron, and those who do apparently don't take the Innerbelt to get there, as I had, and I crossed that spooky empty parcel of America in mental confusion, driving as fast as I could to get to a meeting for which I would be very late and could not even blame traffic.

I learned, later, that the Innerbelt freeway in Akron was so infrequently used that *The Matrix Reloaded* filmmakers selected it for a complicated chase scene that would have required closing the set to real traffic for hours. In the end, the scene was never made, but had it been, the Innerbelt was ideal because no one would have noticed if they had to close it down. The city as I write is working to rip out the highway, or at least a mile of it, and redevelop the land beneath it as something, anything, other than a road.

Dr. Ted Curtis's office was a short walk beyond the converted silos of downtown Akron, in an old industrial site the university had turned into an administration building. Tired and panicky and craving the morning coffee I had skipped because Colby overslept, I was still well enough on task to notice "Wire Furnace" written in faded paint along the office building's brick side wall and "WF Co." carved into the stone above the main entrance. The university had taken over many old industrial buildings, including this one, for administrative offices and other old office buildings around Akron had become student housing; there was a plan for the university to expand into the empty buildings in Opportunity Park—a neighborhood invented in another bold, failed renewal plan in the 1960s. The neighborhood was ghostly. New York University and Columbia University have in recent decades bought up huge swaths of real estate in Manhattan and residents hate it, but in many cities I visited, a university expansion is a godsend.

The public relations assistant brought me upstairs to meet Dr. Curtis, a stout, silver-haired man in a good suit with a big office full of trophies,

surrounded by people who bring him things when he asks. He had returned to Akron after a long career that began with his successful Akron
silo hotel project, then sent him on to both coasts and to Harvard before
Akron snagged him and brought him home. He had a gentle voice; we sat
talking inside his office overlooking the silo hotel he created that was now
a college dorm and looked pretty empty that day.

Ted Curtis told me that when he was a boy, the city smelled like oats.
The smell of oats was stronger than even the smell of rubber tires had
been, which is the commodity Akron is really best known for. Before tires,
Akron was all oats and corn. The city grew up in a key location in the midst
of midwestern farms, alongside a canal that connected farm country to
Cleveland, which was connected by lake to Buffalo, which held all that
midwestern grain, which barges or trains brought to ports, where ships
picked it up and took it all around the world. Whenever Ted Curtis went
downtown as a boy, he smelled Quaker Oats. Not tires. And then one day
in the 1970s after he was grown and working for an architecture firm in the
suburbs, he heard that Quaker was leaving Akron and the silos were going
to be razed. When he heard the news, he realized that like most people,
he had not been downtown for a very long time. The heart of the city he
knew was at risk of being lost forever. He decided to save it.

Dr. Curtis and his partners bought the Quaker site and tried out a
housing plan for it, but inner-city luxury apartments weren't flying with
investors in those days, when all roads led to big suburban houses with
decks and yards. A federal program at that time was encouraging hotel
development in struggling downtowns—pushing the construction of
new hotels just as many existing hotels in city centers were being torn
down, with the help of federal urban renewal funding. The federal government was thus giving grants to tear down hotels and giving other grants
to build new ones even as motels at highway interchanges were taking
the whole industry over. This is excellent evidence that we've known we
were in trouble in this country for at least fifty years, but we have never
known just what is broken or how to fix it. Or rather what hurts and how
to heal it. And just when we fix one thing, something else breaks. This is
how we learn not to work toward an ending; nothing really ends. It only
changes.

The hotel grant Dr. Curtis's team landed changed their project's direction; the only problem left was actually creating a hotel inside huge adjoining tubes of concrete. Each tube was twenty-four feet in diameter, made of poured concrete several feet thick; windows and doors had to be cut into material that would probably stand up to an air raid.

Dr. Curtis showed me an article from *Forbes Magazine*, which noted that when it opened in 1980, the Akron Hilton and the shops around it brought a million people downtown each year and made more jobs in Akron than the actual Quaker mills ever had. It was a triumph. It stayed open for thirty-four years.

The problems Dr. Curtis took on are problems we will never really solve. That is, what do we do with all this stuff we care for when that stuff has lost its usefulness? Is it lost? Do we dismantle what was once built with so much care, or can we somehow make it work again? The problem dogs me, and I'm no one. Finer minds have surfed the giant waves that give us what we want and take it back again.

In any case, the grain elevator-hotel-dormitory stood there proclaiming that we are ever on the verge of destroying things we'll never get back, and sometimes we do save them.

Dr. Curtis and I talked for about fifteen minutes about the project that launched his career and had come full circle by now: abandoned, then salvaged by the entity for which Curtis worked. Again. Then at eleven forty he said he had to go to a doctor's appointment but needed time to eat lunch first and that was that. He dismissed me.

This raised for my consideration another nearly vanished but once almighty phenomenon, and that is the curious matter of Men Who Have Time to Eat Lunch.

When I had arranged our appointment a week earlier, I imagined a university vice president to be someone lean and kinetic and zinging with ideas that tumbled one into another and whose busy calendar, which I had managed to squeeze onto, included meetings with local luminaries and deadlines for making urgent policy decisions and constant demands that might give an administrator of lesser ilk a bleeding ulcer. The college administrators I had worked with had been spread so thin they had been known to break. They had been sent sometimes to rehab; two college administrators I knew got brain tumors and died within three years of each other; one office manager's nervous breakdown reached its climax in a cloud of pot smoke, out in his car in the college parking lot. State troopers took him away. This is what I knew of running a college. Yet there was no frantic energy or evidence of unmanageable stress to be found anywhere that I could see in Akron, least of all in Dr. Ted Curtis; he was a top figure at a university who was busy . . . having lunch before going to the doctor.

I don't question the man's work ethic. He was very accomplished, a man of genuine integrity. That was clear. But also, he embodied a calm and deliberate position in life many of us once aspired to only to discover, once we had climbed this or that ladder, that we would never obtain. No one with a full-time job would get away with being comfortable. Not anymore. Or at least, no one I knew. Dr. Curtis was an accomplished man imbued with the unflinching certainty of a country at a time when one's position, once attained, never really seemed in doubt. In short, Dr. Curtis seemed to me to be a man from Akron, when Akron was still *Akron*, a man whose lunch plans did not reek of sloth; lunch looked like sloth when I ate it, but clearly, I did not belong there.

My grandfather had been a resident of this "men who lunch" universe and he had also been midwestern, like Dr. Curtis; my nostalgia for their world undoubtedly began in Milwaukee, with Grandpa, who ran the family business—a paper company. That is where my own comfort and privilege in this changing world came from, quaint as such a business seems to me today; the success of my elders as much as anything allowed me to take the risks I take with my own fortunes. My grandfather was born in 1900 and his life spanned the American century almost exactly. He died in 1993. As a minor titan of the world he knew, he made sure not only to have lunch, always, but also to visit his mother each day before arriving home for dinner. "Visiting his mother" may have been a euphemism for "spending time with his mistress," another feature in the lives of powerful middle-aged white men at that time and perhaps always, but this was Grandpa's universe to master and no one dared question him. He ran a family-owned manufacturing company in the postwar boom. He took long family vacations on which he could not be reached by telephone. By anyone. He made firm, final decisions that everyone submitted to, if grudgingly, because he was the boss, and this was Milwaukee in the days of world wars and the Rotary Club, the athletic club, the congregational church, ladies in gloves and Grandpa in his big Detroit-made car with tailfins. That was the world as he knew it, a place by now sparsely inhabited by a gang of aging masters; a universe that, when it is finally empty, will certainly collapse into a genuine black hole, a strange phenomenon of incalculable gravity and darkness. Gone.

It is worth noting that I don't think my grandfather liked me. He died when I was twenty-eight and he had never really known me, but he knew all he really needed to: I seemed to lack his good sense, I had not gone to the college he told me to go to, I was twenty-eight and unmarried, I had once quit a job. I was a loser on all counts. Had he known me better, it would have been worse; had he known, for example, that my lovers were nearly all women—or even that I've just used the plural of a word he would never, ever have used at all, "lover," except perhaps to whisper into the ear of his own, which was none of my business—he would have pressed his lips together tightly, turned red in rage, and said, simply, "No." He was so powerful that he would not even have had to say that much; his no would have been understood, and he would have expected the world to obey it. It may sound like I'm exaggerating, but I'm not. Grandpa cut me from his will. He left his money and his business to a son from his second marriage, who in 1999 sold the family paper company to a corporation overseas and retired at fifty, which was the right thing to do. The paper industry was dying. My uncle knew.

Guys like Dr. Curtis and my grandfather are the sons of Akron and Milwaukee and Schenectady and Kansas City and other places like these; they inhabit the photos I've seen of Cleveland when Cleveland was really Cleveland, a first-class city in the major leagues: packed sidewalks, a mansion row, ladies in heels and smart hats waiting to ride a bus downtown. Akron is sometimes called the Silicon Valley of its day, an incubator of industry best known for its tires; Charles Goodyear figured out how to make "vulcanized" rubber (it didn't melt in summer; it didn't stick to things) and Goodyear made tires of this stuff at their enormous factory in Akron, and the world noticed.

Students of human folly will appreciate that Charles Goodyear died penniless, and Goodyear Tire of Akron was named "in his honor" but actually had nothing to do with the guy. Dozens of local tire companies shot up in Akron, and a kind of industrial aristocracy developed around them. The presence of American aristocracy is what marked a city as great in those days; if the rich and powerful were there, the place must matter. There were blue books and social sets and gossip columns in places like Akron. It's hard to imagine real wealth willing to relocate there now.

Harvey Firestone started his tire company in Akron in 1900. Firestone made all the tires for the Model T Ford, the world's first mass-produced car. In 1948, in a kind of American royal wedding, Martha Firestone married William Ford. People cared; it made headlines. It was the industrial tribe's version of peanut butter marrying chocolate. The families stayed linked in various ways until 2001, when the Firestone tires on the Ford Explorer started exploding. After that disaster, Ford and Firestone went their separate ways.

The story of Firestone Tire in Akron is ethically complex but helps explain how things were changing in the country as I came of age, those unraveling years Ron explained to me in Rockford; it is a story of how things never were at all for the students I now spend most of my days with. Firestone as a company embraced values that are hard not to admire—though its values were very unevenly applied; I won't get into the Liberian rubber plantation scandal, except to say that it's easier to be cruel to people from a distance than up close. That's very clear. In its day, Firestone created an entire Akron neighborhood, Firestone Park, full of shops and houses for its employees; it built the Firestone Stadium for local kids to play ball in and the Firestone Country Club for employees to play golf. The company did not merely buy the naming rights for these places. It built them for the community. When American corporations were locally owned and managed, it made sense to be civic-minded; executives invested in the communities they too lived in.

When the postwar boom slowed, Firestone had no interest in going along with the change. Creative disruption, creative destruction: we are watching this story unfold to this day. Change meant closing manufacturing plants. It meant reorganizing; it meant managers laying off workers they had met on the golf course. It meant executives making choices that might hurt the city they had grown up in. Firestone's determination to keep things as they were became the stuff of business school legend because it was such a bad idea, really. Rejecting change does not save you. The *Harvard Business Review* labeled the Firestone problem "active inertia," or "the dynamics of standing still." Inertia was sweet until it was awful: by 1973, one study found, 21 percent of Ohio's manufacturing facilities had become obsolete, aging out twice as fast as the rest of the country's. They didn't keep up, and the lesson of their failure was: evolve. Or die.

Richard Riley started working at Firestone in 1939 and was running it by 1972; he was the company's last homegrown chief executive. Under Riley, Firestone retooled plants rather than close them down and kept employees working even as the U.S. economy tanked in the 1970s. Meanwhile, French tire maker Michelin invented radial tires and with that promptly began to eat Akron's lunch. Firestone fought back with its own radial tires—which peeled apart lethally when driven on. Ask Ford.

Riley retired, and Firestone hired its first outside leader (not a tire guy from Akron but a Zenith TV guy from Chicago). He reported finding warehouses stuffed with tires that Akron's factories had overproduced, trying to keep everyone working. He moved Firestone's headquarters to Chicago in 1980 and from there he dealt with Akron. He closed a dozen plants, cut sixty thousand jobs, and in 1988 sold the whole mess to Bridgestone Tire of Japan. And that was that.

Once, not very long before he retired, Richard Riley appealed to a meeting of Firestone's executive committee to invest in Akron, to continue to provide jobs, which would "eventually dry up" without that investment: "When this happens, it will not be something abstract that we may call 'The World of Business' or 'The Corporation' that will be harmed. It will be companies, and people, and families." And small cities like Akron.

When I left my unremarkable motel in the Rockford motel campus, I hitched up the Scamp and turned out of the motel parking lot onto a densely trafficked multilane road. As I merged into the gush, I heard the awful metal-on-metal grinding sound my brakes had been making for days. I decided to get this mess checked out before towing the trailer any further. I returned to the motel to ask for a recommendation. The woman at the desk suggested Firestone.

The Firestone service center in Rockford was one in a gigantic chain of spit-clean shiny Firestone showrooms selling Asian-made tires, connected to a full-service repair shop run by mechanics who looked to be about twelve years old. No one at the Rockford Firestone Tire Center—not the twelve-year-olds, not the suspiciously happy little woman cleaning the bathrooms, not the large, shaved-headed, impatient man waiting beside me at the service desk poring over his cell phone—none of them had ever known Harvey Firestone, or had likely given any thought at all to his hopes and dreams, or felt a speck of admiration for the Akron aristocracy and the wedding of a Ford to a Firestone; maybe they could not have found Akron on a map. It didn't matter. I needed brakes. I handed over my key and I waited.

Six or so humans and one old dog hardly took up space in Firestone's tremendous airy glass-and-tile tire showroom. Scandalous morning talk-show conversations echoed out of a TV on a table in a semicircle of vinyl-padded chairs that formed a kind of waiting room. An unblinking elderly woman sat across from the screen, cozily wrapped in a pink cardigan that could have been homemade, transfixed by a media professional who was confronting a young woman barely more than a girl, teasing out the details of the sexual affair she had been having with her once-estranged father. The daughter was trying to defend the profound connection of their love, saying there was no one in the world whose arms felt safer than his—him, the man who had incidentally been responsible for her birth. It was a kind of copycat scenario of Kathryn Harrison's incest memoir, *The Kiss*, only without the poetry, and I could find no way to want to hear about all this nastiness and so instead I watched the old woman as she watched the TV, and Colby wandered the showroom from person to person, trailing his leash, looking for his daily high dose of affection. The people in the showroom were otherwise engaged and ignored him.

I felt embarrassed to watch the talk show with the old woman. She was powdered and delicate and not dressed for such a vile world. Sex crimes and other horrors are not new things, but presenting them as entertainment on TV is still freshly appalling to me. What is wrong with us? I wanted to reassure the old woman, but she almost certainly would not have taken comfort from a middle-aged, wanderlusting lesbian. What could I possibly say to fix all that scared her? Soon, the large impatient man paced away from his spot at the counter and joined us, watching the TV with one eye while the other scrolled his cell phone, and somehow, by no specific fault of his own, the presence of a man in our midst made the father-daughter sex thing just that much harder to take.

After a commercial, talk on the television turned to the horrors of methamphetamine, and the scourge of addiction that was destroying not just families but whole towns, especially in the Midwest. The old woman's hands fidgeted in her lap. She stared. I couldn't stand it, so I left to take Colby for a walk through the downcast sprawl around Firestone. I thought I might find some lunch. My choices for lunch that day were a closed strip club; an earnest "theme" restaurant last renovated circa 1958, also closed; and a delivery-only pizza place—closed. All this, surrounded by asphalt sprouting crabgrass, all spread out on a long road with no sidewalks: the world.

Colby and I gave up on lunch and found a side street to walk down and discovered, not even a block off the gloom, a quiet neighborhood of trees and bungalows, and in this place sidewalks suddenly appeared. The concrete was cracked and broken but nonetheless it was there, like a cord stringing together little pastel houses lined up one right next to another. They sprouted along the streets like an Illinois bungalow farm, their age measured by the girth of trees around them. Fifty, maybe sixty years, I guessed; Rockford at its peak: the postwar boom. Tens of thousands of manufacturing jobs awaited World War II veterans in Rockford and that spurred a frantic demand for small houses on tree-lined streets. Maybe the old woman at Firestone had lived in one since 1950. Maybe she couldn't wait to get her brakes fixed and go home, where life made sense to her.

Building houses is supposed to signal a strong economy; it made great sense to build them in Rockford when the factories were booming and workers had income. But Rockford built houses in the boom times and bad. When the country's real estate bubble popped in 2007, Rockford had been bleeding jobs for decades and was nonetheless building nearly three hundred new homes a year—enormous, illogical houses in gated developments on the edge of the city. Then real estate crashed, and in the Great Recession, unfinished developments were abandoned and new houses went unsold. Unemployment reached 20 percent in Rockford in 2007 and soon after that, the home vacancy rate was also 20 percent, and Rockford was foreclosing on houses five or six times more than any neighboring state.

Conditions change. To do what worked in the past made no sense in Rockford, and it makes no sense anywhere when it's not based in the truth of the moment. Now, automation is coming and the whole idea of work may be obsolete. I saw the boys working at Firestone and the old woman and the enormous empty houses on the edge of the city as I left, and I stopped one last time at the empty Barber-Colman plant, and then I remembered the beautiful screw girl. I wished safety for us all in this delicate web, but it seemed clearer to me that the fix we want never comes to stay. The storm is always near, the sky lowers. We want safety, but safety isn't real. I think it's okay to want something better.

9

The Middle

Columbia, Missouri, was as close to the middle of anything as I was going to get, though it is not in fact the middle of anything at all. It is about four hundred miles shy of the true center of the country, which is in Lebanon, Kansas, a place I would have enjoyed visiting; I could have met all two hundred or so of its residents and asked them what they loved enough in that place to stay with it, and whether they missed the other six hundred humans who would have been their neighbors before the dust bowl changed Kansas, and where they thought the other three-quarters of their town had gone. Scattered to the wind. The center does not hold.

But I didn't go to Lebanon. I reached the flat darkness of the Mississippi River without fanfare, at night, hours beyond a painted-sky sunset in the heart of Illinois, a scene beautiful enough to taste. A rainbow sherbet sky. At the river, I felt a lift inside for the experience of passing over this magic line. The Mississippi. A suggested turning-back point on our continent. This is how it felt to me, the way it looks on a map: all the states on the right side of the Mississippi River are crunched up against its bank, twenty-eight of them, as if they had been running hard chasing something and by god they almost had it but then, it got away. It went across the river. Illinois put her arms out crossing-guard style and all the chasing stuff, the mad dash of need and want, crashed up against her, full stop. "No," she said. The chase was over. The West got away.

Those states that got away are all drawn big and simple with straight, clear lines as if, once they were not being chased, they could finally breathe. The land looks like this, as if it were cut up into boxes inside boxes and the boxes were given away. Just given away. Homesteaders took the lots for free. Imagine getting ten square feet of free land today; start by trying just to get a Section 8 housing voucher and see how people judge you. Hand the vouchers out and make us great again. Imagine how rich we would all be if everything were free.

Anyhow, I crossed the Mississippi River near Hannibal, Missouri, with a sense of reaching some point that mattered. After Columbia, Colby and I would head back in the direction we had come from; perhaps we would be changed. Or maybe I would be; dogs are far more constant than people. Colby had remained constant all these years, staying with me no matter where I took him or what I asked. Soon though, he really would be leaving. Even Colby would not last. But for a moment in Columbia, having reached that turning point, I felt the pause of motion that brings about a weightlessness. Somewhere in Columbia, Missouri, perhaps as I was walking Colby in Stephen's Lake Park, I found the vertex of my parabola. I felt the motion stop. All sensation was suspended except that I could hear myself breathe.

Of course, the feeling was almost certainly low blood sugar; I was probably hungry, and anyhow, in that moment, I couldn't remember the words "parabola" or "vertex." I was aware of them; I searched my mind for the words because I had a vague memory from eighth-grade physics that when you hit a place at the top of an arc you do for a moment experience weightlessness. Later, I searched for the scientific words for this feeling. I typed into the Google search bar: "word for top of an arc zero gravity." What happened next describes the opposite of weightlessness, really, because as soon as I typed "word for," Google suggested the following common searches, in this order: Word for Mac, word for today, word for not caring.

I kept thinking I was making too much of the lost feeling that I had noticed, but Google is the oracle; Google showed me I was not wrong about the trouble in our collective mind. There is indeed a word for not caring. I know several of them. They aren't words I care to share with whoever might be searching for them; instead I want to give them . . . what? A lecture? A Valium? A hug?

In Columbia, I had a memorable opportunity to consider the unstrung feeling of weightlessness and the quirks of history and, ultimately, the compelling and freakish nature of love with a journalist named Steve Weinberg, who wrote a biography of Ida M. Tarbell.

Ida M. Tarbell! Native daughter of Titusville, chronicler of the Rockefeller Trust. I had fallen in love with Ida while camped out in a spot near Titusville that I had all but forgotten by the time I met Steve. My host in Columbia, a writer named Mary Kay, had organized a little dinner party for me; Steve was at it, and when dinner ended but I had not divined any cosmic truth from Steve, I invited myself over to his house the next day to try again. I had nothing but time to talk and while he was far too busy for this kind of nonsense, he knew I was a writer on a mission with a trailer and a dog and writers had to be generous with each other in these creative journeys, or at least the ones I know are, though in hindsight, I think he just wanted to meet my dog, so he consented to give me an hour.

Colby, though, was back at Mary Kay's house, lolling happily in the air-conditioning. Her house also had carpeted stairs, which Colby ran right up like a racehorse when we arrived. This was strange indeed. I had been carrying his sixty-pound carcass up every step or staircase we had encountered for at least a year, which extracted from me a major commitment to staying fit. But at Mary Kay's, Colby found the strength to run up and down the stairs, unassisted, barking like a puppy. It may have been senility; it may be that for all the stress of this trip, his mind had kind of snapped and gone back to a time before the troubles, before the arthritis and the egg-shaped fatty tumor and the overall muscular decline. Whatever it was, somehow in that air-conditioned and carpeted house, he had reverted to a dog I had thought was long lost; for all the misery, for all the thunderstorms and carsickness and long boring days driving and still not getting to the pond, it had all turned out to be worthwhile because there he was at last in a really nice house. The next morning he lounged on a rug in Mary Kay's kitchen, with his head raised, panting, a happy bourgie puppy fixed to the ground with no intention of standing for the rest of the day, so I left him.

Steve was pacing on his front porch, in the middle of a phone call that he ended to chat with me.

"Where's Colby?" he asked. "Why didn't you bring Colby?"

He was just back from a tennis match, rumpled and unwashed. I told him Colby was napping and he looked let down. Then he told me his wife was working inside the house and could not be disturbed, so we sat on a short bench on his narrow front porch, side by side, in too tight a space to face each other; we looked out across his long, sloping lawn to the street where cars rolled steadily by. Steve was thick-bodied and shaggy; a gray-flecked dark beard met his gray-flecked hair to make a lion's mane. He turned his head so that his eyes, buried by thick glasses, could land on me from time to time, then slide stealthily away.

I had come supposedly to interview him about something-or-other that made sense the night before when there was wine, but as we sat, the questions taking shape in my mind had mostly to do with my big crush on Ida Tarbell. Before I could ask him anything about anything, Steve demonstrated his superior journalistic skills by asking a question first. He wanted to know how I had met Jessica. I had hinted at dinner the night before that there was a good story in this meeting. Steve hadn't forgotten. He crossed his arms and gazed out across the street and waited.

Okay. If he wanted that story, I could tell him: I was thirty-five and lonely and living in Upstate New York, recently parted from the fairy-tale world of graduate school in New York City. I was now an assistant city editor at a newspaper in all-too-real Albany. The *Times Union* was a serious newspaper, and I was glad to have a job at all, really, and this was a job my grandfather would have approved of, had he been alive, because it was demanding and I had a title. Nonetheless I was, as I said, lonely. I was a single female editor in a pack with eight married, male, city desk editors, and I was the only editor among that group who had to work Saturday nights, always until at least eight and often later, and I was living in a small community north of Albany, where I had already met, dated, and been dumped by the only other eligible lesbian I had found on the grand secret chart of local lesbians—a tool that cannot be found through a simple web search but is available only by word of mouth, and only if you know the password. I did. It didn't get me far. If I was to find romance, I would have to get creative.

I decided to go to New York City for a friend's book release party, which would reconnect me to the city and the people in it who offered more of a life for me. I decided on this, but then none of the five men who were authorized to cover my Saturday shift would agree to work for me that day, or really, to cover for me ever. I begged. I threatened. I would have cried if I thought that would help. I was completely resolved that I must go to this event. My campaign grew so annoying that one guy finally agreed to spell me halfway through the shift, at four. When he showed up he was kind of drunk. He had come from a party and had a red face and bloodshot eyes and a ketchup-stained napkin stuffed in the waistband of his pants. This was not my problem. I left.

It happened to be the night before the New York City Marathon and many streets were apparently already closed off. Between that and regular Saturday traffic, with only ten miles left between me and the book party, I was hopelessly gridlocked. I inched along and hours later managed to get downtown but then couldn't find a parking space. The book launch was at a bookstore on the Lower East Side and I circled those blocks with increasing despair, finally parked illegally (and got a ticket later), ran to the bookstore, and entered just as my friend said, "Thanks for coming, everyone! Good night!"

I found a group of old pals in the room who said, "Lori! You're alive! Albany, right? Is that actually a place? Do you know Jessica?" Then a woman spun around to shake my hand and as she did, she hit me with eyes so blue against a fringe of brown hair that I was blinded. I could see nothing else for what seemed like a long while, only the eyes, which did not exactly sparkle or dance or do anything exotic; they simply spread their blue across the world as if painting a door to be entered. Time stopped and all the other color drained from the room. The voices around me grew faint and distorted, as if my friends were talking through water, and closer to my ears there was the sound of my own breathing: a sharp gasp in, the beat of my heart. The vertex of my parabola. This is where our story began.

The owner of the blue eyes shook my hand. Firm grip. Time restarted. "Nice to meet you," she said. One of my friends asked Jessica to join us for dinner but she couldn't, and that was that. Except it wasn't.

A group of maybe seven women shuffled off through the November gray to dinner at a Dominican restaurant, where we ate plantains and whole fish and talked about Jessica. It was reported that she had recently broken up with her girlfriend, a Jamaican bodybuilder, words that instantly made me feel like a butter noodle: weak, pale. It was also reported that Jessica was very smart. I liked that. Two women at the table were currently unattached. We flipped a hypothetical coin and I won the phone number, then managed to arrange lunch with this woman with the huge blue eyes despite the fact that I lived three hours away and no one would cover for me at work, ever, and also despite the fact that when I met the eyes again they would be attached to a woman I might not actually recognize. I had only met her for a second and I mostly only saw her eyes. In spite of all of this, we did find each other. And it turned out that I liked her. After that, all I had to do was keep showing up in New York City once a week for the next few months, crashing on the couches of friends who were so essential in that pursuit but who are by now lost to me for no special reason; I needed them, they were there, and now they're gone. Eventually I lured Jessica to my home upstate. She came to see me at my house, which I had just bought, and met my dog, who was still a puppy. She liked us. We were in our thirties; it was time to make a choice. We chose. We had been together ever since.

Jessica was without a doubt or hint of hesitation the brightest light that had ever shined into my life, despite a few earnest flashlights. Being her partner was what I was most proud of in the world. Yet years later, sitting on Steve's porch and retelling this story that had always seemed so romantic, I heard in it the possibility that what I had really done was tried too hard to create something that can only, simply, be. A slip of dread shot through me. I wondered if Steve heard that. I did not tell him the part about how, on our second date, I excused myself from the table where Jess and I were having coffee, then dashed into the bathroom to vomit. I was stricken very suddenly with the flu but I did not want to tell her. I didn't want to have to leave, and I didn't want her to see any reason to reject me, as if with the first hint of weakness she would bolt from my life. I was, in a way, complicit in a lie from the very start about our compatibility on some level. But it was, it turns out, what we both wanted so much to be true.

Steve told me stories of people he knew and how they got together and how some fell apart. He told me about two women who had moved to Columbia, Missouri, from the East Coast only to break up soon after they had resettled in this new, uncharted midwestern landscape, which was just then spread out in front of me: wide, flat streets lined with unfamiliar houses and all the strangers who had landed in them somehow, all their strange stories, their strange cars rolling off to places I didn't know and would not recognize. I could feel the surreal dream state of the woman who had been abandoned there, another middle-aged lesbian on a side-walk in Columbia, the prairie wind feathering her hair, waking up after all those years to find herself alone with nothing left of the world as she had known it. This would be like having your tether cut while floating through deep space. It's all so lovely so long as your equipment holds. The connections between people are mystic and miraculous and maybe tenuous too—an observation that led Steve and I to agree that no one can tell you who to love or not love, and when you do find love, no one should ever dare fuck with it.

"I love love," Steve said.

"Yeah," I said. Who could argue? What's not to love? Yeah. I said, "Me too."

I learned nothing about Ida Tarbel in Columbia that wasn't already in Steve's book and I learned very little about Columbia itself except that it was a large college town and that made it an oasis, a bright light in a vast midwestern desert of dry grass and struggle; I took comfort in its light before stepping out again to feel the loss I had come to understand. I found myself in Laddonia, Missouri, where the single block of buildings that constituted Laddonia's downtown held the mark of a once famous architect; what a story those buildings could tell, if every single one of those buildings had not been empty and covered in boards and left speechless. Farmers roll past those ghosts every day bringing grain to the co-op, selling it to storage in the co-op's tall metal silos. I drove in my weightlessness crisscrossing small towns where pickup trucks rode down the center of the road, slow, as if looking for something, as if in no hurry to get where they would go. Eventually they would all get somewhere.

The Mississippi River drains the country top to bottom, ending in New Orleans and the Gulf of Mexico. Mark Twain's hometown, Hannibal, was a Mississippi port city, but it relies on tourism now; Twain revered

Downtown Laddonia, Missouri

"the majestic and magnificent Mississippi; rolling its mile-wide tide along, shining in the sun." He had a way of seeing our young country as it grew that nurtured its optimism; every ugliness would be resolved. And the Mississippi was objectively ugly, no matter what he said. In 1842, when Mark Twain was seven, old-Europe-hardened Charles Dickens rode up the Mississippi in a riverboat and chose these words to describe what he saw: "An enormous ditch . . . running liquid mud . . . The banks low, the trees dwarfish, the marshes swarming with frogs, the wretched cabins few and far apart, their inmates hollow-cheeked and pale, the weather very hot, mosquitoes penetrating into every crack and crevice of the boat, mud and slime on everything; nothing pleasant in its aspect but the harmless lightning which flickers every night upon the dark horizon."

Yes, Charles Dickens! The Mississippi River sounds amazing when you describe it that way, bad and hard and a real force of nature. But Mark Twain's river is what we want to see, a wonderland to be explored on a raft, with your best friend, who just happens to be an escaped slave, and a world of youthful dreaming that we are so deeply reluctant to let go of.

Missouri roads roll along the river through small town after town, many wearing their histories like Dickens's Miss Haversham wore her wedding gown, her great expectation thwarted. Palmyra, Missouri, once had an opera house and still has a jail where, in 1862, ten Confederate prisoners were unlawfully killed. President Lincoln called that "the blackest day in the history of the Civil War," which is a hell of a thing for him to have said, given the number of black days in that war. And yet for all its infamy, Palmyra was still a place I had never heard of.

Colby and I spent a few days along the river, crossing into and out of Illinois and Missouri and up into Iowa. The days turned hot again. Indian summer. A heat wave. I took Colby swimming in the river in LaGrange, an old river port and railroad town of silos, ornate street lamps, and American flags; it is also lately home to the Mark Twain Casino, because Mark Twain was a magic totem and his very name could fix anything, and if any old casino could make a place money, a Mark Twain Casino could make fortunes. The parking lot was full in the middle of a weekday. In town, the sidewalks were empty; the whole world was still.

Colby and I walked across the railroad tracks in LaGrange to the muddy riverbank and he waded in up to his belly, stirring the water by wagging his tail, looking up at me, barking. We had found one place at last where, though it was hot, I didn't even think of swimming myself. The Mississippi River rocks were flat and silted. The water was restless and swift. It had really no appeal whatsoever. We walked back to the car across dry, stiff grass, back across the railroad tracks. Children rolled in and out of a blue house, a sloping wooden box that sat slanted where it fell along the river, its contents spilling out onto the dirt. Had all this been dropped down near New York City, it would have been worth millions. The whole Mississippi would be worth so much more, where I come from. Even muddy. In Brooklyn, people fight for a spot on a toxic trough called the Gowanus Canal. Yet the one home I could find listed for sale in LaGrange, Missouri, was an old farmhouse on some huge amount of acreage west of town, a spread with big barns and a pond. It was listed at $179,900, a number that seemed to me to be missing a digit, and that provides another way to comprehend the wide divide in our country, and the context-bound, fungible nature of nearly everything.

We rode over the bridges and the river proved itself to be no Rubicon, no line that, once crossed, cannot be uncrossed. A car can always turn around. The rivers to watch all flow through the mind. Hate talk kept me company on the radio as I drove; there had been a government shutdown that week, a standoff, so much grist for this mill: ". . . and, oh what was it, oh yeah, the other thing: Obama was on CNBC the other day practically begging the markets to crash so that he could blame it all on the Republicans . . . ," a voice told me in Illinois. As I write, the government is shut down and the markets are teetering and a new president blames it on the Democrats. Change, no change. We crossed the river again and were in Iowa, yet the hate was the same: ". . . he closed the World War II veterans memorial, that was his choice and it's spiteful. That's how he is. Always has been but now you see it . . ."

The first Iowa town I found myself in, Fort Madison, was like the rest and yet not; it looked like any other small town we had seen but something unseen in it alerted me. Words come slower to describe the invisible, and so it was hard for me to grasp what it was but I knew something was wrong. Clouds had rolled across the sun and the darker space held a threat. My GPS was set to a town named Kirkuk but on the way it inexplicably led me and Colby and our trailer to a side road and up a hill. Colby sat up and started urgently panting. I then turned sharply onto a smaller access road that took me to what looked like Dracula's castle, with turrets and stone walls and fences around it, barriers of barbed wire and bars, all rising up gothic and gloomy on the hill my GPS insisted I climb, pointing its boney finger from a cloak and telling me to look where I did not want to look. But I did. Two little girls were playing in a yard in the shadow of the castle and they stopped dead to watch my car and trailer pass; a woman in a housedress on the back steps beside the girls also turned to see, and they all stood blank and strange and staring.

The castle was a prison. The two children playing in the prison's shadow were pieces of a picture that touched but didn't fit.

"That's who he wants to hurt, this is who he is, people," the radio nattered.

The enormous Iowa State Penitentiary in Fort Madison was a maximum-security prison in a nearly two-hundred-year-old building; to see it is to

believe the people locked up when it was new might still be in there, forgotten piles of bone. It was a capital punishment prison. The last inmate
executed in Iowa, before the death penalty moratorium in 1972, was executed there. Three months before some sort of evil magnetism pulled me
to it, a mass murderer named Adam Moss had hung himself in his cell at
Fort Madison. The roadside attractions I had thought to look for included
albino squirrels and UFOs and smiley-face water towers. I had not thought
of prisons, which now seemed like genius. Fort Madison radiated terror.
Fort Madison was terribly unhappy. I wanted to understand Fort Madison.
(It didn't surprise me to learn, later, that the prison was shut down two
years after I had seen it, abandoned like a steel mill or the Beechnut factory
or Silo City, Buffalo, left now as a strange landmark of who we once were.
There is a drive to save it. Old prisons have their appeal: they can host tours,
as do old psychiatric hospitals, asylums that are so like haunted castles
that some now host Halloween sleepovers. Our dark past; our font of
amusement.)

My car idled and the dog panted and the radio declared that "he"
(name your president; pick one, any one) was a sick and spiteful man who
was probably laughing his cruel and evil laugh at that very moment. It was
all so macabre. I felt the balance around me tip for the first time to something irretrievably dark. No light. Castle walls were holding back hordes of
psychopaths fifty feet from a lawn where children were playing. For every
troubled soul locked up in there, many more wander free. And I did not
own a weapon. I was traveling with an arthritic, incontinent dog.

My phone rang.

"Guess what?" Jessica said.

"What."

"I was on my way to the museum but then I stopped at (and here she
named one of her favorite thrift stores) and then . . ."

Oh my god: Jess. How could I let this light slip away?

She had found a fantastic blouse that cost only three dollars but it was
cut funny, though she was built funny in the same way, so it seemed sort of
meant for her; dumb luck. Kismet. And only three dollars! She had tried
the blouse on and people told her how nice it looked and if she didn't buy
it they probably would . . . scritch . . . "funny, but" scratch, blip. "Three
dollars!"

She faded out. I pulled into a small parking lot beside a closed-up ice cream mini-golf place near the prison and its unscalable walls. Perhaps it opened up for kids who come on visiting day.

She faded in: "So then, she goes . . ." and faded out again. Colby stepped forward between the front seats and panted over my shoulder. He said: "hazard hazard hazard." We stared at the dark stones. "But I was like, 'no . . . ,'" Jessica said.

I kept losing her. Then she kept coming back so lightly. She hadn't noticed that the phone call was not really working, the tether between us so terribly frayed. Finally the call dropped and I would have to drive back down to the river to find a viable connection again, and I did do that, but not before I had fully seen the dark spot I was in, the prison I had not known I needed to see. I wished I hadn't had to see it but I did, and once I did I couldn't look away.

I returned to the river and called Jessica back.

"I'm glad you found something pretty," I said.

"It's just a silly thing, that's all," she said.

"No, no. It's not. I'm sorry. I was in a sad place when you called," I said, and I told her about the prison and the children who were playing near the walls. Then there was silence. Then she said, "Oh, Lori."

She said, "Is it too late to take your sabbatical in Canada?"

Interlude

I left Colby with my Cousin Bee in Milwaukee and flew home to New York for a planned visit to attend a special work party honoring Jessica. The flight was bumpy. There were thunderstorms in the East. The ground I had so painstakingly crossed whizzed by underneath me, then disappeared beneath dark clouds. The plane was dreadfully small and was swatted around inside the clouds by unseen meteorological forces and some bird wake and a little engine trouble, maybe, not to mention whatever anxious emotional energy was wafting off of me, all of this turbulence upsetting the ride and reducing my chances of gently reentering what I had left six weeks before.

It's a bit of a sticky situation, going off on a midlife crisis mission, then popping briefly back into one's "real" life as if nothing had happened or was in the process of happening. It is a modern problem caused by conveniences like air travel; we have lost useful transitions. We change in an instant. Bang. Change. Bang, change. It makes me think of a veteran leaving a combat zone on Thursday and finding herself at a welcome home party Friday, drink in hand, Fallujah in her brain. Some change makes no sense without transition.

The very small plane bounced its way from Milwaukee to Newark. The flight attendant strapped into her jump seat and pretty much just threw bags of peanuts out into the cabin. We shook like beads in a rattle, and I came to realize that even though I was no longer young, exactly, I was surely too young to die. I was not at all prepared to die, which struck me as good news. Whatever was happening to me, I wanted to survive it.

The plane touched down unremarkably in Newark, and I slouched off to pick up a rental car and drive into New York City's choked-up metro sprawl, in the rain; all the thronging and very much alive masses had tied the New Jersey Turnpike above all those ports and refineries into familiar knots through which I crawled home.

I know it's sort of wrong to insert this right here, in the midst of my return to Jessica, but the truth is, I missed Colby. Being without him was like traveling through life with a phantom third arm that kept trying to reach for something but failed to exist. My Colby consciousness kept reaching out. I would check for him in the rental car's rearview mirror to be sure he was comfortable in the back seat and then think, "Oh, of course," when he wasn't there. I missed Jessica too, but somehow I knew she was fine; about my dog I had a feeling of our being unable to live apart, ever. It was always hard to leave him and harder still, in that time, because I knew he would soon be leaving me forever.

The fact is I had known Colby longer than Jessica, and while it was likely that she would ultimately win the time test, at the moment he was leading her by at least six months. We met when he was one day old. A friend announced she was breeding her Portuguese water dog, and that I should have one of the puppies. I said I was more interested in a human companion. But then fourteen puppies arrived in one litter. That is a lot of puppies—enough to command a cesarean delivery, which is a frantic matter in dog birth. It's all-hands-on-deck, one puppy to each available human hand, lots of round-the-clock puppy cleaning and feeding and such while the mother remains sedated. I showed up to help in the puppy-birth aftermath, and there he was, less than a pound, eyes closed, filling my palm like a slick black beanbag. It is possible I was the first thing he saw when his eye slits cracked open. Almost from that very day forward I would take him with me everywhere, even places he was not allowed to go: he would curl at my feet under my desk at work; he would steal hot dogs off children's plates at birthday parties; he would get us kicked out of restaurants and sports events. He would be the one thing that I would love, start to finish, and now he was fourteen and the finish part was unfathomably near.

Jessica, who entered our lives when Colby was not yet a year old, heard me coming as I neared our apartment, my suitcase rolling behind, and she peeked out around the apartment door, her blue eyes playing a hide-and-seek game. Jessica presents herself to the world as a person of consequence—no timid thing—a strong, good-postured woman and even a cold woman to some for all that posture and poise, but her soul in a certain light resembles a frightened bird, really, a little frightened blue bird, and it squawks like it's fallen out of its nest sometimes, especially if she thinks someone is mad at her or when she is worried.

Maybe, now, she was worried; even a short time apart is enough to incubate uncertainty, and perhaps we were already in trouble. I had gone away and ta-da! I was back, and it was complicated. Why had I gone away? Did I like being away more than being home? Had being away made me a better person? A worse person? Did I miss her? Come to think of it, did she miss me? What did she feel about me? Was she glad I had been gone, actually? Should we act like I was home now, or only partly home? Was I going to be in a bad mood? Was I going to leave my shoes everywhere? Would she be able to overlook that? Would we collapse into each other's waiting arms or would I kick my shoes off in the wrong place and would that bug her? Would I get angry if she couldn't overlook the way I left my shoes everywhere? Seriously? Shoes? After I had been gone so long? Did we love each other enough to get through the hard parts? The separations? The shoes? Something was wrong. I knew it. But I had been determined to live as if I didn't know because really, I loved her. And how could I abandon anything or anyone I loved?

Jessica peeked around the corner, blinked her blue eyes. I set my bags down and we embraced without, for once, the loudly barked objections of my jealous dog. Jessica was warm and soft and when I hugged, she hugged back. I held her in a way that said I would always come home. I held her in a way that said I hoped that was true. Our arms made a web that contained nearly all I knew of life, then. All the certainty in it was right there, and we held on so tight.

Then in the morning, I left for Utica. True. I made the trip home in part because of Jessica's party but I also wanted to attend the Pioneer America Society's annual conference in Utica, four hours north of New York City. And so, almost as soon as I said hello to Jessica, I left again.

The Pioneer America Society actually goes by a complicated two-part name that also includes the words "Association for the Preservation of Artifacts and Landscapes." Association members attempt to immortalize elements of North America's "material culture" that are in danger of being lost or forgotten or perhaps just ignored to death. They like obscure old stuff. They like to save obscure old stuff from permanent oblivion. A sampling of topics published in the group's journal includes wampum bags from the native Northeast, nineteenth-century beater hay presses of the mid-Ohio Valley, Great Lakes iron ore unloading machinery, and pottery production in the early settlements of Illinois.

It's astounding, when you start to make lists, how much has passed before us that once mattered completely and now matters not at all but is still kind of cool to know about. Even more astonishing is the level of commitment humans have to preserve every last drop of our long-evolving story. The past comes with us, and the longer we survive as a species, apparently the greater our capacity to hold stuff must grow, because we don't seem to want to lose any of it. In my mind I see the inside rack of my parents' refrigerator door, loaded with the two hundred or so butter patties they have brought home from diners. They would tell you they had saved these for some practical purpose but the truth is they do not need two hundred pats of butter. I do not believe Depression-era thriftiness is their motive, either, as is often suggested. I see simply an urgent need to save things, even things that do not need saving. This is the impulse I saw in the Pioneer America folks and that also lives in me.

Utica itself encapsulated nearly everything I had learned so far about change as it shows up in the evolving life of this country. The city was built at the midway point of the Erie Canal and later became a railroad hub; it is a beautifully built but now half-abandoned city with a stately, struggling downtown. Its edges are lined with block upon block of abandoned brick warehouses. Everywhere you look, there you are: long, flat industrial debris rolling out along the train tracks, once grand and charming houses in disrepair. In forty postindustrial years, only the Buffalo–Niagara Falls region of Upstate New York lost population faster than Utica; the city had begun actively courting immigrants and refugees to reverse the trend and it was helping.

The PAS conference was held downtown at the century-old Hotel Utica, which had dodged the wrecking ball, been fully renovated, and had recently reopened with rooms restored to old-school fancy. The day I arrived, the brand-new Utica Sparks ice hockey team was being feted in the hotel's grand lobby. The hotel had been saved and was hosting a conference, and the city was courting Croatians and Rwandans to boost its population, and there was a good brewery in the historic district downtown and even a small college campus. Now the Sparks would play in the new hockey arena. There was a buzz of possibility.

A group of academic supergeeks had gathered for the PAS conference, including a professor from Western Kentucky University who presented her study of how, in the early twentieth century when car travel came along, commercial buildings rapidly took over residential streets, swallowing up Victorian houses in the old neighborhoods of Bowling Green. She really did mean "swallowing." She showed very old photographs of big houses that had disappeared into commercial sprawl but not because they had been razed; generic-looking commercial shrouds had been built over them like devouring mouths. The houses were still there but commercial facades had covered them and left no trace, a phenomenon the professor christened "home-icide."

Later I chatted with the professors in the Western Kentucky contingent, secured an invitation to camp on one professor's farm in rural Scottsville, and, thus feeling I had accomplished something at the conference, went home again to Jessica.

Jess and I spent our time together mostly sacked out on the couch and watching PBS dramas. In a way it felt as if I had never left, except that because I had, we were both trying hard not to pop my road trip bubble or disturb the journey my spirit was on even if my body was home, so there was little talk of "real life" like her job and her troubles parking the car in our parking-deficient neighborhood and the many small worries in her extended family, and to be fair, I tried not to talk too much about my journey, which wasn't over and so I wasn't really sure what to say about it anyhow. Avoiding these things left us little to actually talk about, which was fine. Our apartment felt safe as a womb, a place where trouble hardly ever finds you, and being safe was somehow so rare and so desirable that I was very happy, then, to be there with her.

I did show her some pictures. I had taken thousands. I showed Jessica pictures of Clairton and told her there were hundreds of other places like it that we simply hadn't heard about but that deserved to be seen. I did tell her about how, as I was walking down the center of a deserted street in Clairton, a man appeared, walking toward me from the other direction; he was also in the middle of the street so I could hardly ignore him. What were either of us doing there? As we passed he stopped and asked me for money so he could buy a cup of coffee. It had irritated me that under these circumstances, the man was panhandling in clichés. It's a kind of detail I can get hung up on.

"Coffee, Jessica. They don't even *have* coffee in Clairton. Can you believe he said that?"

We were nestled side by side on the couch and she pulled back a bit to see my face more clearly and she said, "Yes. I can believe it."

"How dumb did he think I was?"

"He wasn't thinking. Obviously."

I stopped on some pictures of Titusville.

"You know how Rockefeller made his money, don't you?"

"Sweetie," she said, "my people are British. How would I know a thing like that?"

"It was oil. Oil from Pennsylvania. As if all the oil beneath the ground in Pennsylvania, sitting there for all those eons, stewing up in the fossils of prehistoric arthropods, was put there for him and him alone to take and make his billions. No one else got to get rich on the prehistoric arthropod fossil fuels. Just him. Like he was entitled to all the earth juice. So now the Rockefellers are rich and the rest of the world isn't. Do you know how many folks live in Titusville that are even vaguely rich today?"

"Seven."

"No. But that's not even the point. The point is it was once really something there, and now it's all lost. And greed. The point is also greed, misery, and neglect. Also, methamphetamine. It's bad. It's really, really bad. Oh, damn it, I'm having another mood swing, aren't I?" I pushed away and started fanning myself. "Hot flash." I went to bed, and Jessica stayed on the couch until after I had fallen asleep.

One night in my small egg of a trailer somewhere near the Mississippi River, swaddled in its carpeted fiberglass pod walls and soothed by a warm, dim reading light, I had composed an email to the old friend I had encountered months earlier in a Wisconsin parking lot, the one I had had such sudden, strong feelings for. Enough time had passed that I thought I could tell her what had happened when I had seen her. I tried to keep it light. I thought at least it would relieve a discomfort I had carried in myself since then, to tell her I had always loved her, that this was a strange and also sweet thing to realize, and that it didn't matter, but I thought I would tell her anyhow. At best, she might say she loved me back, and that perhaps would be a plug in my socket, enough connection to relieve the emptiness I felt. In hindsight I have no doubt she felt what I felt on some level, but what a disaster it would have been to have acted on it, with each other. I doubted she had ever let herself think it. Her response, in essence, was, "Let's never speak of this again."

This answer did not relieve my discomfort—not the discomfort of feeling so foolish over her, and not the discomfort of what that really said about me. What I wanted from that friend was a connection that I did not feel in my life, even with Jess, and to want it so badly woke me up. Waking up would demand things that scared me. And by now it appeared the friend herself was not the point; she was not important and maybe cheating on Jessica was not the point either, though it retained some appeal because, well, plugs and sockets and electricity, that sort of thing. But there was so much more to my finding what I needed and I couldn't turn back and was afraid of what came next. I was living in a liminal space, trying to pretend I was fine, and often failing.

After the big party, Jessica and I took a yellow cab up the west side of the city to the apartment we shared, watching tall and shining buildings pass, lit with dreams of immortality. She was mad at me. I had not been fully present for this big moment in her life. I was angry too, pretending not to be. We rode home in the kind of pained silence that was rare for us, and was so sad, because truly, each of us wanted the other to be happy almost as much as we could want anything. To see someone you love in pain, and know it is your fault at least partly, is a terrible thing.

When it was time for me to go, Jessica kissed me lightly and looked kindly at me and shook me by the shoulders and said I had to have some fun. If I didn't have a little more fun for the remainder of my trip, probably no one would ever want to see my slide show. And that would be truly tragic. And I needed more dog pictures too.

"Not that all the pain isn't interesting," she said. "It's just that people like dogs. And fun." I agreed to take Colby to an Oktoberfest somewhere. Then I flew back to Milwaukee and proceeded to make myself numb.

III

10

Milwaukee

I had left Colby with my Cousin Bee in Milwaukee and when I returned and pulled into her driveway, I saw Colby's hindquarters disappearing slowly into the open garage. He was walking back into the house after a visit to the side yard for a sniff and a pee. I leapt from the car, ran to the garage, dropped to my knees, and called out "Colby!" with the sort of love-lorn drama I would never have displayed for a human.

"Colby! Come here, you beautiful boy. I missed you so much!" I cried.

Colby was a little deaf and he didn't turn around so I tried it again a little louder: "Colby!"

Finally, expending very little energy, Colby looked back over his shoulder, saw that it was me, wagged his tail, then faced front and continued on his way through the garage to the kitchen door and into the airy comfort of Cousin Bee's house.

This lethargy may have been related to despair brought on by our six-day separation but more likely it had to do with Cousin Bee overfeeding him. I knew she had; she liked dogs more than people and she liked Colby more than most dogs, so she gave him treats constantly. I followed Colby into the kitchen, where he flopped on a guest dog bed and I found Bee standing around the granite counter island with her kids, all of them eating cheese-puff balls while sharing some after-school "family time." Bee's kids,

161

a perfect boy-girl pair of blond cherry-cheeked Wisconsin tween-agers, were exceptionally wound up. An alert had been sent out that day to all families in their school district about a strange man who had been observed trying to lure kids into his car.

The pervert alert was so exciting that Bee's kids had to practice their air-karate moves on each other, and they kicked and chopped while giving me the details. No one had been abducted—yet—but the perv sightings had occurred for several days in a row, or at least one sighting had been reported on the news, and after that, by unofficial word of mouth it was learned that a suspicious-looking man with gray hair, in his seventies, driving a silver four-door sedan—a description that fits I would guess about 38 percent of the population in and around Milwaukee—had been seen . . . everywhere. Over the next day or two, even Cousin Bee and I spotted him a few times—at the grocery store, in the parking lot of her gym, rolling aimlessly in his silver sedan through West Allis with its jillion old saloons built of cream-colored brick and hung with Blatz signs. The perv was all around us. We couldn't stop seeing the perv.

Bee and I left the kids locked out of harm's way inside the house and took our dogs for a walk around the block. Bee and her husband, a medical appliance manufacturer, lived in Brookfield, one of Milwaukee's newer suburbs. Her father and my mother and many of our relatives had grown up in Wauwatosa, an older, inner-loop suburb. Brookfield rose in the post-war housing boom as downtown Milwaukee emptied and spread itself out, pushing back the edge of Wisconsin's farmland. The newest and richest neighborhoods in Brookfield are ringed with walls and fortified by large stone pillars at their entranceways. They don't have gates. They have the suggestion of gates and that's almost enough. Cousin Bee lived in a big house in one of those walled places.

Because I asked, not because she was boasting, on our walk she pointed out a few highlights of her neighborhood. I had already seen the pool and the tennis courts and I had seen the gigantic turreted and unfinished ghost mansion where construction shut down after the 2007 housing market crash. All interesting. This visit, Bee showed me the house where a woman she knows killed herself the day Cousin Bee was going to meet her for lunch. Then she showed me a house where the husband had been out of work for years and the family was teetering ever closer to foreclosure, and she pointed out the various other houses where infidelities had occurred, and also the house—a huge one, with odd cement statuary on the front lawn—where a family kept a young woman secretly enslaved for nineteen years until police rescued her. The family was Filipino and very mysterious; no one in the neighborhood had met them, as far as Bee knew.

"They really never came outside," Bee said, crushing her cigarette with the toe of her boot. "I never got a good look at them."

The Brookfield couple who held a woman captive all those years, then went to prison, then were deported to the Philippines in 2010, in fact lived in a development on the same road as Cousin Bee's but a couple of miles directly south, in a palatial 8,600-square-foot house that was not the house Bee pointed to but a house even bigger and weirder. Still, everyone believed the evil family had lived near them and in a way that was the real point; the evil strangers felt close. They felt possible. These modern, walled suburbs had not been able to keep the fear away.

I nipped all this negativity in the bud and told Cousin Bee that I wanted to have fun. We decided to visit a brewery. Thus began my side study of numbing ourselves in the process of confronting the scary parts of life. Hint: it works great until it doesn't. Milwaukee is known for beer, with Harley-Davidsons coming in a distant second. It's not the brewing city it once was, and notably, by the second decade of the twenty-first century, more than a quarter of Milwaukee's jobs were in health care, not beer, but beer is definitely sexier (flabby guts notwithstanding) in terms of urban identity than conventional medicine, so the beer idea sticks to Milwaukee. In the mid-nineteenth century, the city was packed with German immigrants who brewed beer from old-country recipes and built themselves into the city's legendary four: Blatz, Schlitz, Pabst, and Miller. Their grand, stone-walled brewing and distribution complexes sprawled across acres of what has become largely abandoned downtown real estate since the 1980s manufacturing decline. Funny to think of beer as a part of our manufacturing base, but it is. For generations, Milwaukee's four monsters of beer brewed not just any-old pale, thin lager but bona fide beer legends: Schlitz, the beer that made Milwaukee famous; and Miller, the champagne of beers. Big beers. Muscular beers. Nothing so wussy as, say, Canada's

Carling, which, back in mass-brewed lager's glory days, positioned itself by boasting meekly: "When people try it, they like it." Eat dirt! Milwaukee beers grabbed beer drinkers by the collar and slid glory down their throats, and the beer drinkers loved it.

In the corporate reordering of the 1970s and '80s, beer companies began to devour themselves like Russian nesting dolls, one eating another and then another eating that one until in the end it seems Pabst Blue Ribbon pretty much ate them all—and in turn, Pabst came to be owned by a company in Los Angeles that was actually sold to a Russian company (the nesting doll idea really starts to resonate), and by the start of the twenty-first century, nearly all the great old American beers were basically owned by a guy in Moscow. The names owned by Pabst today are a hit parade of no-fuss American working-man's libations, beers my Great-Uncle Harold (also known to Cousin Bee as Bumpa) drank on the patio behind his house in Wauwatosa while he flipped burgers laced with Lawry's seasoned salt. The low drone of a baseball game wafts from the neighbor's transistor radio; it is 1957 and the Milwaukee Braves are ticking their way through the season to meet the Yankees in the World Series, and this city is ecstatic over their team kicking a little effete East Coast ass. In this golden heart-land moment, Bumpa Harold's lower lip protrudes in pouty concentration, pale flapping triceps sprout from his buttoned-up shirt, a barbecue apron wraps the mountain of his belly, and just as he gets the last burger flipped he reaches into the ice box for a can of Schaefer, Schlitz, Schmidt, Stroh's, Piels, Pabst, Olympia, Blatz, Natty Bo, Grain Belt, Special Export, Old Milwaukee, or maybe an Old Style, and he keys open the can. And it is good.

In Milwaukee today, the Miller brewery is the only one of the original big four breweries still active, though to be clear, Miller is no longer exactly Miller; it is owned by Molson Coors. The decline in these big breweries has by no means slowed Milwaukee's pace of drinking. Wisconsin leads the nation in binge drinking—about a quarter of the adult population admits to consuming many beverages in one sitting, regularly; it shares first place with Montana. I don't know what it means that my mother is from Wisconsin and my father from Montana; probably nothing. Maybe everything.

Cousin Bee and her friend Linda and I decided to hit the Miller brewery together instead of one of the newer, trendier microbreweries, in part because I am a student of history but also because to our astonishment, Miller was the only brewery actually open on a weekday at ten in the morning. That was the only time Bee and Linda could sneak out to drink beer and still be home when the kids got back from school. The three of us piled into Bee's enormous black SUV and headed for the brewery, driving the back roads into the center of the city. I sat in the back seat and counted the bars we passed: Mannie's, the Unicorn, Silver City, Silver Spurs, Milwaukee Nights, the Full Moon Saloon, Kegel's Inn—a place that still serves up schnitzel and spaetzle and probably will for as long as anyone knows what that is. (It's fried veal and noodles.) Elderly couples arrive in time for the Kegel's dinner special at four in the afternoon; Milwaukee is old school like that, if you know where to look. Bee drove and Linda wistfully recalled wild times before kids, when she and the guy she eventually married once hit six breweries in a day and then went to a pool party that she remembers not even a little. A flood of beer memories or notions of memories we had been too drunk to recall overtook us after that as we made the ten-mile journey from Brookfield to the Miller compound.

Miller Brewery, true to its corporate scale, gave us a tour loaded with slick videos, led by a dark-haired and very young, very skinny, very well-groomed male guide with a bobbing Adam's apple. He clearly acquired his tour voice in flight attendant school, or else possibly he was a Miller robot, programmed to exude a polished luminescence that is not what I think of when I think of a brewery; I think of vats of roiling foam and of steam that billows up and rattles the vat covers; I think of caverns filled with the sound of boiling liquids and of burly men in coveralls pulling back twenty-foot levers shaped like humongous draft handles, releasing rivers of golden liquid into beer valleys, and obviously the beer flows through the valleys into gigantic funnels, and through the funnels it goes right into big old barrels, and then it is icily cooled. But that's not actually what we saw happening. We spent ninety minutes walking around the sterile perimeter of the brewery and watching videos that provided scintillating trivia such as "no one knows where the slogan 'champagne of beers' comes from" and "Miller's 'girl in the moon' logo—well, no one knows the origin of that," and we saw some empty copper vats and stacks of boxes but never actually saw any beer being made anywhere. Cousin Bee and Linda and I drank our glasses of free pilsner in the beer hall afterward, sitting at a table with a visiting couple who had stopped by to kill time on their way to the airport and apparently had no interest in talking to us. Then Bee, Linda, and I left Miller Valley for a small bar in Wauwatosa, where we ordered bloody marys.

For the twenty-first century's first two decades, beer had been magically becoming more popular than ever, as if that were even possible. In the process, beer has shouldered a heroic share of the job of restoring dead downtowns in America; brewpubs very effectively draw crowds. Name a place; any that are thriving are likely to have at least one microbrewery. The number of small breweries in the country doubled in the fifteen years before I hit the road to go look at the situation out there, but most of the growth happened in a burst around 2010. Unlike other fads, the world never really tires of drinking, it seems, so in the matter of reversing postindustrial decline as well as the need to self-medicate our pandemic anxiety, you really can't lose with beer.

The economic recovery plan for urban centers all over the country, I was coming to see, actually embraces at least six things: sports arenas, beer, casinos, hotel conference centers, loft apartments, and halls of fame. And also sometimes yoga. So in fact it would be a tragedy for the American economy if we all quit drinking now, which of course is a bit of a conundrum. Bee and I had been working on saving the world with beer since we were teenagers, as were many people I know, and by the time I was nearly fifty, some of that drinking didn't look so good anymore. I had another cousin on my dad's side who lived in Spokane, Washington, and he had quit drinking years ago but had, recently, started up again and then apparently taken a leap onto meth. That was the story I had been told just that fall, when my cousin Bill had reached out to my father for money. I noticed Bill had been following my road trip on social media and was surprised to see him there, as we had drifted from each other several years ago, which I now realize was when he had dropped out of recovery. I had a funny feeling about the way beer was sort of saving the world at a time when addiction was kind of killing so many. This was what breweries meant to me, at midlife. Dear god, I was turning into such a drag.

I can confirm that, on that day in Milwaukee, Bee and Linda and I did have fun, and I had the intoxicating sensation that beer could fix anything.

When he saw me hitching up the trailer, Colby knew his time of luxuriating with Cousin Bee was over, a situation he accepted dutifully. He walked slowly to the car with his head lowered and sat down to wait. It was a school day, and when I was all packed up and ready to go, no one was home. So we left as I prefer to—without saying good-bye. I pointed the car south, and within a few miles Milwaukee's suburbs faded like an Emerald City mirage behind us and an infinity of dull, dried cornstalks and gray skies spread out ahead. Flocks of crows flew low crazy patterns above fields of husks and black soil. Colby clawed at his dog bed to get it just right and finally kicked it to the floor and sprawled belly up across the back seat, legs in the air, and I tuned into a radio station that plays only love songs, tipped my seat back, and put on my sunglasses despite the low sky. Marvin Gaye sang all sultry, "Let's get it on," and I agreed, and we sang together as I squinted into the distance: "Baby, please please baby, let's get it on . . . Ooo, ooo . . ."

With the heat in the car turned up high and my sunglasses on I could still feel summer even as fall was digging in and getting harder to ignore. Endless summer. Perpetual summer. If I drove and drove I could believe that summer had not or would not ever really have to end, which may have been what I had wanted all along.

11

Sullivan

I was out in search of the fun I had promised Jessica I would have and, of course, more beer. You would think a girl couldn't swing lederhosen in the German/Polish-dense middle of the country in October without hitting a big beer tent set up in a cornfield. In fact, it was surprisingly hard to find one. This is because, as it turns out, the vast majority of Oktoberfests are held in September. Buffalo Grove, Illinois, actually had its Oktoberfest in August that year. This is baffling. This is another example of distressing decay: we are a bunch of pleasure addicts whose cultural celebrations have grown devoid of meaning. More evidence of this madness: towns that "schedule" trick-or-treating on, say, November 2 just because that's a Saturday, turning the true spirit of Halloween into a meaningless state-sanctioned candy shakedown. Halloween is October 31. Period. An Oktoberfest in August is no longer a glorious celebration of Bavarian Crown Prince Ludwig's wedding on October 12, 1810, but merely the eccentrically spelled name of a boozy street party. When words lose their meaning, a culture dies. Be warned.

Sullivan, Illinois, was home to the only Oktoberfest anywhere near my driving route that I hadn't already missed, so I decided to be in Sullivan by October 18 even though it meant skipping Peoria and Galena and a planned visit to a meat packing plant along the way. Fun of the type normal people understand would be had, damn it; I would go to Sullivan and I would take pictures of the dog.

That day we made it to the Peru, Illinois, KOA just after dark. I set up camp and made a fire. I sat and thought about nothing; to be sitting with my dog in a strange place of no special meaning to me was where I wanted most of all to be: nowhere. Heading into farm country, I would see fewer cities; there were far fewer ruins to distract me and more empty fields, and so all the confusion, grief, and worry I had been staring into would have nothing to land on outside myself. The Peru KOA was not Rockford; it was simple and quiet. I felt simple and quiet. I was alone with my thoughts there, and my dog.

In the morning in the women's bathroom, ladies put on their faces with concentration above the sink. Girls dressed in the shower stalls and talked of hitting Dunkin' Donuts for hot chocolate. The ground was scattered thickly with ugly bumpy green things, osage oranges, known locally as monkey brains. I took a long, slow run down the straight lines of roads that held the land in boxes, facing a hard wind both coming and going.

Back on the interstate, a mustang with Purple Heart license plates driven by a young woman passed me. I wondered how many women have been wounded in combat and awarded Purple Hearts. (It is not certain, but despite the ban that existed on women serving in combat roles, one group reported 106 women had been awarded Purple Hearts from the decade-long wars we were still in, then.) Then I saw an exit for Bloomington, a fair-sized city with a university, and realized I was as close as I would be for a very long time to any place that might serve me a latte; we were heading off the highways and deep into corn. The desire for fancy, overpriced coffee was lodged deep in my infinitely coffee-craving soul, but despite the power of this addiction I didn't stop for it. I couldn't, because something larger was at stake. If I hurried south to Sullivan, I would get to the Oktoberfest in time for Colby to win the cute pet contest, and that was what mattered most in the world to me just then.

I had no doubt that Colby would win this contest, which involved costumes. He was wearing his Green Bay Packers bandana, which seemed good enough; if pressed, I would tell the judges he was a pug dressed up as a Portuguese water dog and then he would not only win but people would be charmed and find us both terribly clever. Even naked, Colby was in my mind cuter than any dog alive and certainly cute enough to win some small-town contest. I had walked him for at least an hour a day for fourteen years; that's more than five thousand hours logged watching him saunter magnificently. That was five thousand hours of holding a leash and looking at Colby's fuzzy rear end, an absolutely princely dog butt, its long tail strong and jaunty like a flag. The wavy black hair on the back of his head parted naturally down the middle and feathered back light and fluffy and glistened as he walked with his confident bounce, and seriously, from my view, he sometimes looked so very much like my preteen heartthrob, David Cassidy. That cute pet prize at the Oktoberfest in Sullivan was ours.

I turned off the interstate without a latte and drove deeper into farm country until we hit the small town of Cerro Gordo; what I noticed first was a large old school, well kept and exuding a kind of authoritative goodness, a school that told of generations of farm children growing up and learning inside, meeting sweethearts there, starting families after graduation, sending new kids to school, continuing the cycles for generations in a pretty little town. In Cerro Gordo, almost everyone finishes high school but hardly anyone goes to college. It suggests a town of bright folks who don't want to leave. Passing through that place I imagined sweet things: Ice cream. Shaded sidewalks where young boys in football uniforms walk home from the game, carrying their helmets, perky girls in cheerleader uniforms chasing them. A place to read Mark Twain and believe him. Dry leaves billowed up from neat lawns in the strong wind that just would not quit blowing. The wind in the leaves blew my visions of innocence right along ahead of me. It seemed I had found an American ideal, intact.

Cerro Gordo is a prosperous farm town fifteen miles from the bigger city of Decatur, and on the radio on the very day I drove through town, the big news was that the big agricultural distributor, ADM, was packing up and leaving its longtime Decatur headquarters and moving to Chicago. The gloom of that announcement had come just exactly in time to taint the sweetness of the place and it troubled me, all this packing up and leaving; then a commercial for Heinkel's sausages came on the radio, promising hunters that if they brought in their deer, Heinkel's would make them some nice, fresh venison jalapeno sausage. That was more like it. I was determined to find some Heinkel's jalapeno venison sausage somewhere in Illinois.

It's another half-hour drive from Cerro Gordo to Sullivan, where I needed to register at a campground and drop off the trailer before getting to the pet contest. Suddenly I felt like I was in a hurry. Since May I had been late for everything I had tried to get to except for two trips to airports, for which being late was not an option. Colby was sprawled in the back seat getting his beauty rest and I was glad for that and glad he did not feel my stress, as this would hurt his performance in the beauty pageant (as it had come to be called in my mind). I rushed on, trying to stick to my plan, but got hung up at the Lake Shelbyville Marina Campground office in Sullivan, where the woman at the desk did not look up, at first, from the paperwork my visit required of her. She just asked me, "You want one night?"

"I was thinking two," I said.

"Okay," she said, and firmly crossed something off the card she was filling out. "Make it two."

I was working up my nerve to ask for three nights but I judged it better to wait on that. The campground was large and more or less abandoned. There were two women in the office, one about my age sitting in a chair, saying nothing, and the other, older, doing all the business. The old woman had tightly curled white hair, a flat, pale face and a pink-lipsticked mouth that was given to such salty expressions as "Oh my lord!" The woman sitting off to the side of the desk was younger and quieter, a more folk-music version of the Midwest, with long brown hair and a touch of makeup and a sweater vest. She was one of the campground's owners, and the woman behind the desk was a regular camper who had, in the manner of many enterprising seniors living in RVs, scored with her husband the job of caretaking the marina campground in exchange for a place to stay.

Outside, the grounds were just about empty of people but still parked with big RVs; most campers had left for the season and the RVs in the lot were being winterized. I asked the woman behind the desk if the campground stayed open to the end of October, and she answered, "Around then, yes," in a voice that sounded wary. My guidebook to campgrounds clearly stated this place was open to the end of October, which was still about two weeks away. I felt like the person who walks into a restaurant and orders a huge meal just a few minutes before the staff would have been allowed to go home, had the place stayed empty. The older woman turned her eyes toward me cautiously, apparently looking to see if I had in mind to camp there endlessly.

At first I thought she must not like me, but that's not exactly it. Her wariness was, once again, a midwestern thing I recognized from my own family. She had the no-fuss manner of a University of Akron vice president, doing business at her desk. She had seen my New York driver's license and she knew plenty well what she was dealing with: someone who thinks she knows but doesn't know. Someone who would expect all kinds of service, then turn around and mock the blue Jell-O with marshmallows in it at the grocery store salad bar. Grow up in Cerro Gordo and raise your children there and maybe grandchildren too, if you want to know a thing about anything. Because of all this, and mostly because my attempts at conversation were met with a politeness that resembled honest-to-god contempt, I decided to sit down and talk until we were all friends.

"Where's the best place in Sullivan to get a cup of coffee?" I asked, and the women looked at each other. The younger one said, "I'll go put a pot on." Really, there isn't any place to go for coffee in Sullivan unless you want McDonald's. There was a family restaurant down the road but they didn't send me there—later I would learn it had been taken over by "foreigners," who in the opinion of the locals had ruined the food. Just didn't understand American cooking. If you wanted food and drink these days, you had to make your own. I waited for my coffee and made myself comfortable, despite my concern over making it to Colby's contest on time, and I started telling the women without being asked about my trip, which drew a silent "Oh" from the older one, who asked, "Don't you have a husband?" to which I said something like, "Shoot! Husband! I never thought of that!" This made her laugh. Only two people on the whole, long trip ever asked me that question, the second being a twenty-five-year-old married boy in Kentucky who took me out to shoot clay pigeons with his twelve-gauge shotgun one day and, when I hit twenty of my twenty-five, said, "Dang! You shoot good for a girl!" When the Kentucky boy asked me, "Don't you have a husband?" I looked at him dryly, shotgun slung across my arm, and said, "No." He looked sorry.

Sullivan, the women told me, is the county seat of Moultrie, the least-populated county in Illinois, though the lack of people should not be confused with a lack of prosperity. The fact that the population in farm country is shrinking is not a sign that the farms are not doing well. It is the opposite, really. Moultrie County occupies a corner of the Midwest with excellent farms and good jobs. But fewer people are needed to get the work done these days, and so the population is falling. There are other reasons to leave. Young people leave the Midwest the same way they leave Albany or the deep south or anywhere that isn't a big city, in search of more excitement. But the farm towns also empty out when people go the other way—moving deeper into the nearby countryside, swept off by better roads and better cars to bigger houses far from the center of things. On so many intersections of the long, straight roads weaving a loose basket on farmland, tiny towns dot the map but when you go to see them, they are half in ruins. The houses are half lived in, half not, empty storefronts, empty laundromats, empty cafés clustered around them. There's a Walmart in Decatur, that's all you need; the rest has been left to die quietly, and if it has died mainly because people have chosen what they like better, it is still unnerving to me to see the shells left behind, and I can't imagine living daily in such a spectacle of loss.

I told my new friends in Sullivan that having seen so many places dying like that, I had lately come to favor the idea of just knocking stuff down. Just do it! Just let it go. Close the schools, abandon the towns. Rip off the bandage. "I now think it's best if we just stop trying to save everything," I said and sipped my coffee.

The older woman, who was a Cerro Gordo native, reached nervously for something near the base of her throat that wasn't really there. I had delivered a verbal solar plexus punch. She turned to the younger woman for an answer to this mischief; here they had confided in me and made me coffee and I replied so casually that I would like to rip their guts out.

The younger woman said: "People do come back to small towns if they're nice. They brought back Sullivan really nice after it was hit by two tornados ten or fifteen years ago and that makes a difference."

Go compare, she said. Go to Paris, Illinois—another county seat, nearby. The shops on the square are unsavory. Around the courthouses in some county seats there's nothing but pawn shops and bail bonders, not nice restaurants or gift shops. A downward spiral takes hold. Every county seat has a town square that can be made inviting; squares were meant to be gathering places, but if a town fails to create that kind of atmosphere, decent people will get discouraged and leave. Good people will start wanting to host their Oktoberfests and chili festivals out at the fairgrounds, way out in the farm fields, when the whole point of a chili festival in a small town is to bring that town some life. It's not like chili actually requires honoring; it's not like you better put that sacred chili festival somewhere safe like the fairgrounds to be sure the celebration goes on. The point of a chili fest was and always will be to show off your town square, your downtown, to bring life back to the center. If the town is so crummy that you can't serve chili in it, you may as well call the whole thing off.

"But people don't always understand that," the younger woman said. "People just want their chili."

"Oh dear, it's nearly three o'clock. You'll miss the pet contest," the older woman said with genuine concern.

"Of course! Better go," I said and stood up and thanked them for the coffee. The older woman left the office and led me by golf cart to the very farthest edge of the vast, empty lawn where in the summer small trailers and tents set up, one alongside the next in a veritable pop-up city of nylon and wheeled-aluminum lakeside living. But the season had long since lost its appeal to all but me; everyone had packed up and left and I was gloriously alone in a vacant, grassy flat the size of three football fields. The land dwarfed my camper and ended abruptly at a bluff that dropped off into Lake Shelbyville. The scene—a browning field, wind-spun waves on a chilly-looking lake, birds catching updrafts in the gray sky—resembled the rugged and wind-whipped meres of Irish lake country, seen by me only in movies, but I think I know a mere when I find one. This was brilliant. It was perfect solitude. I parked overlooking the lake. Colby hopped out and ran directly to a pile of fish bones and heads left in the weeds by fishermen, then fell on them in ecstasy.

"Colby!" I shouted. "You'll never win the contest with guts on your face!" He did not understand these words and so kept smiling and rubbing his head in the gore. Before I could reach him he threw his back down and slid his whole body along the pile of fish heads. I pulled him up and wrestled him back to sanity. Scales clung to his muzzle, and he panted, and a black streak that looked like mud but smelled far worse was rubbed deep into his fuzzy hair. I fluffed him, licked my hand and did my best to gloss it over, then hustled his snorting and death-drunk self back to the car. I unhooked the trailer and we made our way ten or so miles to the Sullivan town square.

The best part about Oktoberfest in a small town is that there are no lines for the funnel cakes. No lines for anything, actually. Hardly anyone was in Sullivan that day by my standards, but if you live there it may have looked like a pretty good turnout. Colby and I parked effortlessly just off the square, where the booths and food trucks were set up, and I leashed him and we dashed out toward a cluster of people that at least resembled a crowd; there were a few dogs in their midst. Colby limped behind me at a good clip, stinky and excited, and we set out to find the cute-pet judging station. Within fifty feet of my car I spied a pair of little dogs coming my way, dressed up as Elmer Fudd and a rabbit, prancing ahead of a woman carrying a ribbon for first prize. It was 3:02 p.m.

"Oh!" I said. "Are these the winners?"

The round, redheaded woman walking the dogs was smiling so big it looked like her face hurt. She nodded. Colby sniffed the little contest-winning dogs graciously. I stood half-frozen in disbelief, sputtering compliments, as another woman came along pulling a wagon with a little dog on it dressed up as what I think was a ladybug. The ladybug dog wore a second-place ribbon. I swiveled to watch the wagon roll by.

Small banners hung from posts down the length of Main Street, each one with the name of a local man or woman in the military. As in all such county seats, the center of Sullivan is a square of roads around the courthouse and the courthouse exudes all the dignity the town's founders could muster. It sat atop a high mound, crowned with bronze, steep steps ascending to it from the sidewalk on each side of the square. It told the world: behold! No one is above the law. Not in Sullivan.

The town square concept must seem obvious to those who have one, but I had never noticed or had much reason to think about them, except that many strip malls and other constructions in the East are named "town square," or rather, "Towne" square, with no regard to geometry or the actual meaning of such a place or the proper use of Anglo Saxon spellings. A strip mall can be named "Towne Square" anywhere in the U.S. and no one will object, so long as there's parking. This troubled me. Beginning with Sullivan, I understood that the true central square design was another element of the vision for this country, when it was new and those planning its future were planning for greatness. It seemed to me that if a small town in the middle of America were to build a courthouse today, it would likely be at the edge of a parking lot that joined the fast food joint to the low rent motel, and they would have to settle for a double-wide trailer. Costs less, gets the job done; still meets the need to fill prisons.

The square around the Sullivan Courthouse was full of shops and galleries and restaurants, and on the north block, the Sullivan Theater marquee proclaimed "*Nunsense!*" The theater was once a major touring venue for shows bound for Broadway, and while the route to Broadway has changed, the theater remains a local treasure. Colby and I walked around the square, then settled in to listen to Christian rock bands on the near-empty Oktoberfest bleachers while eating pork sandwiches. Roughly ten out of about fifteen booths at the fest were set up by local churches. I thought I really ought to visit one. I accepted a wristband at a booth that lured me in with its Free Cookies! sign. The wristband noted a Bible verse, "Eph 3:20." I fought the urge to look it up on the spot and just wore it instead, imagining I fit right in.

Finally, evening came and the chili contest began. I put Colby in the car so that I could concentrate. The chili booths were set up beneath blue construction tarps strung like a tent; inside, everything took on a blue glow reminiscent of the basement rec rooms where I had smoked weed as a teenager. At the first booth, blood-red barbecue sauce cascaded from a five-tiered fountain. Visitors dipped mini hot dogs into the ooze. This set a very high bar for the contest within steps of the entrance. It's hard to top oozing sauce fountains, but every chili competitor tried to best it somehow. A table run by a women's advocacy group based in Sullivan had a big poster of Rosie the Riveter up behind it, and I fully intended to vote for their chili just to support a women's center in the smallest county in Illinois, which seemed downright radical, but then this happened: I tasted some chili made with smoked brisket. I mean, smoked brisket. Come on. When I smiled at the team who had made it, it seemed as if we were touching each other's chili souls. Our eyes softened and our hearts met in a space of pure chili ecstasy and my voting ticket floated gently from my hand. I think my vote missed the point, though. The most popular table, the one where the largest and loudest crowd had gathered, belonged to a group of guys whose chili I tasted and thought was okay. It was fine. But what do I know? These guys had won the contest two years in a row and it looked as if they were on their way to winning again and it struck me, then, that voting against them undermined the firmament of the Sullivan Oktoberfest. When the traditional chili wins, it feels good. When the local high school football team wins, it feels good too but that outcome is less easily controlled. It feels good to pick a winner, so the right thing to do is let the chili guys win, again, and just be happy. Just be happy and stop making trouble, Lori. Lori, who does not grasp the concept of simply feeling good. Lori, who votes for losers. Lori, whose mood still swings without warning, it seems. I finished my tasting and slipped from the tent.

Back at the courthouse, two zombies were being married in a public ceremony, grunting vows before onlookers who ringed them with cameras. I couldn't look away. Was it theater? Or was it a real wedding, in costume? I joined the crowd and the newlywed zombies led us in a staggering march around the town square, then shared their wedding cake with whomever dropped by; it was shaped like a corpse laid out on a long table and they began cutting it by slicing off the head. I had a little piece off the face, then hit the Oktoberfest beer tent for a nightcap, and went home.

At the campground office, the older woman was sitting at the desk long after dark as if she had been waiting there for me.

"Did he win?" she asked.

"No," I said. "Can you believe it?"

She shook her head.

Sunday morning, I sat outside the trailer drinking coffee as Colby lay at my feet on a blanket. I had thought I might go to church that morning, for research of course, but it was 9 a.m. and I was staring at the water and re-considering. The night before, lounging on my Scamp bed in the faint reading light, I had looked up the Bible verse on my Oktoberfest wristband. Ephesians 3:20 said: "Now to him who is able to do immeasurably more than all we ask or imagine, according to his power that is at work within us,"

And that was it. The verse ended midsentence. I had received a sentence fragment Bible bracelet. What could it mean? "His power that is at work within us" what? That night, as I struggled to make sense of the fragment in the stillness of the trailer, Jessica called. I told her I was going to church in the morning. She shrieked.

"Drive around the whole world if you want but I will be so angry if you join a cult," Jessica said. She was teasing; I knew this. It was one of our jokes about me: I wanted to move to every place I ever saw, and I had a collection of obscure history books, and I liked football, and I was fascinated by cults. All of this was weird enough for endless teasing, but this time the joke made me angry. I snapped something like, "I will join any cult I want, dammit," surely a unique retort in the annals of couples fighting.

When we first lived together, Jessica and I had a conversation one morning about faith and marriage that I had never forgotten, and that we had never seriously attempted again. I was in favor of both. My starting point in faith was that there must be more to life than what we see. I vaguely sensed a "power that is at work within us," to borrow words from the bracelet, and I wanted to know that power, but I didn't think I would find it through religion, formally. I figured the power would reveal itself on a need-to-know basis. As for marriage, I wanted to believe marriage joined beings in that same space within us that my vaguely imagined holy power occupied, a point of view that was hard to articulate and that most people I knew, married or not, found to be an overthinking of the contract. Marriage was a construct that was once thought necessary and was now just a formality. Mostly. Still, I believed something else about faith and love. I had never really discussed it with Jessica before our conversation that morning about a year into our living together; our partnership as a gay couple was unconventional, or it seemed so in that time, so big talks about God and marriage, and even about children, and checking accounts, much less joining souls in public ceremonies, seemed beside the point. But these talks really must be had before joining your life to someone, because the answers turn out to matter eventually. Jess and I did not believe the same things, at core. And yet still, I would have married her, as if the fact of being married would make that other part true, the part about something within me having power and value. When I said I wanted to be married, I could not see what I was really asking, so unfairly, from Jessica. What I did see was that we shared an ease and comfort I had never shared with anyone, much less found on my own. It mattered. But there was more, and it kept quietly mattering too.

In my trailer I had been thinking of church, and all the crosses along roads I had seen, driving, and of the changes that could not be controlled or ignored and that frightened me. Jess had teased me about church but she was also right, because I was vulnerable. I might have joined a cult after all, that morning, if only there had been one in Sullivan besides the Baptists, who would send me to conversion therapy. Sometimes I wished God would show up and explain the whole thing, and that I could accept every word of the explanation without doubt, right down to such highly dubious claims as penguins and dinosaurs riding on Noah's Ark together, and the Earth being only six thousand years old, all evidence to the contrary be damned. Certainty is seductive, even when it's absurd.

"I was teasing," Jessica said. "You know I was."

"Not funny."

"But you know you like cults. It's one of your charms."

She had a point. I should not have snapped at her. I was taking things too seriously, as usual, and I had promised to lighten up and church was not the way to do it. I decided to go to a matinee of *Nunsense* instead. Close enough.

I stopped in the campground office on my way to *Nunsense* and there was coffee waiting for me. The younger woman did not come in on Sundays, so only the older woman was there, and the instant I walked through the door she started to tell me about how she and her husband used to spend their winters down in Texas but they had been forced to come back to Illinois because of the drug cartels.

I watched her over the lip of my Styrofoam coffee cup and sipped as she raised her eyebrows and pursed her lips. This was the big bombshell, I supposed. This was the thing she knew and if I wanted to understand her at all, I had better hear this story and listen well. I almost might have guessed that she had not slept the night before, knowing that she would tell me when she saw me.

She was a shuffler, you see. I thought that meant she dealt cards at a casino but she hushed me and went on. She had made the Shuffleboard Hall of Fame (halls of fame: a strategy that draws tourists to broken places) down in the Rio Grande Valley in Texas, where RV parks hold national shuffleboard tournaments (tournaments: another bit of economic genius). She had won a fair share of trophies. Shuffleboard is a game with strategy, if you didn't know. You don't just shove the puck down the concrete and try for all the points you can get, like I did at the municipal swimming pool in Millburn, New Jersey, nearly every summer day that I was not in Wisconsin from 1972 until 1979, whether or not I had anyone to play against. The strategy for my kind of shuffleboard was all shove-and-watch. But the old woman told me it's better to play careful, get a few points, and spend the rest of your shots setting up a defense to protect the points you've got. You play it safe, see?

"What you do is," she said, "you make a barrier of shuffle pucks around your first big score so when everyone else is getting knocked off the court, you've still got yours." She built shuffle puck walls. She sat back in her desk chair and pursed her lips into a closely held smile and narrowed her eyes shrewdly.

She had shuffled in tournaments, sometimes at her campground in Texas and other times out on the road, on the shuffleboard circuit. Many try for the hall of fame, few make it. She made it. She had the trophies. She had the plaque. She brought the trophies and her plaque back to Illinois with her when things in Texas got too dangerous and they had to leave. Those were the very best of times for her and her husband, happy and retired down in Texas, but the good times ended. It was horrible, how things changed. The campground was near the Rio Grande and the land by the river had grown lawless. People were crossing the borders with drugs, and these people did not value life or security or anything that people in the RV parks valued, and the drug people were violent. Too many came. Things changed, and she and her husband had to leave.

This is one of the things that she knew: A missionary couple she was friends with at her Texas RV park went across the river, as they often did, to bring toys and clothes and things to the Mexican children, but then one day on a goodwill trip to Mexico, the missionary man's truck was car-jacked and his wife was shot and killed in front of him. This was a tragedy of unbearable darkness, and yet as I heard her tell of it I also knew that no one in my pretty little Upstate New York town had heard about the murdered missionary, that we did not know this exact pain or anything about what that place was like. The world is far too big a place for news of one tragedy to spread much beyond where it happens. There is enough hurt for all of us to have our own. On the Rio Grande there are bad guys and drugs. At the Texas campground, after the murder, there were rules. You could go to matinee movies only, and you had to go in pairs and be home by dark. Still, one day after that murder, a friend's new Toyota dually truck was jacked. It was simply no longer safe there.

The old couple decided to come home to Illinois and were living in a trailer at the marina now. She brought the shuffleboard trophies with her. Her husband had cancer, and she herself was scheduled to have a biopsy that week for something they had found on her lung. She thinks about the trophies. She said she keeps thinking she ought to give them away to a school or some place that could use them, but whenever she goes to get them and looks at them again, she knows she isn't ready to let go.

I listened to this story and she watched me to see if I understood. Such sorrow, such loss, and even in that moment perhaps she feared there was yet more to lose and she had no power to stop it.

I said, quite logically of course, "The trouble is drugs. If we could stop people from wanting drugs in the first place, things would begin to get better."

She studied my face. I had missed the whole point, clearly. I was not whom she had come to hope I was—a woman who listened and so would understand her pain and thus would agree with her. The people doing this harm had to be stopped. Simple. How could this be misunderstood?

The old woman said: "Well they're making half the drugs legal now anyways."

"Good," I answered. We looked at each other. I raised my hands in a kind of surrender. "That would get rid of the criminals."

A moment passed. "Aren't you going to be late for your show?" she said.

On Monday, I walked with Colby down to Lake Shelbyville and had a swim. It was October 21 and sunny, but not really swimming weather. As November drew near, it seemed to me that my chances to pretend it was still sort of really almost July were growing very slim. So I dunked, and Colby barked me back out of the water and we wandered the beach, watching ribbons of pelicans drift across the sky and turkey vultures circle over husks of washed-up fish.

I wanted to explore Lake Shelbyville but when I asked in the campground office if I could rent a boat from their marina, the old woman told me they had stopped renting boats a few years ago because "too many drunk idiots" get into trouble on the water and then I heard a few stories of drownings. Apparently, people like to rent several pontoon boats, or "party barges," lash them together like tails to the rat king, and float around the lake like that, all day, drinking. I just wanted to go fishing. The only boats I found to rent were twenty miles away, down at the Lithia Springs Marina on the south end of the lake near the dam, and because I had a dog they would only let me take their smallest model, a rowboat with a little ten horsepower engine on it.

It was a cool day and cooler still in the wind when the boat got going. I made a blanket bed for Colby near my feet on the bottom of the aluminum boat and motored us through a channel and up the bleak water. In his younger days, my dog would stand up on the bow of whatever boat I put him on and let the wind whip his ears back. He would hold his nose in the air and grasp at the rush of scents we plowed through. He was a water dog, and though he did not like to go into the water, by god he loved to go on it. Now, Colby was laying on the blanket at my feet, where it was a little safer and warmer. When he looked up at me, his fuzzy face rustled in the breeze and his eyes squinted and blinked and his nose tried to recapture a scent of the old days. Then he gave up and lay his head down to endure his discomfort.

Lake Shelbyville was created in the late 1960s by the Army Corps of Engineers as part of a regional flood control plan. They built a dam on the Kaskaskia River in a region of loose shale, digging up Indian artifacts and old coal mines as they worked. This dam created a seventeen-mile-long lake that on local maps looked, at least to my eyes, like an elongated uterus with fallopian tubes attached and also many nubs of cut veins and arteries hanging off it. Or, if you prefer, it looked like a decorative dragon drawn on a medieval scroll. From boat's-eye view, riding on it, the lake was a long, wet seagull feather, with clumps of feather hairs arranged into slivers along the feather spine, in a series of narrow bays to either side of the lake's center. It was sweetly desolate. I steered our boat north and then into one of those countless narrow bays. The shores rose up from the narrow bay sharply, making a thin canyon. Deeper into that crevice, tiny fish started hopping in silver arcs all around us. They would splash up as if a school had been disturbed by the boat and then just as quickly settle back down for a while. I shut the engine. Colby sat up and we spun our heads left and right, watching fish jumping, then not jumping. When the fish did not jump, all was quiet but for the wind. Then a few fish would dart out again and sprinkle back into the water like rain.

We were having fun.

I baited up my hook and tossed it out. In about five seconds a little striper bass about five inches long bit it. I threw it back and tried for the bass mother but she never came, only the babies. I caught a few and in a while I gave up against the cold and I motored us back to the marina.

The woman behind the rental counter was my age, maybe fifty, maybe younger, but she also seemed so much older somehow; everything about her from her short, neat hair to her simple dot earrings to her clean pleated jeans spoke of the common sense and security that come with surviving to a certain age without embarrassing yourself in front of your neighbors. I stood before her in my camouflage coat, wind-whipped hair sticking out from my orange cap, my dog on a rope (I forgot his leash) beside me. I chattered on about the pair of five-inch bass I had caught. She seemed familiar, like a high school friend who had stayed behind when others had gone off into the world and changed, and when we came back, we saw her as simple; she judged us for judging her. What did we know about how hard it was to stay? If she thought anything about me at all she never said, and her silence made me lonely. She took my money without a word and I tipped my cap, and Colby and I went on to Shelbyville.

Much of Shelbyville is made of bricks; some of its streets are, and many of its houses are too, and so is the courthouse (it is the seat of Shelby County). It was really very pretty and I liked it there, except that the shop that sells cupcakes and coffee was closed, because in small towns, apparently, shops keep the hours they feel like keeping. I like this in theory but I wanted my coffee. Abraham Lincoln practiced law in Shelbyville. It was a stop on the Eighth Judicial Circuit, a route lawyers traveled together as a pack through fourteen counties of Illinois, county seat to county seat, courthouse to courthouse. Roads were awful then so the lawyers walked and without motels, they camped along the way. Lincoln said those rugged, traipsing years were the happiest of his life. I can see why. I would have liked to spend a few years traipsing the country in my trailer with my dog.

Eventually I asked what I always asked about all of these places— "Why is there even a Shelbyville at all?" This time truly I was mystified, because the town was not on a large river; it had no oil well. Trains didn't make the place; trains came decades after the courthouse was built. So what was Shelbyville doing there at all? Simple: When new states were organizing themselves in the nineteenth century, the authorities cut the map into counties, and put county seats near the center of each. It was a shift from the days of exploring and growing up alongside what was found into a more strategic way of planning. Shelbyville was ordained. There was no other particular reason.

I was losing daylight and I had one last mission in southern Illinois: Heinkel's sausages. Maybe venison jalapeno. My old lady friend at the campground had told me that I should go to a butcher shop in an Amish town called Arthur, where all the meat is raised and processed old-style. But I wanted Heinkel's. I had heard about it on the radio. I wandered from sleepy Shelbyville into the town of Windsor, where, across from the Windsor farm co-op and silos, a giant manlike pig in a blue vest and chef's hat was mounted on a platform, waving a flag above the Windsor Food Market. Was the pig not there to beckon me? I went inside the market and marched straight back to the meat case to find me some Heinkel's. I saw all kinds of things in there but all I found with a Heinkel's label on it were red tubes of "Chili Con Carne." I didn't want those, but I did find them odd, so I decided to break out my camera—meat tubes were no less noteworthy to me than spelling errors in public art, which I had documented exhaustively.

The meat picture was a mistake. The butcher came out moments after I took it and asked, "Can I help you?"

I was glad to have his help and I began to ask about Heinkel's sausage and whether he had ever heard of their jalapeno venison kind, and about what other kinds of sausage he carried and also about whether he cut all this meat up himself, and if it came from local cows. The butcher was dressed in white with an apron and cap. He was a stout man, beefy even, and not smiling. He only answered in monosyllables and never took his eyes off me, and I got the feeling pretty fast that he did not really want to "help" me. He said they didn't have any Heinkel's and I shrugged and tried to explain why I wanted to find that type in particular, that I had heard about it on the radio, and as I was talking I turned and saw a standing freezer case and realized, they DO! They DO carry Heinkel's!

"Look," I said, "here it is," to which the butcher said, "Oh. Yes. Yes, but it's not breakfast sausage. I thought you meant breakfast sausage."

We stood there looking at each other, and I don't know what he was thinking but in my mind I heard Sean Hannity, a right-wing radio personality who had been keeping me bad company in the car, saying that the threat to America today is not barbarians at the gate but our own internal stagnation; "The enemy is us." The enemy was me; it was him; it was all of us. Sean Hannity had been going on about this in the car while I was driving, how we had become a welfare state like the French; in the parking lot of the Windsor Food Market a bumper sticker on a truck said, "Annoy a Liberal / Support the Second Amendment," which did annoy me, but only because I didn't understand why it was anyone's goal to annoy me just because I'm a liberal and anyhow, I sort of like shooting. I'm a natural. I didn't know it just then but in about two weeks, I was going to hit twenty of my twenty-five clay pigeons at a shooting range in Kentucky, as I've said. I was at a loss to understand why the butcher did not like me, but he didn't, and I thought it must have something to do with all of that. The enemy was me. It was the strangest feeling.

I thanked him for his help and bought a little store-made beef jerky, a New York strip steak (which is known as a Kansas City strip in that part of the Midwest), and grabbed some all-natural homemade real chicken dog treats for Colby, and of course, one pack of Heinkel's polish sausage. They did not have venison jalapeno, sadly. At the checkout, to which the butcher and another woman who worked at the store followed me at a distance, I decided to ask if the cashier could break a large bill. I held up a hundred; I knew this would upset her. "I'm sorry," she said, eyes locked on me. "We just changed the register." So I paid for my meat in dollar bills and quarters.

Not wanting to disappoint my old lady campground friend, I then raced up to Arthur in time to bang on the door of the closed Amish butcher shop, which a woman in traditional dress opened. She sold me a frozen lamb steak. Mission accomplished, I headed for home. On the radio, the classic rock station I had tuned into had begun to annoy me by replaying the same classic rock songs that stations play everywhere, over and over, as if the world were determined to relive an endless loop of hits from the same seven or eight years we had lived in the 1970s, just at the dawn of industrial collapse. It seemed like no coincidence to me. It seemed like a longing to stop time before disintegration gained speed. This urge to remain in the past had moved from delusional to dangerous, to my mind. If this obsession with the familiar was intended to feel safe, it did not. I like Bob Seger and Foghat as much as the next tail-end boomer but this soundtrack was growing warped. I switched to NPR, which, as I sped through vast plowed-under fields, reported to me that the average age of the American farmer was now sixty. All around farm country, the young had left and the old held on, but also, apparently, the young have started to come back, because farming is a good business if you can get in, if you can buy the combines that cost six figures and patch together enough land. It is a way of life that people have started to think they might enjoy, again; maybe, out on the land, things can be simple. I don't know if that's true or just wishful, but I do know farm country is lovely.

On the road to the marina near Lithia Springs I had stopped at an abandoned farm—not a failed farm, it seemed to me, but a finished one; an old family farm with a collapsing silo and a fence strung with vines, and a name still on the mailbox, Birney F. Canfield. I thought maybe Birney

Windsor Food Market pig

had possessed something essential that had been left off my list of demands
for a happy life, or for a forgotten place attempting a comeback, as I had
been thinking of these things on my drive; anywhere I might live must have
a good coffee shop, high-quality dog care, some kind of arts presence that
would bring vibrant neighbors, and a truly open door to "others," which
in my case meant an open gay community. Also, an availability of craft

beers and maybe a wine shop would be helpful. An actually delicious vegetarian option on at least one local menu, also desirable. And good cheese.
Those were the things I would have said I needed; not a casino or hockey
arena or a hall of fame, not a metropolis. But I had the things I wanted
where I lived, and still, it was not right, and maybe Birney knew why. Certainly, he knew how it felt to have stayed in that quiet place not for minutes
but decades. His old farmhouse was another empty building in such a long
string of them I had seen, certainly abandoned, but this one looked different to me. It did not feel as sad. The stillness was the thing. Even with
people living in it, I thought the Canfield farm would be still. It had become hard for me to sit still long enough to even read a book; whatever else
this life offered, the sorrows and frustrations and trips to the vet and flat
tires and soured milk and crop failures, death, cancer, furnace explosions,
bee stings, bankruptcy, maybe a wedding now and then, maybe some fun
stuff too, whatever the stories were in this house, on this farm in such fertile
farm country, I imagined Birney F. Canfield, whoever he was, returning
always to this stillness. Out in the fringes of the smallest county of Illinois,
with no hip culture to hide inside and no distraction to be found: to be so
still seemed really hard, mind numbing even, but something in it felt
right.

Back at the campground, I pulled up to the office just to use the bathroom
but as I stepped out of the car the old woman dashed outside.

"My husband said he saw someone so I knew it must be you. Did you
have a good day?" she called out.

"Yes, I did!"

"Did you see some Amish?"

"It's hard to miss them."

I showed her the picture of the little fish I caught on Lake Shelbyville
and she tipped her head and looked at me admiringly. I don't know why.
Maybe just because I was alive and did things that suggested I was not tired
of living, or that I had better ideas than to lash my boat to other boats and
get drunk; whatever it was, she said, "Bless your heart," and when she did,
my heart warmed noticeably. Then she told me that she and her husband

were moving that night from their trailer to their rooms above the camp-ground office, and that there was supposed to be a frost.

"See you in the morning," she said.

That night, Colby got wild. I think it may have been from eating too much meat. I had ended up with an awful lot of meat that day and had to cook most of it on our fire to keep it from spoiling. There was far more food than I could eat, so Colby got a belly-full. He tossed his snout back and chewed and chewed and snarled and hacked and chewed some more until he was exhausted. He walked to the Scamp door and barked. He pre-ferred by now to be inside the trailer most of the time, his fear of it long past and his general preference being anything but sitting in the dirt.

All night, he had meat dreams, his legs kicking furiously, small yips forming in his throat; he awakened from his meat slumber at odd hours, apparently craving more meat, panting, not wanting to go outside, just wanting to eat. He barked at the refrigerator. I persuaded him to settle down and then cranked up the furnace, which I had finally learned to use, discovering it had just one little switch I had to slide to get it started, and then it warmed us up remarkably.

We were heading south toward Kentucky the next day. The cold that had come seemed to have settled in to stay. If I could make it south to Kentucky soon enough, I figured, I would stay on the right side of the sun, the warm side. I stopped by the office on my way out to say good-bye to the woman and to wish her good luck with her biopsy. This woman had said things I couldn't bear about the mass of Mexicans being dangerous, and she had worried about "foreigners" taking over American athletic teams and the local restaurants, and she was afraid of changes in the world that she could not understand. Yet still I liked her for daring against her judgment to show something of herself to me. I believed she had simply wanted to be happy and had found that to be as hard as anyone does. I tried to push back on her fears; where she lived, no one else would do that much and so those fears had hardened and they wouldn't change over a few days, but at least we had been able to talk and I was fond of her, and I think she was fond of me. When I stopped by the office, she wasn't there. I left without saying good-bye, and for the first time I can remember, I was sorry.

12

Scottsville

It was getting cold. I headed south to camp in a field owned by Sarah, the Kentucky professor I had met back in Utica. I was trying to hurry but kept getting distracted by things like the diner in Matoon, Illinois, which had "froings" on the menu—a combination of french fries and onion rings. I couldn't resist. Before long it was dark and I was still driving, the misty rain on my windshield fracturing taillights ahead of me into red stars. The night glowed with every stripe of neon as exits passed. A white cross as tall as a skyscraper appeared in a quadrangle of spotlights in Effington, flexing its biceps in front of me and then above me and then behind until it too was gone, and after that, dark again.

Colby and I arrived late at the Benton KOA, where unlit roads threaded through the cramped campsites; I nearly backed the trailer into a deep ditch in the dark but stopped just short of the abyss and did not dare unhitch. There was no cell service, but there was Wi-Fi. I made mint tea and because I had no cell phone service, I tried using Skype for the first time to talk to Jessica. Seeing her, I felt a rush of warmth and I touched her face on the screen and then it froze, stuck with her mouth rounded into a vowel, her eyes blinked shut. And that was that.

In the morning at the KOA dog run, I met a guy who said he had retired after thirty years in the army but was too wrecked in the back to work and couldn't make ends meet, so he had been living at the KOA in a little trailer for three hundred dollars a month. He told me about all the KOAs he had camped at in summers as a boy and how much fun they had been, like the KOA in Bowling Green, Kentucky, where for a dime you could go to the amusement park. Those were great summers, none better. This might have made living at the KOA seem like a childhood dream come true, but it wasn't. Then he and Bean, his Chinese crested powder puff terrier, left to go make coffee, which I normally would have tried to muscle in on but I want to do this with everyone I meet and for that, I needed more time. I needed forever. That's the thing: time was passing.

Next stop south: Crab Orchard National Park, where the park host in the office trailer was whiskery and had a drawl that sounded like a wad of tobacco was stuck in his face, but it was just bad teeth. He had sweet blue eyes. As I filled out my paperwork, he said the park had been closed until a week before because of the federal government shutdown, which is what had been causing right-wing radio voices to call Obama "hateful." The host had pulled the gate to Crab Orchard park shut but he had needed to stay on anyway, for security, and he had told all his friends he was living in a gated community with his own lake. Har har. He was playing solitaire. When I asked who was winning, he studied my face like I must be dumb. He said that out above Crab Orchard Lake the pelicans fly in ribbons like long Chinese kites, and there's an eight-point buck he had seen almost every day except the one day he went out bow hunting. I think he told me this because I was wearing a leafy camo hunting jacket. It's funny about the men I met everywhere; they all wanted to tell me things but then stopped listening when I talked. It's like they had been saving up all these words for someone, sitting in their lonely offices or sitting in their retirement or stuck in some other solitude. The men wanted to be heard. And outside of my stay in Sullivan, the women were nowhere to be found. Maybe they were tired of listening.

In the news was a story from just outside Boston: a fourteen-year-old boy had murdered one of his teachers. The story was horrible both because it was unfathomable and because such unfathomable violence was happening so often; missionaries from El Paso get murdered, cops kill black men for no reason, and dear god, not one year earlier, a shooter killed all those children at a school in Connecticut, miles up the road from the school where I worked. You would think we would all be numb by now and yet we still feel. Hearing about a child killing his teacher as I set up camp on the edge of the lake, I had a feeling that nothing observed closely can continue to make sense. I felt that way about violence. It went on and on; more evidence of our sickness only made it harder to understand.

Later I was walking Colby, and the camp host was standing outside his RV smoking a cigarette. I thought I might ask him for some firewood so I stopped by and we stood and watched the night come on. He said I missed his turkey chili by half an hour. Damn, he said; it was good too. He told me that he and his wife (What wife? Where was the wife?) go to free cooking classes at the community college and then he named about seven things you can do with pork loin. "By the way," he said, "if you like good food, Murphysville, Illinois, has the best Italian food, great little restaurant there, real Italian family from Italy runs it."

"How'd an Italian family from Italy ever decide to start a restaurant in Murphysville, Illinois?" I asked, and I noted to myself that in the middle of America if you are Amish or Italian, you are not considered a foreigner.

He ignored me. He said the "Fruity Delmari" was the best dish. He told me the pelicans were out flying like ribbons again and he had taken some great pictures. He and his wife (I know, right? Was there really a wife?) had just been to N'orleans for a wedding in an old abandoned-industrial-park-turned-wedding-palace. He had pictures. Then he told me about his favorite funny signs, like one he saw on a front yard that said, "House For Sale. Will Trade For Cash." Then he turned to go inside and watch the Red Sox game. I didn't get a chance to ask for firewood. Colby and I curled up in our trailer, with the little furnace working hard to keep us warm.

In the morning, sunlight came in through the opaque roof vent first and when I pushed the curtains open, our world lit up and glowed orange like the color of the leaves around us; the seasons had changed entirely now—a change you can do little but accept, once it comes, and that is its own kind of sweetness. Surrender to the fall. We sat in the light and the quiet until we were ready to keep going.

To Kentucky. By way of Carbondale, Illinois, a university town just beyond Crab Orchard Park, and far from any cultural center or big city,

which makes Carbondale itself a beacon of light in its part of this heart-
land, and a countercultural beacon too; the National Guard was sent into
Carbondale in 1970 to quash a student riot just days after the Guard killed
four students at Kent State. I had never heard about the Carbondale riots;
I didn't know the Guard had been sent to any campus aside from that one
in Ohio. There's a song about Kent State; history must have its songs. In
Carbondale, six months after the Guard quashed a protest, city police shot
up a house they said was occupied by student Black Panther leaders. The
students fired back. Nearly eight hundred rounds were fired that night.
None of the six black men the police were trying to kill was ever convicted
of anything, but no one died, either, so history forgot it. No song. Hardly
anyone I know has ever even heard of Carbondale. We know this: Detroit
is the failed city, and Detroit and Newark had the race riots, and Kent
State is where students were shot. That's what I had learned, at least, as if
each struggle were anomalous in the otherwise forward march of time. But
I was visiting these places to try to understand and what I was learning was
this: there are no events; there are patterns.

I ate at a locally sourced, Sufi-affiliated vegetarian café in remotely
groovy Carbondale, where there had been not only riots but a "radical
feminist commune movement" back in the day; I read up on this appealing
history and studied my maps, trying to decide whether to head for Kentucky
by way of Paducah or by way of Cairo. Paducah is home to the National
Quilt Museum; in 1997 a kid shot up his Paducah high school. On the
other hand, Charles Dickens called Cairo "a dismal swamp" when he did
his literary rock-star tour of the country in 1842. Cairo is the southernmost
city in Illinois; it sits at the confluence of the Ohio and Mississippi rivers.
During the Civil War, it was home to a Union port and a prison that held
thousands of Confederate soldiers and was home to a huge population of
freed slaves; thousands of freed black men and women had been sent there
as refugees. In the 1970s, the city of Cairo filled the public swimming pool
with cement rather than let black people swim in it. One night in that era,
police stopped a black driver, a Vietnam veteran, and shot him dead. After
that, Cairo did not have a race riot so much as a protracted race war, with
gunfire and retaliations and marches that carried on for years until at last,
everyone lost. I had never heard of any of this.

But I was late for Kentucky and in the end I had no time to stop in either Paducah or Cairo if I was going to make it to Sarah's farm for dinner. I crossed the river, the Mason-Dixon line, and then did not even stop at Patti's 1880s Settlement in Grand Rivers, Kentucky, where I could have eaten flowerpot bread and boo boo pie. There was no time for that, and no time to stop for gas, even, which was a mistake, because really, there is always time to stop for gas. There has to be.

Kentucky Sarah lived deep in the countryside between Bowling Green and Scottsville. It would be hard to find her property once it was dark outside, and I was running late, so I hurried but the dark was gaining on me. Once I left the interstate, pretty much everything in Kentucky disappeared except for road and trees. The road was the sort that rolled with so many ups and downs that its contour added miles to the fly-over map of the region, making the drive longer than I had guessed, and despite weeks towing a trailer, I still hadn't quite gotten used to how much faster it made my car burn fuel. Simple fact: towing burns fuel; this is somehow especially true when driving in remote or potentially dangerous places where it would be really bad to run out of gas. That is paradoxically just exactly the kind of place where gas burns its utmost fastest.

Somewhere well beyond the Paducah-like buzzing of civilization, past the interstate tarmacs laden with pump-your-own-gas travelers' oases, the empty gas tank warning light on my dashboard lit up like a little orange barb. The road I was on was very narrow with no shoulder for breakdowns, and my cell phone, I had noticed, had no signal. The sun was setting and the woods around me were dimming, and that last little bit of gas was disappearing faster than all the bits before it had, like water that rings a drain and then suddenly—*sssslurp!*—is gone.

I became worried. I realized I had put myself and my dog in danger. Did Colby know we were in danger? My heart started beating faster because I didn't want him to know we might die in the next hour or so. If the car just stopped, right there, in the middle of that shoulderless road in Kentucky, certainly a tractor-trailer would appear on the crest of a hill behind us and bear down, horn growling, Mac cab smashing into the Scamp and running us completely over because I couldn't move and it couldn't stop. Or no, no. This: walking down the road to find a house, ringing a doorbell, facing a shotgun. BANG! Or this: walking down the road in the dark, being grabbed by big brutish hands, being thrown into a pickup truck, Colby crying from the road, strange-smelling hairy men smuggling me off into the hills to become a human sacrifice. I was in Kentucky. I confess I thought of this in Kentucky *because it was Kentucky*. I didn't trust Kentucky. It was not fair of me. In most ways the road was the same as any road I had ever seen, yet as familiar as it was I knew it was strange and I could not quite read it because I was in Kentucky and so it was *not* the same. It was unknown to me, and so it scared me. And fear is underneath mostly all of our problems, even the problems of cars and gas.

I clung to the steering wheel, leaning forward, pulsing the gas pedal to conserve fuel, and then Colby noticed something wasn't right and so of course he started panting. He stood and began to pace in the back seat, his pink tongue lolling from his mouth. His face pushed up now and then beside my own face, and he panted in my ear. He sensed my anxiety, and probably had to pee, because we hadn't stopped to do that in too long, either. I wanted to give him a Benadryl to calm us both down but the road had no shoulder and so there was no way to stop even for Benadryl, much less to pee. We kept going.

I searched in the fading daylight for "the road just past the community church that you don't turn on; just pass that road and wait till you see a house with a barn down a driveway. Pass that too but you'll be close, then." GPS did not see these things; GPS kept blinking around as if it too were lost. Three or four times I thought I may have passed this church and the house with the barn but I wasn't sure. I had to make a decision about going on or turning back but it was hard to think with so much fear banging on my head. The way through is always forward, I decided; always forward. Drive. I did, and I also did the only thing that ever really helps when I freak out in my car. I sang. This time, the song was the Johnny Appleseed song: "Oh, the Lord is good to me, and so I thank the Lord . . . for giving me, the things I need, the sun and the rain and the apple seed. The Lord is good to me!"

Three rounds of that and then a key change, then three more rounds, and so on. I can sing this thing up and down the scales for a long, long time. I have no idea where I learned it and while it does memorialize an

actual historic figure, I don't even care. It's my fear song. It once got me
through seven hours of gridlock in an ice storm and it somehow got me
and Colby safely to Sarah's house, engine running on fumes, the last fading
gray sky still showing through the treetops and lighting the way. Colby
jumped out of the car and let out a long stream of urine, then straightened
up, looked at me, and wagged his tail. I lifted him back into the car and
climbed the steps to Sarah's door. I knocked. It opened. I stood there,
rattled, nervous, road-weary, hoarse from a dozen frantic rounds of the
apple seed song, bug-eyed, untucked, desperate, scared, my whole self lost
in Kentucky. I blurted out, "You said I could camp down the road so tell
me where to set my trailer up and if I don't make it back in half an hour,
you might need to come find me because I'm out of gas and it's a wonder I
got here at all . . . aren't I a wreck." I stared at her without blinking. She
stood in the door with a quizzical smile. "Hi, Lori," she said. She was really
very nice.

Sarah had warned me in an email that Scottsville was a prosperous spot so
I would be disappointed in my hunt for distress. I confidently replied that
I find trouble wherever I go. Scottsville may be prosperous but surely, for
example, the local grasp of basic science was suffering greatly. While she
cooked dinner, I showed her a list of twenty-five meth labs recently busted
in a small region around Scottsville, including several within a mile of her
house, to which her response was a small, quiet smile. I had won my point
but I kind of felt like an asshole.

Dinner was pasta and garlic bread and enough wine for me to notice
that Sarah was really smart and cute and lived in a big house all by herself.
My single-woman-what's-her-story radar perked up. She told me Allen
County was doing well because it is the home of the Family Dollar chain,
and the local family who owns that chain had been generous to the town
of Scottsville. I had mentioned in our email exchange that I was interested
in schools—the troubles of rural Illinois were fresh in my mind, where
towns don't want to consolidate their school districts because without
schools proving their existence, the towns really might just die. So they've
kept the schools open as the population falls and the result is a world of

badly underfunded schools. That's what I had learned in Illinois, but Allen County had its own story. It had made a wise choice to consolidate its schools not long ago, and now they had new buildings and great teachers and were doing very well. A colleague of Sarah's had made me an appointment with the superintendent of the Allen County School District, who was going to bring me the next day to a Rotary Club luncheon.

"The Rotary Club!" I gushed. "That is so perfect."

Sarah, who grew up in an academic family in Georgia, smiled her wise smile and gave me a little bit of a warning. Not this kind of warning: "Watch out: if you turn down the wrong road, isolated pockets of rural hicks will kill you." Not that. She warned me about the opposite—people would fear I actually thought Kentucky was full of rural hicks who might kill me, and therefore they would not trust me. Members of the Rotary Club would be suspicious of my motives for studying them. The man who had arranged my lunch invitation was a climatology professor who did not see a link between human behavior and global warming; he had vetted me thoroughly on the internet, where he would have found scads of pictures of Colby but no pointed anti-America, anti-God commentary under my byline, no guest appearances on liberal cable news. He had decided I was safe enough to invite to lunch in Scottsville, though he still believed that no one would have driven all the way from New York without ulterior motives and so he still did not really trust me.

"People in Kentucky are sensitive about being portrayed as hillbillies," Sarah said.

"What? Wait. What?" I said. "I would never . . ."

"They think northerners aren't interested in who they really are," she said. "They're only interested in Appalachia and expect the woods are full of rednecks."

"No! But also," I said, "Appalachia really is kind of interesting." I was just being honest. I said this to Sarah and took a slug of wine and decided I liked Appalachia very much because it was super weird. This made me the jerk they thought I was, but it's true. I liked Appalachia and hillbillies and I liked Sarah too. She had an Obama bumper sticker on her pickup truck, which struck me as brave under the circumstances, braver even than my cousin in Vermont with his Republican bumper stickers; the Vermont liberals he was provoking were not, in my view, as dangerous as the conservatives in rural Kentucky that Sarah might provoke. When I told Sarah I thought she was brave, she shrugged as if there were no reason to hide one's liberal inclinations in this land of people who were not hillbillies even if they were. I thought this even as I swore I did not think it. Also, I now know what a truly ugly word "hillbilly" is if you live in rural Kentucky, but I would be lying if I didn't say it is the word I was thinking before I learned; it is not a word I use lightly anymore.

At some point over dinner, I began speaking to Sarah with a new earnestness, which came from a mixture of wine, loneliness, and the scent of opportunity to finally cheat on Jessica. After all, there we were, drinking wine and trusting each other like liberal doppelgangers in the land of right-wing hill people, and she would let me camp on her land and bathe in her bathroom and she had fed me. Sarah was brave, and really smart. She was the first person on my trip who, by the simple facts of her life, reminded me of what had sent me running to begin with. Desire. Another woman. Awakened feelings. I sipped my wine and decided Sarah and I should fall in love. It wasn't like an awakened feeling but more like a thought; it was nothing like what I had experienced in the parking lot months before then but was instead a wine-inspired decision to just do something, finally do something, about all the feelings I had been hauling around. But if it were to happen I would have to get busy, because it was November already and I couldn't stay long. The drama would really have to erupt right then. But how? I was not someone who had ever really had what might be called trysts; I had never even watched porn, which I had heard was full of narrative suggestions for cases like this. Unpracticed in seduction, I decided to go with love. I would love-bomb this woman until she surrendered and we ended up doing who knows what; I did not know. But I could figure it out.

The word "love" spilled from me according to plan. I told Sarah that I was in love with America, troubled as it was. I didn't want to give up on America. I told her I thought it was a beautiful country full of loving people with amazing stories that I loved, people whose lives my father found worth fighting for in World War II, and I loved my father. (Extra points for family values and patriotism, both sincere, proving that I was safe to sleep with.) I told her that most of my friends found it distasteful when I said I loved this country; it was like loving an abusive spouse, they said, a bad relationship that I needed to get over. But I loved the country nonetheless and while people in Scottsville might be suspicious of me, the truth is I had come all this way with my dog because I loved them. All of them. I honestly wanted to know the people there. I wanted to . . . share love. I didn't come to judge but to know and to love, and telling Sarah this, I began foaming at the mouth a bit, I think, going on about love as the cure for the sickness in America; what we need (obviously) is love, lots of love. We've all taken up sides against each other and the real issue—the real issue, Sarah, I can tell you—under all of this pain, the real issue is that we can't let ourselves love ourselves, or love each other because . . . because why . . . because the Civil War. It never ended. We still live it every day; we relive this wound of hate; we are at war with each other and that makes healing impossible. Go to Cairo and ask them. Who loves Cairo? I would love Cairo, given half a chance. I would go to Cairo and love Cairo if that were my mission on this Earth but it's not; I have to love someone else, I mean thing, love some-*thing* else, excuse me. I need to love something else and we are still fighting that damn Civil War.

Whatever I said, what I really meant was, "On a scale of one to ten, how attractive do you find me?" I had had a fork full of pasta hovering near my mouth for ten minutes and a wineglass waiting in my other hand. As some point I realized there was no chance I would ever sleep with Sarah and that was okay because I didn't want to, and with that I began to understand how, while I was open to finding plenty of it, sex was not really the point of the crisis at the middle of my life. I could keep trying to make it the point because, what the hell. It's a great point. But it wasn't the point, really, and it refused to cooperate. I put the fork down and drank the wine. A silence followed, during which I looked across the table at Sarah, who smiled wisely.

"By the way, I really love the Rotary. Love those guys. I hope they won't think I'm a jerk."

"I'm sure you'll do fine with the Rotary," she said.

After dinner, I went back to my trailer alone.

It grew very dark and very cold. Very cold. This is not what was supposed to happen when I fled to the south. On Wikipedia, the climate for Kentucky is described as "humid subtropical," yet all day wherever I had stopped I had caught bits of conversation, ". . . not ready for winter . . ." and ". . . dread it," as if this place below the Mason-Dixon line, this place whose southern bona fides included former plantations, could also have winter. It was time to send a warning home about my predicament but that only underscored the predicament itself: Cell service was spotty and I had very little phone juice left, and the trailer was not hooked up to electricity on Sarah's farm, and my car was out of gas, so I couldn't run the engine to charge my phone or even sit in the heat for a moment. I couldn't walk back to Sarah's because she for sure knew I was a creep by now—and how much creepier would it be to come back in the darkness and say, "Lead me to a bed"? And anyhow, she had offered me a spot to camp on her farm. Period. That was the deal. I mustn't burden her, I knew. I walked far enough out into a dark field to get a few bars of service and managed to call Jessica. I told her about my situation, the impending death by freezing. Back in our warm little apartment in New York, she said, "Okay! Stay safe, sweetie! Have fun!"

Fun? Did she say fun? Why was this always her advice? She knew nothing about the awful thing that was about to happen to me in Kentucky. I hung up to preserve my last drop of juice.

The temperature dipped down to 20 degrees that night. The furnace was useless. I had no lights. Inside the trailer my breath puffed out in bursts of steam as I set my bed up by flashlight. I had flannel sheets and a light polyester-filled comforter and a thirty-five-year-old snuggle sack that, when I was a girl, my mother would snap herself into, then watch *The Love Boat* on TV while drinking apple spice tea. The snuggle sack had found new life as a backseat blanket for the dog. I tossed it onto my bed in the trailer. I wore two layers of clothes. The good news was that a bit of Moultrie County steak I had left in the fridge remained frozen even without the power of refrigeration, so I had not yet wasted all of that. The bad news was that for the second time in one five-hour period I was pretty sure I would die.

I lifted Colby up onto the mattress and made it clear to him with the guttural human equivalents of alpha male barking that not only was he to stay up there that night, he was additionally required to sleep lengthwise pressed up completely against me for warmth. Then I lay down in our nest and Colby wrested himself from my grasp and curled into a tight ball near my feet. I wiggled down to his end of the mattress to wrap myself around him and pulled the quilt over my head, leaving a small breathing hole, releasing a slow pulse of steam into the darkness.

What kind of love gets a body through winter? Not the fast-flame-that-burns-out kind. In winter a body needs a good furnace, a warmth that endures. But what kind of love is that? Colby was better equipped for the cold than I was and his breathing soon grew heavy and deep. I looked toward his face in the dark and wondered what love is like when you're a dog and if he had ever been in love with anyone, aside from me. Perhaps the little cat he had once known. Butterscotch. I gave him a nudge. He ignored me. I nudged again and he breathed in deep and sighed. When Colby was a puppy, he had been in love with my friend's kitten, Butterscotch. He would start crying when we pulled into their driveway because he loved Butterscotch. The cat would torment him, reaching her white paw up to swat his smiling furry face, or waiting atop a chair for him to walk by, then leaping on his back. No matter what she did to him, Colby adored Butterscotch. When my short relationship with Butterscotch's mom ended, Colby never saw Butterscotch again. Yet for the longest time he looked for her, everywhere. Anytime he saw an orange cat he would cry in a way that only one who has loved and lost could understand. He would sit and refuse to move, waiting for the familiar-looking orange cat to acknowledge him, which it would never do, because of course none of these cats was ever Butterscotch.

I poked a finger up through the breathing hole in my blanket and stroked Colby's nose. The hardest part for me was to see him, at last, stop expecting all these cats to love him back. He had grown older and wiser. Or maybe he had just forgotten, over time. I really hated for anyone I loved to be disappointed, including my dog. I am so sorry that the things we believe very often turn out to be wrong, or that good things, wonderful things, don't last. For many reasons. Things come and go. But even if I knew this, my instinct was always to hold on, to insist on happy endings. I wished I could have made it work for Colby and Butterscotch so that they could have stayed together. I said this through my breathing hole to Colby; Colby, as usual, didn't understand a word I said.

In the morning, once again, we were alive.

The water was frozen in Colby's bowl and, in the farm fields around us, frost covered big rolls of hay and wide blades of grass bent over with its weight. It was the first I had seen of Allen County, Kentucky, in the full daylight and it was beautiful. The colors were pure fall: matted yellow-green turf, a red-and-gold canopy above the tree trunks, a pale-pink ribbon of early sun across the sky.

I stopped by Sarah's for a shower. She had a *New York Times* on her kitchen table. This glimpse of news provoked a long frothy caffeine-fueled current events rant from me and it was not even eight in the morning and Sarah had barely said hello; when I finished, Sarah was looking at me with that smile again. She emptied a container of gas for her lawnmower into my car and I drove off past the shells of a few shuttered old general stores and abandoned gas pumps and into the heart of Scottsville, where the new, modern, quickie-marts with fuel pumps awaited. As I pumped gas, a Shriner in a red jacket and a fez—an actual big, red, gold-tasseled fez—sold me some candy. That is a thing we do not have, back home.

Scottsville, Kentucky: population 4,226, nestled up snug to the Tennessee border, home to many proud and hardworking Amish, birthplace of the evangelist Mordecai Ham, whose preaching at a 1934 revival converted the great and powerful Billy Graham. The road out of town led to Dollar General's headquarters, a cluster of low buildings and parking lots that keeps Scottsville thriving. I drove past that, then turned around and went back through the town square, got mixed up and a little lost and finally managed to arrive late for my appointment with the school superintendent.

The superintendent was a gentle, round-faced man with a quiet voice who shook hands softly and smiled and blinked. His hair was fine and swept across his forehead, and he held his head always to the side as if listening, waiting for his turn to talk. When I told him I was sorry I was late, he said it didn't matter, we still had time to get to lunch, and with singular focus we set out in his Lincoln Navigator to feast at the Rotary luncheon in the basement of the Scottsville library.

The monthly Rotary luncheon, he told me, was the best food around, a buffet prepared by local Amish ladies. When we arrived at the library, the superintendent made his way to the buffet with casually masked panic, working his way across the room saying hello here and there, shaking a few hands, keeping one eye on the prize, pressing forward until at last we were at the serving table. We loaded our foam plates with Salisbury steak and potatoes, chunks of chicken in casserole, green beans and corn (both, I was assured, homegrown and home-canned), salad drowning in a mayonnaise thick dressing, sweet tea, and a fluffy white dessert thing with home-canned cherries on top. As we shuffled along the feed, I met Sarah's friend the climate professor who had set up my visit. He was gray-haired and plaid-shirted, bespectacled and narrow-eyed. He looked me over. We talked about the weather. This is never a light undertaking with a climatologist, and it was especially fraught that day because everyone was cold and not happy about it.

"It's my fault," I said. "I brought it."

Back in 1973, I had learned by example from my great-uncle Harold in Milwaukee to take credit or blame for the weather when traveling and I had fallen back on this device often in life. It was familiar and comforting banter. A common language. Taking responsibility for the cold spell made the men I was talking with in Kentucky laugh but still I could not shake the feeling that they all thought I was a spy who should not have been allowed to eat there, and worse than that, I knew this was more or less true.

The superintendent and I took our plates to a long table where as I ate, I was asked over and over to explain—by my neighbors at the table, by the luncheon host when I stood and was greeted by the room—who I was and what my project was about.

I know well by now the real answer to that question, "What have you come here to learn?" I know now that I needed to learn about ruins, why they happen, how to survive them. But when they asked me, "Why are you here?" I could not reasonably have stood up in front of a room and said: "It started with a midlife crisis. I felt a powerful and unwanted attraction to an old friend one night, and after that, I couldn't lie to myself anymore. My partner—she's great, you'd love her—we deserve more than we're giving each other. It kills me to face it and, well fuck me, what if I'm just flat out wrong? I'm driving around, trying to think about something else, but everything I see looks like the same problem." Shrug. Feel the silence. Sit down.

When I stood up, I said: "I'm a professor on sabbatical interested in several things, including how schools in small towns like yours are faring; I've driven thousands of miles and met all kinds of people, but it's really been one big excuse to go camping with my dog."

The dog remark drew earnest applause. I sat down. A man two seats over from me leaned in and said, "Tell me. Are you here to learn what our schools are doing right? Or doing wrong?"

I chewed my Salisbury steak as I looked at him, blinked twice, and said, "Yes."

He laughed. The table laughed.

The guest speaker was a climatologist for the commonwealth of Kentucky. He had come to discuss the Kentucky Mesonet, a severe weather tracking and data-collection system that was using sixty-five local monitoring stations around the state to help stay ahead of dangerous storms. The guest speaker wanted to see this expanded to 120 stations but the state needed money to do that and yadda yadda yadda la la la; finally he said, "I'll take your questions."

Hands shot up.

"All this talk about climate change," a man began. There had been, it should be noted, no talk in the past hour about climate change. "Al Gore goes on and on about how we're on track to have another ice age, you hear him talking about that. Do you agree?"

The speaker said, "Well, if it happens I won't be here for it," and the room laughed. Then he gave his real answer, one that hewed to a cool, rational talking point about the "conservative" way to behave when faced with a possible problem. The "conservative" course is to prepare for it. He said there is wisdom in acting to mitigate any clear, undisputed climate change that would harm people or property, regardless of cause.

Questioner #2: "Don't you think there could be a correlation between these climate change figures and the Earth shifting on its axis? Or, sun spots? Electromagnetic fields?" The answer, once again: "conservative" response requires us to mitigate changes that would be harmful, regardless of cause. Lunch ended. The superintendent worked the room for a few more minutes and we left.

A generation ago, the schools in Allen County, Kentucky, merged. There had been a Scottsville High School and a County High School just a mile apart, but now the whole county has one high school, shiny and new and doing well. I got a driving tour of their new facilities and then asked the superintendent and his head of curriculum questions for an hour. They assured me there had been no controversies at the school, no fights over what could and could not be taught, and I was satisfied with those answers and let the real tension remain unspoken.

The whole weird distrust over anyone scrutinizing the schools in Kentucky is a simple matter, really. The problem is science, especially evolution but also more recently the science of climate change. There is a divide over the core tenets of science that leaves humans, truly, engaged in a simmering battle over the very nature of reality. Addressing this head-on seems impolite in a place like Scottsville because the conversation is pointless; it can lead only to insults and arguments. In fact, the state's science curriculum is strong. It explicitly instructs that the Earth formed 4.6 billion years ago, that changes in the climate can be observed, and that species evolve; public schools are forbidden to present religious views with equal weight. But conservative leaders still openly reject these ideas, and anyhow, whatever the schools may teach, no one can undo what gets taught at home. Fewer than 30 percent of Kentucky students, including those in Allen County, meet the state's science proficiency standards. It doesn't seem to matter what the teachers say; truth gets swept up and lost in an unyielding darkness. I understand darkness. In that very time I wandered through Kentucky I was skirting the edge of a personal void, a dark spot at my core that looked increasingly like the darkness around me. I saw despair; I saw loss and grief and discomfort, a reckoning upon us, the grinding hell of transformation. And I could work with that. But ignorance is something else. Ignorance has a quality of darkness that sets in and hardens. It is epoxy darkness. It cannot allow itself to change because when a wrong idea changes, it ceases to exist. And nothing wants to cease existing.

I visited Mammoth Cave, near Louisville. It's a really big cave—the longest cave ever found, four hundred miles of it explored so far and many more miles to go. A dark hole in the ground, one of so many in the world, giving spectacular form to all the darkness one can ever know; it consumes us, and we are bound to panic. The rangers who guide us into this dark nearly beg us to turn back if we fear getting hurt, because deep in that cave, it will take a long time for help to find us. My Mammoth Cave tour guide was Ranger Darlene, all Kentucky twang and sass in a green park service uniform. She led a pack of us through the cave for two hours, streaming forth a charming cocktail of history and common sense. Toward the end of the tour, we all gathered in a large dark chamber where Darlene invited our questions, and I thought of my friends in Scottsville as I watched the first hand pop up. The question was, "How old is this cave?"

I would like to say that a hush came over the group and that as the last echo of the question stilled, a torch lit Darlene's face and she peered out at us and said sternly, "Now listen, people, and listen well," and began telling us the scientific truth about the millions of years it took to form that cave, telling us this in the clearest and firmest possible terms so that we would leave knowing the facts—or not leave at all. But really, the group was restless. Fidgety. Darlene stood up tall, repeated the question. "How old is Mammoth Cave," she said, not as a question really but as some kind of admonishment, a thought we should not let distract us from the joy of the thing. "I will tell you," she said. "There are geologists who say this place began forming ten million years ago. But you know what? I glaze over when I hear that. I don't know what to make of all those zeroes. So this is what I like to say: this place is older than your great-granny, and it's still forming."

She dodged it; she knew. There are some for whom the only acceptable answer is six thousand years, the time that has passed according to the Bible, but the time and place to take up that fight is not in a dark hole underground, when the kids are getting cranky. We queued up and made our way slowly back out to the light.

13

The Garden of Eden

What's with this need to reject science? I think it's an ironic fear of evolution on the cellular level. Ceaseless change generates ceaseless insecurity. Clear, firm, biblical answers don't evolve; big relief.

The epicenter of mass anti-change hysteria is the Creation Museum ("Prepare to Believe") in Petersburg, Kentucky. I made a point of visiting the museum while I traveled through the state, curious to learn exactly how the theory of evolution can be denied. Petersburg is an unremarkable spot in the quiet hilly tip of Boone County, where northernmost Kentucky pricks its spiky border up into Ohio like a dental probe—as if it would like to find a soft spot to infiltrate and keep going, move its Kentuckiness ever forward. Yet there in Petersburg, at the river, Kentucky stops.

The Creation Museum opened in 2007. It is run by an international group called Answers in Genesis. It is a sleek, modern, glass-and-stone building surrounded by parking lots; its companion museum, the Ark Encounter (also known as Ark park), is in nearby Williamstown. I approached the Creation Museum with an attitude of humility because I was pretty sure that the museum's staff and the other visitors would, like the Scottsville Rotarians, judge instantly that I had come to mock them, and also, once again, I was pretty sure I had. I felt bad about it. I wanted so much to keep an open mind; I could roll my eyes all the rest of my life but just then, in Kentucky, I wanted to feel Kentucky. I wanted to know and to care. Yet clinging to lies rather than accepting a clear truth—that life is full of change, that evolution is with us always—that's a position I just can't respect. It's dangerous. I cracked the car windows for Colby and walked toward the stone building with its peaked wings and glass doors, and as I did I felt somehow conspicuous, and then I realized that I was also scared.

It's true that I feared many things, but not the things people seemed to think I should fear; I feared a deep loneliness for example, but I did not fear spending months alone. I feared how dangerous our world had become but I did not fear for my own safety in it. I feared that, desperately, I might look for answers in risky places, but I was not afraid I might accidentally join a Christian cult at the Creation Museum that day. At that moment, what I feared most was being yelled at. Not sure what for. Maybe for leaving Colby in my car unattended? He liked the car. He practically lived in the car. For letting him pee out front, in the Garden of Eden? But there were dogs in the Garden too, weren't there? And other animals. Surely, they all had to pee somewhere.

Or was it that I was afraid for not believing? I was afraid it would be obvious, and that this would somehow hurt me. Most likely the hurt would come in the form of a judgmental comment or a shaming human glance. I cared for some reason about how even the most narrow-minded people saw me, but mainly because I wanted them to try harder to accept me for who I was. Not who they thought I was. As for God, the God of this place seemed to select people to punish on a whim. A staffer had recently been struck by lightning while he was clearing kids from the zip line. Struck dead. No one said it for the record but we all knew what that meant: God was angry. Right? Not sure why. Doesn't matter. In fact, it's best to simply know these things can happen and give thanks daily for being spared.

I attempted nonchalance as I walked past the guard directing traffic in the Creation Museum parking lot; he was dressed like a state trooper with leather boots and a wide-brimmed hat and a buzz cut, but he was not a trooper. He was a museum guard. Bible people, to state the obvious, appreciate power and authority; they aren't afraid to dress the part. The guard nodded and smiled at me as I approached the museum entrance with trepidation. I had an Eph 3:20 wrist band on but I still was not saved and they knew it. They all knew. I lowered my eyes. Here is a quote from God that I saw: "If my people . . . will humble themselves and pray and seek my face and turn from their wicked ways, then I will hear from heaven, and I will forgive their sin and will heal their land. 2 Chronicles 7:14."

I myself wished to be forgiven; I wished for God to somehow heal our land. Our land needs healing, and I was willing to pray for that. I would listen for the truth in whatever form it came, but I could imagine no honest way to deny evolution. Everything on Earth will change.

Thus sensibly girded, I went inside. The openness of my mind felt exhilarating. The Christians at the Creation Museum were, despite my fears, super nice to me, which made me feel awful. I focused on examining the story of creation that this place was built to promulgate, which is basically this:

- Everything made by God in six days (and a seventh for rest);
- all done about six thousand years ago;
- life disrupted by a catastrophic flood but not annihilated;
- Jesus coming back very soon;
- dinosaurs not in conflict with any of that.

In the words of Answers in Genesis founder Ken Ham (an Australian Baptist evangelist with no apparent relation to the Mordecai Ham of Scottsville, Kentucky), the organization "exposes the bankruptcy of evolutionary thought, including the concept of millions of years," meaning that it's ridiculous to think all this stuff around us could have existed for so long. It's just a dumb idea. A frequent refrain at the Creation Museum is this: "Millions of years? Ha ha ha ha!" Who knows what to make of all those zeroes.

Alternatively, the Bible is the "history book of the universe," whose truth is irrefutably supported by "observational science."

"Observational science" is a crucial concept. In sum, you have to be able to see something for it to be true. Unless of course you're talking about God. But we have the Bible, a historically accurate account of God, so that's covered too; it is full of witnesses to God's work. "Observational science" redefines the scientific method to turn nonscientific argument into science, and actual science into nonsense, and the commensurate brain fuck contorts into an infinity loop of overturned reality that I can't seem to grasp well enough to explain, which seems to make me too ignorant to even reject science properly; I don't understand how this nonscience works. This is what I mean by brain fuck. I try to follow and get bamboozled. False syllogisms, non sequiturs, tautologies, all the classic forms of logical fallacy have been studied so that they can actually be put forth as truths in the effort to undermine scientific truth. Why do this? What is the value? I see it at work in politics too, and so can only suggest that perhaps it is useful for some Christian fundamentalists to create an army of willfully ignorant people to maintain their own power. I really don't understand, and can't truly believe the chief manipulators truly believe the story they're selling.

The Creation Museum's mission includes "taking back the dinosaur" from secular culture. The real dinosaur problem for fundamentalist Christians is that nowhere in recorded history do dinosaurs coexist with humans. If God made dinosaurs in the same week he made everything else, someone would have mentioned it. And yet there is no record of their coexistence.

The Creation Museum's response is, "Nonsense!" It is the kind of fact-free answer that is difficult to argue with. We know the Bible is true, and we can observe evidence that dinosaurs existed, therefore the dinosaurs were around when the Earth was formed six thousand years ago. We have the cool dioramas to prove it. At the museum, exhibits mimic New York's Museum of Natural History, with three-dimensional life-sized dioramas of things like Adam and Eve and the dinosaurs, and fantastic depictions of critical events like the Earth being made by God. Creation scholars assure us in slick multimedia presentations that the Earth is, in fact, about six thousand years old.

The best part of the museum is all the gigantic swooping, running, pouncing, chomping dinosaur models. Not actual dinosaur fossils, not skeletal remains, which anthropologists must be loath to lend them, but big plastic models of creatures that are what dinosaurs probably looked like. It's cool to walk through them.

The museum tries to explain how, if dinosaurs and humans showed up together, one disappeared when the other didn't. Yes, there were dinosaurs on the ark. But bad things happen. And as any scientist, any real true scientist, will tell you, things go extinct all the time. It happens. It's not evolution; there are other causes. Look at the passenger pigeon. Here one day. Then, gone—extinct. So, yeah. No more dinosaurs either. Correlation obvious, problem solved.

I want to talk a little more about the pigeons. Science does not throw up its hands and say, "Well, it just happens." There has to be a cause for the effect. Regarding the pigeon extinction, we definitely witnessed the cause: hunters were wiping them out in mass numbers in the late nineteenth century. News accounts tell of a hunting industry in the Midwest that sent dead pigeons by the barrelful every day to cities all around America; there were roost burnings and poisonings and mass netting of the birds. The last passenger pigeon died in 1914 in the Cincinnati Zoo, right across the river from the Creation Museum. Dinosaurs disappeared much sooner than the pigeons and we either weren't there to observe the cause or, depending on your belief, we just somehow forgot to make a note of it. Scientists have worked hard to determine what happened. Many think a meteor struck the Earth sixty-six million years ago and annihilated them. To agree with the meteor idea but say it happened sometime less than six thousand years ago would open biblical theories up to scrutiny—why is there no human depiction of the event? Why did nothing else die then?—so Christians at the museum simply say, "Things disappear all the time," like that's a full answer.

Here is another example of fundamentalist thought: Noah couldn't have kept polar bears cool on the ark, so he couldn't have taken them along. Agreed! But it's okay, we're told, because Noah only took a pair of the bear "kind." Which means that after the flood, varieties of bear must have developed from the pair of bears of "the bear kind" that Noah did take. That's how that worked. Except . . . that would be evolution.

The fundamentalist rejoinder: "No, it's not."

These examples can go on forever without getting anywhere.

I'm not surprised that I disagree with nearly everything in the Creation Museum. What does surprise me is how guilty I feel for mocking that place simply by writing, as plainly as I can, what is in it. It all sounds so dumb. And I don't like mocking people because it is the exact strategy the creationists use to dispute science, and I don't want to be guilty of arguing like they do, of saying: it just sounds dumb. Science is absurd.

Wait: that's true. I agree. Science is ridiculous. Little shell creatures pressed themselves into shale in the Allegheny Mountains hundreds of millions of years ago and turned into gas we now use to fuel buses. Wait, what? That's ridiculous. And it's also really stupid that animals eat each other to live and that our waste functions are located right alongside our sexy stuff. We could perhaps all agree that on the face of it, everything is dumb. Except we're unlikely to all agree on anything, ever.

I've observed this: the life cycle of a body is a kind of evolution, and I could not have been more aware of that than I was in the year of that visit to Petersburg, Kentucky, when I was living through The Change. My body was changing, my life was changing, the country had changed. We want certainty; we get disrupted. We don't know how we will survive but we do survive because we adapt. We change. Or we fail at that and we suffer. Science tells us the planet is 4.5 billion years old, and in another 7.5 billion years, the sun will change; it will grow enormous and destroy the Earth. Nothing survives. Come to think of it, evolution is terrifying. I hate it. But hating a thing doesn't make it untrue.

14

Louisville

Thump thump thump. It's 5:38 a.m.

"Louisville police." Thump thump thump. Bam Bam.

The last time I had been startled out of a sound sleep was when it thundered on the Erie Canal, and Colby had stood up and peed on the bed. Ten weeks later at the Baymont Inn and Suites in Louisville, I was awakened again. It was warm and dry there, and we had a nice bed. Colby did not stir. I awoke unsure of where I was for a few minutes.

"Lori? Police." Thump thump.

My first clear thought was, "What did I do?"

Commence inventory of conscience: Colby and I left Sarah's farm after a quick back-slapping tent hug and I drove off feeling creepy as ever about my misdirected romantic impulses but that was no crime. Or was it? Were gay thoughts banned in Kentucky? I made my way to Louisville and spent a few hours walking the dog around a part of the city called Old Louisville, as in, the original Louisville, the once gracious mansion district that had evolved from its creation through its slumification, then through urban renewal, now gentrification. A nineteenth-century Louisville social directory I found included important information about life in that city in its youth, such as the proper days for calling: Tuesdays were Fourth Street, Thursdays were Second Street, and so on. Ladies did not just butt dial any old someone any old time; ladies did not show up uninvited with a six

213

pack to hang out on the neighbor's porch and watch traffic. What changed? Why had the heathens prevailed? What would evolutionary theorists say about the decline of Louisville society?

Near lovely Old Louisville was a neighborhood of pubs and coffee shops and streets lined with cottages, a hip enclave with a ubiquity of stray cats, a place once known as a "streetcar suburb" because a hundred years ago, light rail came along and opened up the neighborhood to riverfront factory workers, who could now commute cheaply and could get away from the barracks they had lived in near their jobs. They made compact neighborhoods of small worker-houses and shops, inland from the fouled Ohio River and its smokestacks. The factories are shut now but the old workers' neighborhood is the hip part of town, bumped up against the historic, bucolic Cave Hill Cemetery, resting place of past masters, where Colby and I only lasted about five seconds before a guard stepped out to say dogs were not allowed. He did not care that I, personally, would totally want dogs to walk on my grave if I were dead.

So I dragged poor Colby away from those pretty green hills and we tried again to take a walk in the grassy park that rolls along the Ohio River, where the ports and warehouses are long gone and an old railroad bridge is now a walkway to Indiana. There were not many people on the walkway; we wandered onto it headed for the far shore, and each time someone approached from the opposite direction, I prepared for the usual "aw, what a sweet dog!" fuss that was always what walking Colby brought. This time, everyone we passed looked sour, until one finally said, "No dogs allowed on the bridge, didn't you know?"

I didn't know. There were no signs. There had apparently been newspaper articles and a big flap about dog piles not being cleaned up. Colby and I would never be so thoughtless, but Louisville didn't know us. We reached the center of the bridge, where we looked down into the rolling Ohio, a busily churning brown river, and then we apologized to everyone we passed as we walked back to Kentucky. I left Colby exhausted and sound asleep in the car while I had barbecue and a beer at a downtown microbrewery, watching some of the World Series, Red Sox versus Cardinals. At closing time, Colby and I returned to our room at the Baymont Inn, a humble place off a side road, where I was staying because I was in a

Colby

city and the nearest campground had been maligned by the usual urban campground reviews. Anyhow, Colby hadn't had a bed with a pillow since his vacation in Milwaukee with Cousin Bee. So I parked the Scamp in the lot, got a room, and my dog and I went to bed.

When the police started banging on the door at 5:38 a.m., I thought it all through until I was sure I had not gotten drunk the night before and plowed someone down on the highway. My conscience was clean; I had done nothing wrong, except for crossing that damn bridge with the dog.

Bang bang bang. "Lori? You in there?"

Had they seriously come in the cover of night to enforce dog regulations that weren't even posted? What should I do now? Was running an option? The Baymont provided us with a king-sized bed with three feather pillows so Colby was down for the count. Maybe I could hide him, I thought. His fuzzy upper lip chuffed as he breathed.

Pound pound pound. "Police."

"Okay, hang on," I said and stumbled to the door. "I need to see badges," I shouted, which I was pleased with myself for thinking to say, as it suggested I knew how to handle a raid. I looked but couldn't see anything through the peephole.

"We're in uniform, ma'am," the voice said.

"Right. Okay." I opened the door.

The police in Louisville, Kentucky—at least the ones who drew the overnight shift on a Sunday—were apparently all fresh-faced, young, and just totally adorable. In the next thirty minutes, I would meet about ten of them and they were all good-looking, capable and focused, earnest in the execution of their duties. I retain an impression of the pair of sweet blond officers at my door as smiling big gleaming smiles like the king and queen of the Louisville prom as I stood there in my Green Bay Packer jammies. Probably this is all colored by a sleepy memory but I recall that I liked them instantly and that if they hadn't been there for work I would have wanted to invite them in to maybe watch Netflix. We could make popcorn or something. I found myself immediately enjoying the crime they had come to investigate, of which I was apparently the victim.

"Someone broke into your trailer, ma'am," one officer said. "We need you to come outside and identify any items the perpetrator took that might be yours."

Again, memory shades things; I can't be sure he said "perpetrator" but he looked like the kind of officer who would say that and anyhow, the exciting part was, the perp had been arrested and was sitting right outside. A trucker who had been sleeping in his cab near where the Scamp was parked saw the guy climbing into the back window of my trailer and called 911; minutes later every squad car in the city of Louisville was in the parking lot, the sneak was in cuffs, and it was over.

I put on some clothes, marched out with the two cops, then doubled back to grab my digital recorder, camera, notebook, and a pen. In the lot behind the building, the night was warmed to a pale orange by the buzzing efforts of halogen street lamps, and inside the circle of light thrown by one of these lamps, the burglar was sitting on a curb quite low to the ground, hands cuffed behind his back. He was gangly and lean, and his bent knees were nearly up around his ears as he sat there. He was in his burglar outfit: all black clothes and a black wool cap, and gummy black shoes that he must have acquired expressly for burglaring. As I approached, he looked up. He was mopey and very sorry-looking, with a bit of stubble like he needed a morning shave. Really, he looked like my community college students, young but old enough to know better, with that stunned look on his face like he didn't realize the final exam was today.

"I'm real sorry that I done got you up out of bed, ma'am," the burglar said.

So he was a sweet burglar. The stunned expression could have been a put-on, of course; it could be the same confidence game I play, half real, half not, when I don't want, say, the Scottsville Rotarians to know that I secretly do think they're ridiculous to doubt climate change; sometimes it's in one's best interest that the world believes one is guileless. Sometimes it's even true.

On the sidewalk beside the burglar were two neat piles. In one pile were a screwdriver, a pack of cigarettes, a small pick, and some keys; in the other pile were a little orange bag with a drawstring that I keep my jewelry in, and Colby's Benadryl.

The back window to the Scamp had been pried open and was open still and a policewoman was shining her flashlight through it to see inside, checking everything out with interest. Maybe she was asking herself if it was big enough in there for her and her boyfriend or if they would need the sixteen-foot model.

From the sidewalk, another officer asked, "These your things, ma'am?"

"Yes—that's my Benadryl, and that's my jewelry bag."

The mention of the jewelry bag, which was empty, created a riot of activity. Heads lifted from smartphones. Bodies turned and drew near. Two cops started shouting into radios, and the questioning cop squared off to the seated perp. He bent forward at the waist, leveled his face Marine Corps–style to the young man, who raised his wool-burglar-capped head from its sad lilt between his shoulders, revealing the full stork length of his bare neck and the aching grace of his Adam's apple. The cop shouted threats into the lifted face at close range, punctuating his verbal assault with gestures, telling the burglar to cough up the jewelry he was obviously hiding or get his ass kicked: "I'll strip you down right here on the ground," the cop shouted. "I swear I will, I will strip you down in about two seconds if you don't tell me where the jewelry is," and the dopey perp, perplexed, crunched his face and answered back, "I ain't got nothin', I'm telling you."

This went on for a while and as it did, I entered the trailer with the cutest of all the police girls and together we looked through my cabinets, just to see what else might be missing. That's when I found all my necklaces and bracelets and rings; they had been dumped out of the bag and left in my storage cabinet. The perp took only the drawstring bag. I went back outside and told this to the big, yelling cop and the yelling cop asked me a few times if I was sure, and then, perhaps disappointed, calmed down.

"There really wasn't nothing in it I could do nothing with," the burglar said, looking at the cop, once things were quiet again. He had been pulled to his feet and was standing on the sidewalk now. He looked at me. "Nothin' personal about your jewelry, ma'am."

I didn't really know what to say. The storyteller in me was dying to interview this guy; that's why I stopped to get the recording gear before I came outside, but then, standing out back of the camper at 5:41 a.m., seeing that the only thing I possessed of any value to him was a half-used box of Benadryl, that this was the one commodity in my private space worth risking his freedom for, the situation kind of depressed me. All this commotion for a guy who steals little pills. The burglar was not menacing; he was pathetic, and when I looked at him, again I thought of my students, the way they behave when they have made mistakes, as if they alone are smothering beneath whole painful worlds and not part of the universally crazy disorder of things. They look at me hopelessly sometimes like the burglar in Louisville, pleading their own special story to explain or excuse whatever they had done, but I already know the story and don't want to hear it anymore. All I want is for them to stop being lazy about their lives, go read a book, just follow my instructions one time, maybe start to see what's really going on and how they are a part of it and then, maybe, start to change. Maybe then, the world will be better for it. My hope for them can turn to anger, and then I am a student too: I have to soften my heart. We are faster to fear than we are to hope. We are all always learning.

According to the police report, the perp was thirty-one years old. They took him away, presumably to book him and for him to enter a plea, presumably guilty, so that he could bargain his way out of trouble, be freed, try all this again and be more careful next time. But instead of waiting for that chance, three days later, the perp picked his wrist and ankle shackles in a Louisville Metro Police transport van and when the van door was opened, he rushed the attending officer and bolted.

The cop chased the perp and as he tossed him to the ground, the cop tore his uniform pants. So then he booked the kid for evading police, criminal mischief, and resisting arrest. The incident report noted that the cop's pants cost sixty dollars, far more valuable than anything allegedly taken from me, which is what got the perp in this mess in the first place.

After the burglary, I became obsessed with reading police blotters. All over Kentucky, people were being arrested for possession, for stealing, for making, for buying and selling methamphetamine. Drug addicts steal stuff. Stealing cold tablets is part of the cycle, though not necessarily Benadryl. You need a cold medication with the right key ingredient, starter fluid, rubber gloves, a few other things. Get that stuff. Cook the stuff. Get fucked up. Start again.

The methamphetamine scourge and the home labs that fed it was biggest in the Midwest and the Pacific Northwest, like Seattle and Spokane. Other drugs had started coming in, but the meth epidemic opened the doors, and that's what I kept reading about, and had been seeing from the start of the trip, and then in Louisville some kid tried to steal Colby's Benadryl, and it really shook me.

I was heading to West Virginia, which was losing whole communities first to Oxycontin, then to heroin. I had bought my Scamp in Vermont, where a local official told me 25 percent of the population of Rutland was using heroin. I had been touring around the broken places looking mostly at buildings, which told me so many stories. In Louisville the pain had a face, and the face kept coming back to me.

Later that morning, after the burglary, I packed up and left the motel and drove right to a hardware store to buy a bar to secure the trailer's rear window. While I was out shopping, I also bought a few bottles of bourbon at one of the largest liquor stores I've ever seen. One entire long aisle was dedicated to bourbon, a veritable runway of glittery booze bottles filled with honey-brown sauce, and after reluctantly, but I think prudently, skipping the many and mystifying commercially bottled varieties of moonshine, I took the bourbon on-ramp and bought a few souvenirs. After extensive hand-wringing, I settled on a label that seemed both sufficiently local (read: exotic) and of high enough quality (read: expensive) to give as gifts, and I bought a lot of it. When this brand of bourbon turned out to be a mass-produced staple served at every bar on the planet and sold all over the country cheaper than I had bought it in Kentucky, I consoled myself by remembering I don't like bourbon anyway. It was just a thing you do in Louisville.

I was heading up to Indianapolis for the annual conference of the National Trust for Historic Preservation, an event for which I would again be stuck in a hotel, and knowing this, I had already scheduled some Scamp camping time beforehand. But when I arrived at Charlestown State Park on the Indiana side of the Ohio River, I was scared. Aside from the usual purely self-inflicted anxieties I experienced now and then, I was usually brave in the world. Now, I looked out on an utterly neutral landscape of roads and trees and was genuinely frightened. My home had been invaded. The pain I had proposed to go out and study had made a clear step closer to me, and I had been shaken.

Charlestown State Park marks the spot on the Ohio River where a large Civil War munitions plant churned out bombs, a major economic staple in those days. Now the town outside the park has an enormous Amazon fulfillment center. Charlestown Park's gatekeeper was an older man whom I had called in the morning so that when I arrived after dark, he would be expecting me. He was especially gentlemanly, trim and a little crookedy, snowy-haired and bushy-browed and reticent, like an Indiana man is bound to be, but pleasant enough. He met me at the office and then led me in his truck back to the actual campground. It was growing dark early and getting cold at night, and this was another near-empty campground in the off-season, but this one was different; this campground was deep inside a large, lonely, forested park and so hard to find that the man had to lead me to it in his truck. Then, I would be left.

I was not only scared but worried in advance of the fear I knew would come later. It was like entering Mammoth Cave and, while not panicking, worrying that I might panic once I got too deep into the earth. Darlene the Ranger had said as we entered, "Please please please turn back now if you think you might end up needing rescue because that will just ruin everyone's day." I felt fine in the cave, but in Indiana at this campground, I was rattled. Suddenly it was not clear whether camping alone with my very old dog had ever been a good idea at all. It had been Russian Roulette all the while, like the most horrifying torture scene in *The Deer Hunter*. BANG. Eventually the troubles will catch you. Eventually your time is up. I saw a parade of slowly shaking heads with grim expressions uttering warnings and asking me if I had a gun. Clearly, an exterminating force was on the hunt in this world and it always had been but I had been running two steps ahead with a dumb smile on my face, like a yellow bulbous smiley-face water tower. Ridiculous. It was closing in on me.

"Uh," I told the fella, "I'm a little scared to camp back in there."

He looked at me like for all the world he could not understand what the hell, then, I had come for. He said, "You've camped before, haven't ya?"

"Well, yes, but last night I was robbed."

"In your camper?"

"Yes. But, no. I wasn't in it at the time. But tonight I'll be in it and I'll be worried."

We considered each other. This was highly psychological talk, clearly not his milieu. He likely felt most at home puttering in the workshop in his garage, refinishing an old rocker, waiting for Mrs. Fella to call him to dinner. That's sweet. That's the Indiana we once had and now don't. That's my grandfather's Midwest, my late great-uncle Luther of Indianapolis's Indiana, and now that Indiana is long gone and the fella didn't realize. Maybe, I thought, I should tell him about Indiana's meth lab ranking—number one last year! Top of the meth heap!—but this was not a chatty fella and so I cut right to it.

"Look, is this place safe?"

He wrinkled his brow. "Well, I think nothing bad will happen to ya, but then again if you stay and something does happen to ya, you'll think to yourself, 'Oh gee, I shoulda listened to myself!' Ha ha."

"Exactly."

We were at an impasse. Ideally, these debates end before arriving at the park gate at 9 p.m. The man huffed. "Well, I'd say, come on up and see the campground and then you decide."

So that's what I did. I followed his truck up the winding road deep into the lightless woods for what seemed like twenty miles, though it was probably only one or two, and by some miracle my phone worked for a while so I called Jessica for a gut check. And because she had been worried ever since the morning call in which I had gushed out many fascinating details of being robbed by a probable meth addict, she began suggesting ways I could turn back without losing face. This whole adventure had gone far enough, hadn't it? The danger was closing in. Was I sure of what I wanted?

"It's not like you can't change your mind," Jess told me. "Tell the old guy you got an emergency phone call. Tell him your dog is sick. Just, stop right now and turn around. Can you find your way out alone?" Poor Jess. I am really sorry for all I put her through.

"No, I can't find my way out, that's the problem. What's done can't be undone, and, shit, Jessica. Okay look, I might die," I was saying, or, something equally frightened and irrational. After the words, "might die," of course, the call was dropped and I couldn't get her back again.

At the campsite deep in the park, I looked the old fella in his bespectacled eyes and opened my mouth ready to ask to go back but then found that I simply couldn't do it. I could not go back. There were many reasons for this. One is that I just don't believe in going back. I am a big believer in forward. And here's another thing: I wanted my idea of Indiana to still matter; I wanted it to be an innocent place where apples grow on the trees and kids toss frogs in your pants and have sack races and stuff, and more ice cream and less methamphetamine because that is both safer and more fun. We might be in a dark patch in this world but I believed in a goodness still. That's the world as I wished to see it. Fear of my own mistakes, like running out of gas, like walking out on love if I really thought I had to, that was one thing but aside from howling coyotes, I had never before feared that the world intended to harm me. It was not what I believed, and I did not want to begin fearing the world then.

And also, I wanted to reclaim my Scamp. I loved the Scamp. The burglar had sullied it. I had fixed the window with a little spring-action curtain rod; it was good to go. If I let the fear win that night, who knew when I would ever feel safe in there again.

"I'll stay," I told the guy. He smiled a tight-lipped smile and nodded at me. It was the kind of smile old-timers give young guns in action-adventure movies at the start of the climactic final battle, in which the young hero has chosen to engage the existential threat—fight the beast, defeat the aliens, intercept the approaching asteroid—despite the likelihood of dying in the process. It was a final-act smile that also said, "Better you than me, kid." The old fella smiled and I smiled back. Then I heard a loud rustling in the woods.

"Listen," I said. He picked his head up and looked around like the killer I feared had caught up with us. In a moment I placed the sound. "I think it's a raccoon."

"Well, you're not afraid of them too, are you?" he asked.

"No," I said.

He left. I drank a tumbler of bourbon. I can't remember if I got a text through to Jessica or not but either way, she had good reason to be worried about me. I was facing down fear like a Jedi. And I had just begun.

15

Indianapolis

Yet again, Colby and I survived the night. We had a perfect record so far for waking up in the morning and not being dead. It may not seem like much but I think we ought not to take it for granted. We stayed in Charlestown long enough to savor light's triumph over dark, had a little breakfast at Waffle House and a little meander at the old munitions plant by the river, then had to press on. We were scheduled for a few nights of obscene luxury that could not be avoided. I was going to a conference in Indianapolis, and we would be staying at the gleaming new Omni hotel and conference center downtown.

The Indianapolis Omni was a hotel finally worthy of Colby's breeding; rarely had he looked so right, so pert and perfect, as he did in the Omni's sparkling lobby. As we entered, time slowed and the light softened; all eyes turned to watch as he trotted regally at leash's end, sunlight pouring down through high glass walls to dapple his shifting black withers. Uniformed attendants tipped graciously to bid him fair day as I signed in at the front desk. They watched over him and fed him treats while I worried about our luggage and arranged for a place to leave the trailer.

Our room had a minibar and a view of the city and a thousand small touches aimed at restoring us to a more refined station—drapes, decorative runners on the bed, a couch across from an enormous TV. Golden fixtures in the bathroom. A long, deep, sunken tub. A bottle of water that would cost twelve dollars if I opened it to fill a glass or, more likely, a dog dish. So many amenities to which Colby was clearly entitled but had for so long been deprived. This trip had been hard for him, but the fantastical existence of professional development funding had come to the rescue, providing comfort to my dog far above what the vast majority of humanity will ever experience. And doing this for him pleased me. Making one creature on the planet happy pleased me. The conference would start the next day. I left Colby to nap while I went off to do our laundry.

The laundry facilities were not in the Omni but at another hotel several blocks away, attached to my hotel by a mall and an enclosed glass walkway. Indianapolis maintains its status as a world-class city at least in part because it is a good destination for conferences. It has multiple sports arenas, microbreweries, Imax theaters, an aquarium, and a zoo. Conference center/entertainment economy secured, it also is a state capital with all the attendant courthouses and state office buildings and government jobs. There's a lot going on in Indianapolis, which surprised me; I had thought of it as a city in the sticks where my great-uncle Luther had lived. He had been one of my favorite people when I was a girl, a stalwart engineer with a firm jaw and a sturdy disposition, and so much love in his enormous heart, but he had been sad, that was what the family had told me, and when I was too young to have any better guesses, I blamed strange, distant, Indianapolis. Who would not be sad to live there? I had never been but believed this.

The city as I found it was hopping. Thousands of people were in town for the National Trust conference on historic preservation; thousands more were attending various other conferences. People with name badges on their shirts wandered the sidewalks looking for barbecue, and sports fans lined up outside restaurants after the stadiums emptied out. Kids rode skateboards around the downtown fountain and a marathon raced through the streets one morning. The place was alive.

The next day, Colby got groomed in a mobile grooming van, and I got ready for the conference. The opening party was at the Rathskeller, a German social club where Indianapolis native son Kurt Vonnegut allegedly used to drink. And why not? The place has on its walls the taxidermic heads of more horned creatures than you would find in your average primeval forest. I drifted away from the conference party and ended up in a jazz bar in a hip little neighborhood around the corner with another conference attendee, Bill, from St. Louis. We were watching the Red Sox beat the Cardinals in the final game of the World Series. I liked Bill right off because we were both rooting for Boston, we were both gay, and eventually, we were both drunk. The bar we found was about the best jazz bar I've ever been to. Christmas lights were strung to light dark-paneled and decrepit walls, and regulars in polyester stretch pants parked themselves on bar stools and packed the tiny tables; a beautiful woman was wailing on the saxophone and the Sox won the series up there on a TV so old it had some kind of weird crooked line flipping over and over across the middle of the screen. My god, what a place for the National Trust conference; Indianapolis had preserved the past perfectly. It was 1970.

Another conference attendee joined us to say hello and Bill introduced her to me and she was cute, and young, and I liked her. And I had been drinking a little and I thought, "She will come with us to the gay and lesbian opening night dance party, and at last I will have my road trip affair," because as if my episode at Girls Week was part of some state-dependent memory, whenever I got into the drink, this seemed like the answer to my problems. I needed an affair to resolve the tension I had set out with; that would fix everything. Fortunately I lacked skills in seduction, or I might have been dangerous. I thought of the possibility of going off with this very nice, attractive, smart young person, of bringing her back to my super-fancy room, and under the influence of drink it all came clear to me once again: this is how people solve the problems in their lives and soothe their agonized souls. They drink too much! Then have regrettable sex! And I sat there thinking of my upcoming reckless near-anonymous encounter with this fantastic creature and thought, "Wow! So this is it! So this is what people do!"

Only, it turns out, it isn't what I did. Bill and I never even made it to the LGBT dance party because when we got into a cab to go there, we realized our tickets didn't have an address on them; he looked up "Preservation Conference LGBT dance party" on his phone, then gave the driver an address that took us thirty minutes to reach, which turned out to be a really remote location far beyond the bounds of the city—a small blue house on the side of a hill where a woman in pajamas was out walking her dog. At this point Bill checked his phone again and laughed: "This address was for *last* year's party, in Spokane." Apparently Indianapolis and Spokane share some street names. The cab turned around and seventy dollars later we were back at the hotel and I went to bed alone.

At 5:30 a.m., I awoke from a restless sleep with no new solutions to the troubles of the world but a strong premonition that Colby had to pee. I took him out, and then back in the room I felt unhappy. I was stuck in patterns that made no sense, and the answers I grasped at made much less sense when sober. Really, I had wandered for months and confirmed that the country was hurting and I was hurting, but I did not know yet how it would get better except that I feared what I felt would get worse first, because change must come, and change is hard. Disruptions hurt. I knew that much. I put Colby back to bed and opened up my laptop to explore that day's selection of conference panels; maybe I would find some answers there. As I worked I received a Facebook message from my cousin Bill in Montana, though he no longer lived in Montana; he lived near Spokane. Near *last* year's LGBT dance party! So that explained it; clearly all night he had been beckoning me. His note said, "Lori, call me," and gave me a phone number.

Curiously, I was just then thinking of going to a panel on preserving industrial heritage in Butte, Montana. Butte, though it is in what can truly be considered the middle of nowhere, became an enormous and briefly very rich city when copper was discovered in a silver mine there. Silver is great stuff, no question; I happen to wear it on my person daily, but copper has a few more functional uses than silver does, and the copper in Butte was found just as the nation, or actually the world, was electrifying. That meant the planet was wiring up its grid, sending these long alternating current lines out across the Herculean towers of Charlton, all across the planet; electric cable was scrolling out copper by the fathom. Incredible timing. In the 1890s, Butte had the copper all the world just then wanted. It was Butte's turn.

I read about the Butte panel just as I received that note to call my Montana cousin, whom I had not spoken to in years, and I wrote a note

back promising to call a little later. It was about 6 a.m. in Indianapolis
when he wrote that message, which would have made it 4 a.m. where he
was, and he had contacted me on Facebook's live chat function so I knew
he was awake, but I did not feel right calling anyone so early. I should have
thought more about what it meant that he was up chatting at 4 a.m.

I had a special love for Montana and for my cousin, but the last I knew,
he was in a bad way. He had come into money and lost it, been married
and divorced, sailed the Pacific on a boat but later lost the boat, been sober
for years and then, his friends feared, lost his sobriety. He had drifted away
rather dramatically. His behavior had become erratic, and then, it did not
seem like booze he was into but something more dangerous. Some of his
friends thought it was drugs. Specifically, methamphetamine. Spokane was
struggling with that scourge.

On the other hand, I had heard, he had not admitted even to drinking,
much less using anything, so maybe he had just lost his mind. It was possible. Truth is, he and his brother and my brother and I all shared something that I think dogged us; we had all been adopted shortly after birth,
and sometimes I think that first separation had left us all wounded. But
who could know. My brother had been an addict and he died young; my
cousin Bill's older brother had committed suicide. Last I had seen Bill,
seven years before, he didn't look well. Word was, he had been hitting
people up for money, saying he didn't expect to live long. He had recently
reached out to my father, whom he had not contacted for at least twenty
years. My father and I had discussed it, and he had given Bill an amount he
was willing to lose, no strings attached, enough money to get a man back
on his feet. That was about three months before the morning my cousin
contacted me as I sat in a posh hotel in Indianapolis. He had been following my travels with Colby on my Facebook page, and I had been happy to
know that he was still out there, somewhere. In the morning, just before I
left for the panel on Butte, I did as he asked: I called.

"Hey, cousin."

"Lori?" He sounded confused.

"What's going on?"

"Oh wow, where to start," he said, and didn't hesitate. "First off, I've
been clean and sober eight months and that's certified, I got the paperwork

to prove it." This was an alarming first sentence. I wondered what sort of certification one could get for sobriety and made a note to look into it, but more importantly, fears that he had in fact started drinking again at some point were now confirmed. "I'm in a terrible way and things are looking real bad and basically I had my identity stolen and I've had so many problems around that mess, they took everything, I mean, I lost everything. They're gonna shut my cell phone off in two days."

"Well, at least you've still got internet."

"No, they're going to take it."

"Well, at least you can still use free Wi-Fi."

"No, they basically took all I've got," he said.

I would probably have kept going like that if he had let me. (At least you're not naked. "No, cousin, they're gonna take my clothes." At least you still have skin. "No, they'll take it.")

"I can't even pay the court fees I need to pay to fight this thing and what it is, is, I'm going to die. I'm going to die in jail."

"I'm sorry to hear that. I really am."

"Yeah, well, I'm sorry too. I'm completely fucked."

My cousin's complaint was succinct and businesslike, both nonsensical and a little too practiced. The presentation was dispassionate, an outline; the dying in jail part was its grand conclusion. Not just dying—dying in jail. He almost forgot to add that. He had doubled back to clarify: "I'm going to die—in jail."

If my cousin, a grown man capable of surviving many things, I knew, was merely struggling with going to court, living without internet service, getting his stuff stolen, this sort of thing, then he would be okay. That was regular tough shit. We all have that. Name anyone who doesn't. He had to be dying in jail for this story to be truly dire and yet it felt obviously wrong and contrived. It was 6 a.m. in Washington State, where he lived. My cousin fed me ninety seconds of bullshit and then stopped, as if he also sensed his mistake. The moment came when we both knew this was a bullshit plea for money to buy drugs.

"I'm sorry things are still bad because you know, my dad did send you some money a couple of months ago and we were hoping that would fix some of this."

There was quiet. His voice softened: "Uncle Jim. I love Uncle Jim."

I started to say something else but my cousin just said, "Bye, Lori," and hung up, and that was it. Disconnected.

I turned the ringer off and put the phone in my pocket and went off to get coffee and go to my panel on Butte, which was so interesting. Butte and nearby Anaconda are a case study of what happens when corporations own the local media and run the local government. Even though the copper mine and smelter devastated the environment, if you lived there in 1910 or so, then you were raised on a very different narrative; the major newspaper in Anaconda was owned by the Anaconda Company and the story was always what you would expect: Mining Makes America Great. No one questioned the mess that was growing all around them. The land between Butte and Anaconda became the country's largest Superfund site, exhibit A in how high fortunes can rise and how hard they must fall.

Butte was in its day such a large and cosmopolitan city that it was home to Montana's only synagogue. Not even Billings had one. Butte was a destination city, really, except that it was so full of miners and bars that it was not exactly Paris. It was no Buffalo. It was Butte. And Butte was really something, boy. It was dug out and drained of minerals, a sort of giant sandy disease in a crease in the otherwise majestic Rocky Mountains. After the copper mine shut down, its demise was swift and thorough.

The ways in which this region became contaminated range from the typical to the truly imaginative. In Butte, they used waste matter, called "slag," from the smelter to build their light rail lines, a clever form of recycling/reuse in its day that, in effect, strung toxic rails right down every main street in the city. Despite these and so many more challenges, preservationists do amazing things; they are turning that Superfund mess into an industrial heritage site, with a bike trail. People love Butte now. It's hipper than Buffalo, and warmer too.

The phone in my pocket began buzzing even before the first speaker started explaining all of the above. I did not need to look. I knew. At first, the vibration alerted me to phone calls and voice messages. In a little while, I felt the special buzzing that indicates a text message. The texts came frequently. I knew they would. I really tried to ignore them. My pocket was rattling, though.

In Butte and Anaconda, as with so many "industrial heritage sites," like the Rivers of Steel heritage area across the mill towns of southern Pennsylvania, one of the most complex questions people face is what, or how much, should be saved and for what purpose. It was one of the central questions of my own journey and it was exciting to think there were ways to answer it. When do you save what you've loved? When do you let go? You don't have to just knock it all down; you don't have to feel guilty to lose some things. Preservationists look at steel mills, power plants, mines, or even whole cities whose existence was predicated by a single industry that eventually left, and they ask, Why save any of it? What matters most in what has been left behind? And they found answers. I loved this. It was at last hopeful.

Buzz buzz. Each new message buzzed several times to let me know it was there. The buzzing grew disturbing. I imagined my cousin completely freaking out. It was possible, though, that rather than heaping on abuse, he was trying to apologize for hanging up on me. I peeked at my phone.

"If you had said this to me," the first text said, "I would have been ass spent to beg borrow and steel [sic—and, interesting too, given my industrial mind-set] for you."

And the next one, "Fuck you."

And the next, "Enjoy your dog trip."

Places like the mines in Butte, and the miners' homes around them, the small neighborhoods with churches and corner bars, and all the institutions that rose in relation to these places, all of this is our common history. This stuff, good or bad, tells us who we are and how we got to be us. We need to read these places like history books and if we are to keep reading them, they must somehow exist in the future. It seems that covering up the ugly things does not make them go away. Not really. They are in our DNA. Failing to preserve is like saying those places and the people in them never mattered, but they did, they do, and anyhow the past doesn't disappear. It follows us.

"Here," my cousin wrote. "I got an idea. You take your sabbatical to me now."

And, "Dumb ass."

And, "Don't pay attention your cousin is stupid."

And, "Write this down."

"I have been fucked."

I wrote: "I am at a conference sitting in a presentation on industrial archaeology. The speaker right now is talking about Butte. It's very cool. I have my phone on vibrate. . . . I want you to stop the texts please."

"Yeah I bet you do," he wrote.

And, "How's the trailer to live in? Wish I had one."

And, "Fuck it."

And, "Do you know how?"

And, "BANG!"

It continued like this, with stops and starts. I imagined him in agony, one outlash followed by a rest, and then another and then rest, how his suffering had a target but nothing would be soothed. It was purely horrible.

One of the artifacts preserved in the Butte-Anaconda region, after a hard debate about it, was the smelter stack itself. The smelter stack is ugly but also in a way stunning. It was built in 1918, is 585 feet high, three times the height of the Marine A silo in Buffalo. It spewed a cloud of poison into the sky for decades. The smelter is iconic, a powerful symbol visible for miles around. The smelting operation ran until 1981. The region was like a moonscape by the early 1990s, part denuded and largely cleared out. It had taken only a few years for the population to exit Butte, and for the region to find the size of its future.

"Right sizing" is what the presenter called it. "Right sizing and population shifts" are inevitable, but just because something is inevitable does not mean it's easy. Of course not. In any case, people left Butte and Anaconda; the smelter stayed.

"I am going to die cous."

"Get this on paper."

"Bye."

I ran back to my room after the session on Butte and blocked my cousin from my Facebook account, which he had also been posting messages on. Facebook asked if I was sure I wanted to block this user, and suggested less drastic measures I could take—as if the person I wanted to cut off had simply forgotten my birthday, not as if, after months of looking, I had just encountered probably the hardest lesson I could have found about the pain our country was suffering. I had seen it, I had studied it. But then, it got personal. I sat on the luxurious couch in my luxurious paid-for hotel room in scrappy Indianapolis and thought of my cousin, and how hurt he was, and the grief that comes with loss, or with change, and I did not see what I could do about any of it, except see it. And cry. And then, keep going forward.

16

West Virginia

The crying I did for my cousin was the first I had done in ages that involved something in the physical world, as opposed to the baffling hormonal flash-cries that had for so long been mugging me like demons; this change felt like progress.

Light snow was in the forecast for West Virginia, where I was going next. The wandering would end soon. It was November and something about my trip had changed and the change was more than the weather. The mood had changed; what I felt was more despairing than curious. The balance had shifted. Sometimes this happens in November, but that November, I had been alone longer than I was used to being, and I was not sure what it meant to go home, and my mind was full of worry for my cousin; I was so troubled by the things he had said to me that in the days that followed I couldn't concentrate. I took no joy in seeing ruin, or in the stories of how and why things that come together later fall apart. I was sorry. And I wanted to see something else. But I had planned my last stop in West Virginia, which I had saved for the end believing it would be the hardest place of all to see, the least welcoming, a kind of grand finale of failure that made sense back when I had plotted my course. By the time I got to West Virginia, the sorrow I had come to study had touched me in ways I hadn't foreseen, just as by then I understood I carried my own despair, just like these places I saw, that I had carried it always but I didn't want to anymore, and I would have to change my life to relieve it. This idea, that I was not simply enduring changes but that in fact change was required, I had never wanted to see at all. But I could not unsee it.

I drove to West Virginia by way of Cincinnati, east along the Ohio River and then across it to the south. I listened to WIMV Christian contemporary radio, broadcasting religious music from Owingsville, Kentucky; I was soothed and delighted by the gentle psych-ward harmonies of a pretty song called "I Wish We'd All Been Ready." It spoke to me in a way no song had since the Grateful Dead turned up on my radio in the very first minute of the trip. It had been sunny then, still summer, and Colby and I looked forward to a long journey. The song "I Wish We'd All Been Ready" tells about life being filled with guns and war, we all get trampled on the floor, some leave but most are left behind to suffer because Jesus has returned. The melody is syrupy beneath a message meant to terrify, an "oh, what a shame sweetie, Satan got you" song sent to mock me. I've since watched the video of this song many times on YouTube. Well-dressed men and women with tranquilized bliss on their faces serenely describe how damnation will actually look, in the end times. Connie Hopper of the Hoppers sings the verses outside a shuttered brick warehouse that resembles thousands of abandoned places I had seen, all over the country, like the old tobacco warehouses I could see right there in Kentucky. This is the background music to lives in the middle; seeing these places while hearing the song could make anyone wonder if the Rapture really was upon us. We are ruined, and only Jesus can fix it. And Jesus is not coming to heal this world, by the way; he will flight-evac the chosen to paradise while the rest of us writhe deeper into pain. Trampled on the floor, even.

"Have a Holly Jolly Christmas" came on the radio next. It was a sunny day despite the forecast. The houses and horse farms along the highway in northern Kentucky began to grow smaller, then receded from the road and disappeared altogether, and then the hills were not rolling and grassy but large and wooded. I crossed the river into Huntington, which is West Virginia's second-largest city, named for a railroad magnate as big as Cornelius Vanderbilt was, but somehow, I had missed all the Huntington bits of railroad history. Coal overshadowed the train part of West Virginia's story anyhow, because without coal there would have been little need for all the trains, or even trucks, or really much of anything that came to pass here. Even the medical industry thrives in West Virginia partly because so many people were so damaged by coal. There's no story, or no history, or no poetry in West Virginia without it.

I had planned to camp at a state park near Charleston, but as I read about the park on a break to let Colby pee, I learned that a steep narrow road with switchbacks led up to that campground; the road was described as difficult to pass in daylight and would probably be dangerous at night. Dark was coming earlier and earlier and bringing a chill with it and camping at the park at the top of that dangerous road seemed unsafe. After three months of this ride, I wanted to be safe. I did not feel as I had in Buffalo, when the days were longer and the ruins were a new idea to me and far more alluring. In order to make a good decision, I asked myself, "What is the first most stupid thing I could do right now?" hoping to hear a very clear answer, like, "Driving up a dark, desolate, winding road pulling a trailer would be the stupidest thing for sure; do not do this." Instead, I heard myself say I hated motels, and would probably be stuck in a really bad one. I whined about having lost my travel mojo as I walked the dog around Marshall University, the school made famous when its champion football team got wiped out in a plane crash. The whole team. All that youth and vigor gone instantly. Such grief. I considered sleeping in my trailer in a grocery store parking lot in Huntington, West Virginia. But this, I was certain, would demonstrate the utmost stupidity. I started to berate myself unfairly for not sticking with my plan to camp; I hated knowing just how scared I was.

I stayed at a Motel 8 south of Charleston. The more comfortable motels would not take my dog. I took the seedy option as a consolation badge of honor; I was very strong and I could hack awful. I would be okay. The Motel 8 offered mooring in an ocean of conjoined parking lots on a low-rent commercial strip. As I walked Colby through one especially desolate patch of asphalt between a gas station and a pancake house, a grinning face approached in the dark; the man wearing it asked me if I had a lighter. He was not holding a cigarette. He was unwashed and unhinged and he grinned in the dark, and as we stood facing each other, I understood this to be the first volley in a drug deal or, perhaps, a slow-motion mugging. Bill flashed back through my mind, a shot of grief. BANG!

No, I said, I did not have a lighter, and Colby and I kept walking. When I turned back, he was still standing there, grinning.

It was cool but a mild night really, so folks in several of the Motel 8 rooms had left their doors open, letting the kids run in and out to play in the asphalt sea. Through the open doors I saw the grown-ups sitting on beds, in tank tops or oversized athletic jerseys, in flannel pajama bottoms or basketball shorts, sitting still and looking blank, stoned, bored, watching television quietly. A bone-thin woman smoking a cigarette outside her second-floor motel room leaned over the balcony into the night; she smiled down at me as I walked by and said, "That's a real perty dog you got." Yes; he was a pretty dog. I looked up to see a halo of bleached-blonde hair around a face deeply creased and leaking cigarette smoke, bare skinny arms folded on the balcony rail. Her eyes were deep sparkles, shining to me across the dark. I still see them.

"Thank you," I said.

"Sher," she purred.

There was a dead cockroach on the mattress in my room. I called Jessica.

"A cockroach. On the mattress," I told her.

"Well, at least it's dead," she said. That did make it better. "When are you coming home?" she wanted to know. I thought I might never. I thought I didn't know. I thought home was the wrong direction. But also, I missed her. I really did love Jessica.

"Soon," is what I said. When we hung up, I cried.

I sat in that room, alone, staring not at television but at myself in the mirror wondering what my long road trip was really meant to find. All this grim fortifying of my tolerance for loneliness, building up my empathy for lives in despair. How could it be that so many had lost so much, and how would they survive this? They would, wouldn't they? Not everyone, no. Not everyone does. People wanted happiness but what they got was change: changing world, changing jobs, changing loves, changing bodies, changing cities. Change takes from us and gives us what we didn't even want. Sometimes. I know it works both ways, but in this moment in time, the beautiful parts seemed lost. I had taken all this on because I was as scared as anyone, and I don't sit still when I'm scared. I run. In West Virginia I examined my face in the mirror. I saw my lines, my jowls, my disappointments. I saw my cousin looking back from Spokane. BANG! I could not save him. "Hey Lori," he said. "Act like you give a fuck, cousin who I love."

I'm sorry.

What was there? A child's skin, my lost time. The daughter my mother dreamed she would have. The son my father wanted. The face of Joan Didion, fantastic fabled author. Deer slayer, screw maker. I wanted to see what was true. Someone to be proud of. Someone to help me.

"Hey, Lori," the face in the mirror said. "Why don't you love yourself the way you love your dog?" Good question.

I went to bed.

In the morning, I drove myself south to the coalfields in search of the hell I had heard of there. I passed the Soggy Bottom Tavern and another called the Top Hat and I knew I would never go in because the bars in southern West Virginia had no windows and I could not see if it was safe inside. I passed countless small churches along the narrow roads, apocalyptic messages on the boards outside their doors. One church sign in Rhodell said simply, "TICK TICK TICK."

I listened on the radio to a sermon, in which the preacher said the church has got to stop preaching fear. He said young Christians are turned off by that antiscience attitude, and then he said, "I don't believe in evolution, of course I don't, but we can't tell these people, 'Hey, if you don't believe what I believe about this then you can't be a Christian.'" So, hook them first, *then* talk them out of evolution? The signal faded; Glen Campbell's voice mixed in with the sermon. "Like a Rhinestone Cowboy." Hell, hell, hell. "Star-studded rode—" EE-vo, LU-shun.

West Virginia's old coal towns swelled up along the narrow roads in the hollows and were gone in a blink, lost beneath hilltops ridged or sheared off from mining. Abandoned mining equipment was easy to find, still and rusted now. Ozymandias again; the Buffalo silos again, but harder. I wondered what it had been like when it was all still alive. Busy, grinding. Dangerous, polluted. Something so many want back desperately. There is no back.

Church in Rhodell, West Virginia

Roads rose and fell in unhurried curves; southern West Virginia has no major highways, which is largely why it feels so isolated. Because it is. The poverty is so deep, the people so definitively cut off in tiny towns in dark hollows that some will never leave, not for anything. You could be hurt worse, if you leave. People stay. The population of Rhodell is 173 but I saw only five, and only by accident, and with the distinct feeling that neither they nor I had wanted to be seen; I stopped in Rhodell to take a picture of a gutted stone church perched high above a narrow creek. When I stepped out of my car to look closer, two children in a yard across the road stopped chasing each other and faced me. One shouted at me to go away, that her daddy was coming to shoot me. I waved. They did not wave back.

Rhodell, West Virginia

A kind woman named Jill showed me around Beckley, the biggest city in the southern part of West Virginia. Jill worked in the mayor's office and she talked to me at length about how she and so many people had been fighting to preserve their historic downtown but it was a hard battle; they had lost their national "Main Street America" status because some non-preservation-minded choices had been made, and could not be unmade. A rich local man had different ideas, and so buildings were torn down. Parking lots paved. Factions disagreed about the best path forward. She showed me a "Made in West Virginia" craft outlet and sent me to a ballet that dramatized the history of coal; she suggested I might try going to the ecumenical church service at the community center. She set me and Colby up with a campsite in the closed-for-the-season campground at Beckley's Exhibition Coal Mine, and at least once a day while I was there camped out alone, walking Colby around the deserted park, she called to make sure I was safe. She was kind and an incredible ambassador for Beckley, which was her hometown and the only place she had ever really known. Her kindness was the sort that grows from deep roots and loss; it was rich with compassion. She invited me to a turkey dinner fundraiser; she invited me to a barbecue at the Wildwood House Museum. I went to all of this and I adored Jill for her kindness. I was not quite ready, though, to see the hope she offered. She offered hope kindly and persistently. She had answers to my questions; she seemed to say, "It also looks like this, like this." But I wanted to see Rhodell, Mullens, Beeson, Lashmeet. The loneliest places in all the world. Towns that people created with hope. Things changed. And the people could not see their way forward, and were afraid. And this is how I felt, and so finally this was all I could see.

My last night on the road was in Cumberland, Maryland. I told Colby we'd go home in the morning and the way he looked at me, it was clear he'd forgotten we ever had a home at all. Oh, but wouldn't he be happy when we got there. And first thing, I promised, we'd go for a walk at the pond. I ate dinner in an old house with local beers on tap and a wood fire in a fireplace. I found this genuinely comforting. I was relieved to be out of West Virginia. The man at the bar next to me was a large-animal vet, which seemed like a fulfilling and caring thing to be. When I told him about my dog, and our journey in a trailer to see places we didn't understand, his brows met severely in a point above his nose, and his whisker-speckled jaw worked a bit of food for a moment. Then he said, "That's a foolish thing to do. You say you don't have a gun?" Then he told me a story of driving to Harrisburg once and it was a good thing he was "packing" because he got lost and stopped on a side road and a black guy walked up to his car window and said, "What you doin' here, honky?" ("That's what he said," the man told me, "honky." I didn't believe him.) The vet flashed his pistol at the black man and said, "Just driving." And that fixed that, apparently.

The veterinarian said he wanted to move to Hawaii because things just have to be better in Hawaii; surely life would be safer and happier on a sunny island but he couldn't move to Hawaii because he would not be allowed to bring his guns. He had thought about it but could not come up with a plan to get all his guns to Hawaii and of course, no way would he leave his guns behind. I asked him how many guns he had. He looked me over silently for a good little while. "That's not a question you ask," he finally said.

The veterinarian was afraid, and afraid for me too, whether or not I had the sense to be afraid for myself at that moment. Fear is a condition in the middle, both geographically and personally. It is supposed to be sweet, there. It is supposed to be Mark Twain in Hannibal. Instead, we are gobsmacked by loss in the middle of life, like the middle of the country. Take flight. Anesthetize. Find something to blame. Point your gun out your car window and find a target. BANG BANG! There are multitudes of targets to hang your fear on. The targets are not the problem. The problem, really, is the fear.

17

The Change

A wooden rowboat with a deck of yellow pine and a small engine on the back sits, right now, on a trailer in a damp garage way up in northern Wisconsin. My grandfather gave the boat to my mother when she was sixteen. That was in 1947. I imagine my mother as a girl in the relief of those years just after the war, when the boys were home and the country was, finally, booming again. Depression, then war, now this: the best years. She grew up in the middle of the century, in the middle of the country, and whatever came before and for all she suffered in life after, she knew how good it was to spend so many hours over so many summers in that pretty wooden boat of hers, in Wisconsin. She was fortunate. Her father owned a small business, a paper company; he was a minor titan in the center of his life, forty-seven years old, giving my mother a birthday gift she would love for as long as she lived. And because she loved it, I loved it too. I still do. But now it's mine and I'm not sure what to do with it.

A wooden boat is a fussy thing. It needs a lot of care. Over the years some of the wood in the boat rotted and had to be repaired. Even healthy wood soaks up water like a sponge when it goes into the lake. Launching the rowboat means bailing out that water, bailing off and on for hours until the wood expands and stops leaking, which seems like much more work to me these days than it once did; bailing was worth giving my own summer days to, when those summers seemed endless.

243

I want to save this boat at the cabin in Wisconsin. I want to preserve everything anyone ever loved there. Or anywhere. Science won't allow it. Evolution. Decomposition. Entropy. The life and death of cells. The sandcastles we build and the tides that come get them.

All through the Northwoods there are boats sitting in the weeds, waiting to launch, and the weeds grow up around the boats, and time passes, and gravity works the hulls down hard against their metal cribs. Then comes the rust and the rot, and the small nesting creatures, and the rain and the snow, and the seasons that change without pause. The boats do not launch but turn into planters. The planters are left to grow wild. Sometimes it hurts to see what's left behind, but it has become my habit to look anyway. I used to think the work was to save all the lost things, but now I've tried to make peace with them instead.

My fiftieth birthday arrived in the springtime, despite my objections. There was no choice left really but to celebrate, so I held court at a bar on Madison Avenue near Grand Central Station, and I sat there waiting for friends to drop by. Through high plate glass windows, I watched the evening light fade. Lawyers and bankers in expensive suits and leather shoes ran to catch trains. I sipped Prosecco and spent much of my evening telling an old friend about my trip into the middle of the country with Colby, and especially about West Virginia, about how starkly depressing I found the coal towns. Certain hollows are empty of all but the most desperately poor. They must be insane with boredom. There are so few jobs. In November when the trees have lost their leaves, you can see it all too clearly: the mess and the loss and the loneliness. West Virginia has nothing, without coal. It's terrible.

My old friend rolled her eyes. "Coal is West Virginia's bad boyfriend," she said. "They need to get over it." That woke me up.

My friend had lived in East Coast cities all her life; she was well educated, she worked for an environmental agency, and she evinced absolute certainty. Don't bother arguing. I thought she was right in a way, since there is really no going back, but "getting over" coal in West Virginia was next to impossible. In a dark, high-ceilinged watering hole in Manhattan, when you have more or less made it in life and you have something to celebrate and you have friends to celebrate with, and the bars have large windows and a woman alone is not afraid to sit there, it's easy to feel right about everything. Yet something about a pair of aging urban lesbians using a bad boyfriend analogy to describe West Virginia maybe, just maybe, underscored the futility of trying to grasp anything as distant from us as Appalachia.

I asked my friend where she thought people would find work in southern West Virginia when all the mines were closed.

"I don't know. Maybe they could put up some nice wind turbines," she said.

It happens that this woman was responsible, so many years earlier, for introducing me to Jessica at the bookstore where Jessica's blue eyes had knocked me off my feet. The night of my fiftieth birthday celebration, Jessica stood at the bar, glowing in the light of votive candles. She was so bright and so lovely, and she stood tightly beside me; I thought we fit. I thought everyone could see. It was a role she knew how to play for me and she liked it as much as I did. It would not have been a party without her there; she had the most appealing way of making life fun. One long-lost friend had shown up by surprise, drunk before she even arrived, and grabbed me at one point to slur in my ear, "Your girlfriend is so much hotter than my husband." I loved that. I was proud. And also in that moment I thought to myself, "I think it's time to put my glass down." And I did put it down, eventually, seeing it as one more thing coming between me and what I really needed.

At the bar, I told my friends stories: "How old is this cave? Older than your great-granny and still forming." We laughed about the fear in the world, the way people hid from the truth. We were wrong to laugh; we didn't see the depth of the pain that was coming. We did not realize that it could get worse. But that night we laughed about a lot of things. I told people I had known Jessica almost as long as I had known Colby, and Jessica added that I loved them in that order: Colby first, then her. We laughed. I think of this now and remember us standing in the dark with candles glowing, on my birthday. I remember loving Jessica because the world, which is so dangerous, felt safe with her in it. I did not want to be in that world alone.

A few months after my birthday, Colby died. He had lived a good life, a long one. He was ready to leave. Still, it was hard to accept that anything I'd loved so much could, all at once, be so thoroughly gone. It hurt, and it seemed to touch off a process of required hurting that would last for a very long time. But not forever. I'd find my way.

Later that summer, Jessica went with me to the cabin, the very site of my imagined affair, the most life-changing event that had never even happened. We had been fighting. I was angry at her for everything, or for nothing. I had been hoping for so long that these feelings would pass. But I was really struggling. One night I showed her a picture of us, taken by a friend who had sent it to my phone. This picture caught us down by the water, sun soaked and smiling, two women in full summer thrall. I thought we were beautiful in that moment, and the beauty I saw gave me hope. I held the image up and called Jess to come see, and she glanced over my shoulder and said, "Meh," then walked away. It crushed me. Such a small slight, maybe even comical to think of it now, but in that tender time, I knew ineffably that we were done. Our life was not without a certain beauty, but something essential was missing for us, and we would never find it by staying together. We both knew this, and as hard as it was to do, we finally parted.

But what about my troubled country? Would it also fall apart? The stark, sad places in the middle hurt in ways I understood to be deadly. Not everyone survives. I heard from my father that my cousin Bill died, that same year I lost Colby, the year I left Jess. Such darkness. A deep soul night, dense and acrid, like 3 a.m. in Bethlehem where the mills have been gone for decades by now. I'm sorry. The changes can bring pain. I only know to feel it, and to not be afraid. For every one of us who finds her way, the whole will grow lighter. They project movies up on the high walls of the silos sometimes, in Buffalo, and people do come back to small towns if they're nice. They rebuilt Sullivan real nice after those tornados. I should add that I have a new dog. She's naughty. I don't know what will happen to the coal towns, but something else will come along. Only, this may take longer than anyone likes. It will take years, perhaps millions and millions. That's evolution. That's the truth. We like our answers to ring with such certainty. But the only certain answer is change.

Epilogue: Dark and Light

Ihad to go back to West Virginia. I was not done with it. I was sad when I got there, and so preoccupied by my sadness that I had not really figured the place out. And I had wanted to be brave enough to really see West Virginia. The coalfields were just seven or eight hours away from New York. Not so far out of reach. I could go back to try again.

I made plans to connect with some administrators at Southern West Virginia Community College, hoping this time I would find more people to talk to and really learn something, and I hooked the Scamp back up and hauled it six hours down the interstates and two hours more beyond that, stopping ritually at the last known chance for latte, then twisting into the mountains and arriving, finally, at the Buffalo Creek National Park campground ten miles outside the small city of Logan. No girlfriend, not even a dog this time; just me.

Logan is the epicenter of the "War on Coal." The "War on Coal" is what today's West Virginians perceive as a liberal plot to dismantle the coal industry and replace it with things like wind power. This plot has much truth to it, except that it doesn't seem to me like an actual plot; it's just the source of power changing. As wars go, the "War on Coal" is a very cold one, fought with politics and words and signs in people's yards. The "coal wars," on the other hand, also centered around Logan and had involved weapons and blood; these wars were a series of violent clashes between coal miners and their industrial bosses in the early twentieth century, when the miners were trying to unionize. Back then, liberals supported unions and the miners considered liberals their allies. Conservative government officials, on the other hand, sided with industry and literally dropped bombs on workers. A century later, it had all flipped over: liberals still liked workers well enough, but the environment had become an existential concern, so liberals turned on coal, and West Virginia workers turned on liberals. The coal workers aligned themselves with the powers that, in another era, sought to murder them without apology but that, now, promised to bring back coal jobs.

In Logan County, for about a week in August 1921, a small army of ten thousand miners took up arms against the anti-union Logan County Sheriff. The whole bloody situation started with the "Matewan Massacre" down in Mingo County; Sheriff Sid Hatfield killed a Baldwin-Felts agent who had been hired to evict unionizing miners' families from their houses, which the coal company owned. Fury was unleashed. Eleven people died in the streets of Matewan that day, but that didn't end it. The situation escalated over time and spread, reaching its macabre zenith when actual bombs were dropped in Logan from actual planes hired by the county sheriff. The sheriff defended coal management with the aid of federal troops, who opened fire on coal miners. It's said that a million rounds were fired and as many as 150 or so men died in the "Battle of Blair Mountain" in Logan, just one battle in the coal wars. I had never heard of it. I don't believe we ever learned this stuff in school. President Warren Harding threatened to send military planes to bomb the uprising workers in West Virginia, but the fighting stopped before he could.

Chief Logan State Park campground is laid out alongside Buffalo Creek, which is a trickle that runs fast down the steep hill of the state park but turns into a river later on, and I did not know this when I parked my trailer there, but Buffalo Creek is famous, actually, for a flood that sent 132 million gallons of water and coal slurry through a hollow in 1972, after a shoddily built coal dam burst. A twenty-foot wall of water and coal sludge wiped out whole towns along a seventeen-mile stretch of Buffalo

Creek. People running up the hills to safety looked back and saw faces in
the windows of houses swept off by the water; people rode on their roofs as
their houses careened downstream. One hundred and twenty-five people
died. It lasted only minutes, but this thing was about the worst disaster
that ever hit West Virginia, and West Virginia has suffered more than its
share of catastrophe. People at the community college would refer to this
flood in conversation later as if it were 9/11, as if everyone knew. I had no
clue. I made camp in the park on a site by the creek, which tinkled sweetly,
and at night I slept to the gentle music of the water and owls and peeping
frogs of all kinds. It was beautiful. The campground was well maintained
and patrolled. It was early in the season and for a while I had the place to
myself and down in the city of Logan there was actually, incredibly, a really
cool coffee shop that served lattes and any other kind of fancy yuppie drink.
I was just one bookstore and one specialty food shop away from being able
to live there, except that peaceful as it was, it was still hard in West Virginia
to get anyone to talk to me. I was working hard for it.

One morning, a couple arrived and spent about two hours moving
their thirty-foot trailer back and forth to find just the right level spot in the
campsite across from mine. I sat in my chair outside watching this spectacle of spousal cooperation and thought surely one of the two would start
screaming, eventually, but neither did. They were in their sixties. The
man, Gordon, saw me watching and when our eyes met I waved and said
hi and within minutes I was over there for coffee. Later on, when we were
friends, he told me he was sure I would have preferred to be left alone.

"I saw the license plates and didn't think I should say hello," he said.

"I was just waiting for you to invite me to dinner," I said.

"Well, I didn't know if we ought to."

"Why not? I love dinner."

Gordon's wife, Donna, was a retired teacher; Gordon had worked for
the railroads, then later he was a safety director for several coal mines, and
now he was retired too. Donna and Gordon were both widowed and had
been married to each other less than two years. They did not hesitate to
begin my coal country education by telling me West Virginia can break
anyone's heart. I wonder now about their own broken hearts—losing

spouses from long marriages before it seemed fair, and grieving, and finding love again in a small town, late enough in life to make it seem perhaps
impossible. It's never impossible. Nothing is, I think.

Gordon and Donna were well off and had a swimming pool and of
course a thirty-foot travel trailer and they clearly were holding down the
local middle class, but they acknowledged that comfort was complicated in
Mingo County, where they lived. People want prosperity but all the steps
between wanting and having are so hard, Donna said. In Southern West
Virginia, about every other person I spoke to told me a story that ended
with tears. It's that full of grief there.

I had coffee with Donna and Gordon and later on we had dinner and
then we sat out by their campfire with Donna's mom and brother, who had
come to visit them at the campsite. Donna's mother, Beulah, had moved
to West Virginia from Ohio more than sixty years before and that made
her an outsider still; Beulah was a Buckeye. Her kids were born in West
Virginia so they were hillbillies.

"We're hillbucks," Donna said.

"Buckbillies," said her brother.

Point is, you could be born there and still not quite fit in. West Vir-
ginian roots are miles deep. I told them I thought the mountains had a
dark feeling to them, such long shadows buried the hollows. Donna and
Gordon said that could be right, but it was once darker, back when the
soot and coal dust ran through everything. The water was black, back
then.

At their urging, I took a day trip down to Matewan, population 484,
famous for its coal war massacre. There are still bullet holes in the walls
of the post office in Matewan. I was a little scared to go, but Donna and
Gordon told me not to worry because it's actually a real nice day trip now;
it's been all reconstructed and they've got a nice new restaurant and an
inn. The coal war days are over; the past ten years, Mingo had not been old
Bloody Mingo anymore. It was changing.

Of course, a year or so earlier the sheriff in Williamson had been shot
point blank in the head while he sat in his patrol car. But that was random.
That was not over coal. Most of the violence in coal country now is over
drugs. Drugs are everywhere. Government officials in one Mingo town

had sold drugs for years out the window of a trailer on the main street, as if it were an ice cream truck. You can still find pain without trying very hard in Mingo but there are good things to see too, now; Williamson is a sweet, sleepy city where dogs bark up at the top of narrow stairways and trains park across a dozen tracks in the valley below, and in Matewan, tourists—not many; it isn't easy to get there; the nearest interstate is two hours away—tourists come for the history. They can come see a reenactment of the Matewan Massacre on its anniversary each year. It's fun. Gordon and Donna told me all kinds of places I should go see if I wanted to have fun in southern West Virginia. Like, the Dingess Tunnel. It was built as a one-track train tunnel, then later turned into a one-lane road tunnel and it's long, and dark, and if a car is coming at you, there's no way to know until it's right there.

"Oh, the tunnel, you have to drive the tunnel!" Donna said. "Go to Matewan the long way and drive the tunnel!" But of course I couldn't go to Matwewan the long way because I spent the morning in Logan, drinking coffee. I was running out of time.

Back at the campground that night, I was walking on the park road as Gordon and Donna and Beulah were coming home from a bluegrass jam down at the community center. Gordon pulled his car up next to me and said, "Hey! How was Matewan?"

"Fine," I said, "until I ran into some snotty New Yorkers." In the back seat, Donna's mother, Beulah, nearly spit out a mouthful of iced tea. But it was true. A van pulled in with New York plates; filmmakers had come from Brooklyn to shoot a Matewan Massacre documentary. It felt surreal to have traveled so far only to bump into a van full of New Yorkers in Matewan. It is still such a desolate and isolated place. When I approached to say hello, they ignored me.

The next day, I went to a Baptist church picnic that Donna and Gordon and Beulah had invited me to. It was at a picnic area in a large park and I hauled the Scamp to it, because after the picnic, I had to start for home. But when the food was put away and people started leaving, Gordon convinced me to go for a drive. He wanted to show me an abandoned strip mine, he said. He wanted to show me the view from the mountain. So we drove off, Gordon and Donna up front, Beulah and me in the back. We drove up the side of a mountain and found a dirt road to turn on and we got out and saw the old mining equipment and looked out on a bright grassy slope. We started off for another spot but somewhere along the road, Gordon got nervous. You don't really know who might be up there; you don't really know if you might make a bad turn and get lost. It is still West Virginia; it is still a place to beware. We drove back down to the road in the hollow, then rode through the budding countryside. In the back seat, me and Beulah opened our windows and turned our faces to the breeze. It was a pretty day. Then Gordon said, "Surprise!" We were at the Dingess Tunnel.

The tunnel's mouth is a small stone arch, the shape of a cartoon mousehole, like a church door painted black. It was a portal to darkness on the side of a hill. There was no way to know what was in there. Gordon's car idled. He and Donna and Beulah and I looked around at each other, waiting for someone to speak first. Then Gordon said, "Well, here goes!" and gunned the engine. The tunnel was only inches wider than the car, and our headlights cut only a short way into the dark; we were driving almost completely blind. The only safety was knowing that the driver coming at you, if there was one, must be afraid of dying too. You had to hope so. You had to believe you would find light on the other side. The four of us with our windows down stuck our heads out and whooped real loud. It was like a West Virginia theme park ride, only it was real, and free. I shouted, "Beuuuuulaaaaah!" into the stone walls to achieve maximum echo. Gordon drove fast, but the road seemed to go on and on, and we were in the dark for the longest time not knowing if it would ever end. But then, the light appeared and we drove to it and passed back outside. We were alive.

It was a warm afternoon just turning to evening when Gordon drove me back to the park to drop me off at my trailer, which was hooked up and ready for me to head home. I was sorry to go. Donna gave me a plate of leftovers from the picnic and told me to be careful, and I promised I would and thanked her for the food and walked off, but I took only a few steps before Donna called me back. "Momma has something to tell you," she said.

Beulah got out of the car so that she could hug me. She said, "I'm glad I knowed you." It was a moment of pure love; it had no other purpose. To feel it soothed the late-day sense of loss that had begun setting in; such love showing up was worth all the sorrow of every inevitable good-bye.

Acknowledgments

This book was a journey in more than one way that required help from friends, family, and many total strangers. I'm especially grateful to people I met on the road, who will recognize themselves in these pages but whose names I've withheld for privacy. I trust they know I'm indebted to their openness. Help in revision has come from readers of this and other projects over the years, including Tzivia Gover, Gail Hall Howard, Laurel Peterson, Sarah Durham, Kerri Gawreluck, Renae Edge, and Suzanne Parker. I am grateful to Norwalk Community College and the entire construct of college education and its sabbaticals, which gave me the time to create and funding to expand the possibilities for travel. I'm grateful to Margie and Bill W. for helping me find my story. Deep gratitude to Katherine Van Acker, who gave me the world's best boy, Colby. Raphael Kadushin has been an indispensable voice for LGBTQ literature at the University of Wisconsin Press and he will be sorely missed in his retirement.

The original version of the Buffalo chapter was published in *Bluestem Journal*, and a variation of the West Virginia material was published in *Terminus Journal*. I gratefully acknowledge the work of other literary road trip warriors, especially John Steinbeck and William Least Heat-Moon. Now, it's finally time to have that piñata party.

Living Out
Gay and Lesbian Autobiographies

David Bergman, Joan Larkin, and Raphael Kadushin
Founding Editors

Just Married: Gay Marriage and the Expansion of Human Rights
Kevin Bourassa and Joe Varnell

Two Novels: "Development" and "Two Selves"
Bryher

The Hurry-Up Song: A Memoir of Losing My Brother
Clifford Chase

The Pox Lover: An Activist's Decade in New York and Paris
Anne-christine d'Adesky

In My Father's Arms: A Son's Story of Sexual Abuse
Walter A. de Milly III

Lawfully Wedded Husband: How My Gay Marriage Will Save the American Family
Joel Derfner

Midlife Queer: Autobiography of a Decade, 1971–1981
Martin Duberman

Self-Made Woman: A Memoir
Denise Chanterelle DuBois

The Black Penguin
Andrew Evans

*The Man Who Would Marry Susan Sontag: And Other Intimate Literary Portraits
    of the Bohemian Era*
Edward Field

Body, Remember: A Memoir
Kenny Fries

In the Province of the Gods
Kenny Fries